# THE LIBRARY-COLLEGE

*Front row: (L to R) John Harvey, John Terrell, Dan Sillers, Louis Shores, Lamar Johnson. Second row: Gilmore Warner, Sister Helen, Patricia Knapp, Betty Brown, Father Jovian Lang, William Westley, Tom Minder. Third row: Harry Mason, Charlotte Fletcher, Rodney Bell, Robert Gaylor, Bruce Lee, Colleen Halverson, G. M. Armstrong, Robert Jordan, Theodore Samore. Back row: Dale Shook, R. W. Witt, James Holly, Bruce Manwaring, Franklin Faust, John Coyne, and Franklin Grady.*

*A part of the discussion of the Jamestown College Library-College workshop occurred in small, informal groups such as this one. Participants pictured here are: (L to R) Theodore Samore, Louis Shores, Colleen Halverson, Dan Sillers, Robert Jordan, and Lamar Johnson.*

*Dan Sillers (L) visits with Lamar Johnson and Louis Shores at the conclusion of the workshop.*

# THE LIBRARY-COLLEGE

*Contributions for American*

*Higher Education*

*at*

*THE JAMESTOWN COLLEGE WORKSHOP, 1965*

*Edited by*

LOUIS SHORES     ROBERT JORDAN     JOHN HARVEY

Drexel Press

## 1966

"The whole educational system is about to do a great flip-over from instruction to discovery, with the students as researchers." Marshall McLuhan interviewed in *Newsweek,* February 28, 1966, pp. 56-57.

"The educational function of the college library is a concept of the 20th Century . . . Today the teaching function of the academic library is still in its infancy."

*Encyclopedia of Educational Research,* 1960.

MANUFACTURED IN THE UNITED STATES OF AMERICA

*$7.00 per copy postpaid*

vi

# Table of Contents

## PART THREE

### THE JAMESTOWN LIBRARY-COLLEGE

## APPENDIXES

# *Preface*

*The purpose of the Library-College is to increase the effectiveness of student learning particularly through the use of library-centered independent study with a bibliographically expert faculty.* (from the Jamestown Charter)

EXPERIMENTING COLLEGES are preparing the United States for another historical first — the higher education of all the people. As millions of students pour out of our high schools in search of learning, post-secondary institutions struggle with several urgent quandaries: the impersonality of numbers; the wider range of individual differences; the accelerated torrent of information; the unlimited commitment to specialization; and perhaps problems which others would measure more threatening. Current experiments deal with all of these aspects of higher learning.

To contend with the inevitable numbers several of our so-called "multiversities" with student populations approaching 100,000 are taking a cue from the British university and reorganizing into small, personal colleges. To match the range of individual differences in young people a wide range of learning resources is being acquired, organized and disseminated by the library. To counter a zealous, national worship of the specialist many colleges are offering "integrated" or "inter-disciplinary" programs encompassing broad segments of knowledge.

## INDEPENDENT STUDY

For the student, these new programs are characterized by independence from the lock-step pre-digested oral informing in average measured doses. Labelled in experimenting colleges variously as honors reading, autonomous courses, tutorial instruction, preceptorial teaching or just independent study, the central theme is that each student is a unique individual who works best at his own pace toward his own objective at an individual "work bench" in the library. The instructors are bibliographically competent counsellors available for individual counselling, for group discussions and for periodic lectures that provide elements not available in print or other formats.

The logical conclusion of this trend toward independent study is the Library-College. Several of the experimenting colleges today approach this conception. Over the years Antioch has hovered over the idea. At Stephens for years the Dean and the Librarian were the same person; today, an advanced library-instructional complex reveals the potential for learning in all formats from textbooks through television. Monteith at Wayne State has demonstrated a new relationship between those who teach in the classroom and those who teach in the library. Florida Presbyterian dismisses all classes in January so the students may concentrate in the library.

And now a Library-College is about to be born. From December 17 to 21, 1965, 30 exponents of the Idea gathered at Jamestown College, Jamestown, North Dakota, to design a Library-College for that campus. Led by Dan Sillers, a President with vision and courage, and, above all, a talent for working with faculty and students, an uplifting experience occurred. For many of the participants, it was the best conference they had ever experienced; for others, it was a turning point in their lives. From early morning until late at night people talked, read, designed, displayed elements of the new college for challenge, revision, remolding. Some of these components are on display in Part III.

In preparation for the Jamestown meeting each participant was invited to describe an ideal Library-College or any of its components, and these essays are offered as Part II.

Those who accepted this invitation had been brought up on a developing pre-Library-College literature going back at least to the often-quoted but frequently under-estimated Carlyle statement from his essay on the *Hero as Intellectual*: "The True University is a Collection of Books." Representative parts of that literature comprise Part I.

Therefore, this collection of essays, papers, committee reports, and appendices is offered to college and university presidents, to classroom and library faculties, to public and private supporters of higher education, to students pre, in, and post-college as a prediction of things to come in the nation first to commit itself to universal *higher* education.

The present book is an anthology of various kinds of papers concerning the Library-College idea and covers many different facets of it. The reader may be concerned about some repetition of ideas among the papers included here. Obviously similar ideas have occurred to several leaders in librarianship and higher education at different times and this should give added impact to their importance.

In sharing the task of preparing the volume for publication Louis Shores and Robert Jordan have compiled and edited its contents from Workshop contributions, while John Harvey did final revision and editing. Acknowledgment is made to the publishers who have allowed quotation from their works.

The editors thank all concerned from Dan Sillers who planned the conference, to Barrie Lind who typed and re-typed it, and Robert De Farges who printed it.

LOUIS SHORES
ROBERT JORDAN
JOHN HARVEY

Easter, 1966

# *Contributors*

Where available the last two degrees and the previous two full-time positions are included for each contributor. *Not at Workshop.

Rev. Gilbert M. Armstrong
Assistant Professor of English
Jamestown College
Jamestown, North Dakota 58401
    M.A., University of Kansas City.
    Licentiate in Theology, St. John's College, Winnipeg.
    Chaplain and Vicar, St. Peter's, Harrisonville, Mo., and
        Roanridge National Training Center.
    Rector, Grace Episcopal Church, Jamestown, North Dakota.

*George M. Bailey
Executive Secretary, Association of College and Research Libraries
Chicago, Illinois 60611
    Reference Librarian, Northwestern University.

Rodney E. Bell
Professor of History (on leave)
Jamestown College
    B.S., Jamestown College, 1955.
    M.A., University of Michigan, 1956.
    North Dakota State Supreme Court Law Librarian, 1960.
    University of Michigan, IST, Research Information Leader,
        1960-61.

*Daniel Patrick Bergen
Chairman, Department of Library Science
University of Mississippi
University

Betty Martin Brown
Instructor of Library Science
Graduate School of Library Science
Drexel Institute of Technology
Philadelphia, Pennsylvania 19104
> B.A., University of Vermont, 1950.
> M.S. in L.S., University of Illinois Library School, 1956.
> Catalog Librarian, Drexel Institute of Technology Library,
> Philadelphia, 1963-65.
> Doctoral Student in Medieval History, Bryn Mawr College,
> 1965-

*Maurice Brown
Professor of English
Oakland University
Rochester, Michigan 48063

John R. Coyne
Reference Librarian
University of Denver
Denver, Colorado 80210
> M.A., University of Alaska, 1963.
> M.A. in L.S., University of Denver, 1965.
> Marine Corps.

Franklin P. Faust
Instructor of Art
Pratt Institute
New York, New York 10024
> B.A. and M.F.A., State University of Iowa, 1950, 1954.
> Instructor of Art, Sacramento City College, 1961-63.
> Residence in Spain, 1964-65, to paint and study Renaissance
> Spanish art.

*Blake Fishburne
Administrative Assistant
Goddard College
Plainfield, Vermont 05667

Charlotte Fletcher
Librarian
St. John's College
Annapolis, Maryland 21402
    A.B., Hollins College, Virginia, 1935.
    B.S. in L.S., Columbia University, 1939.
    Librarian, Talbot County Free Library, Easton, Maryland,
        1941-44.


Robert G. Gaylor
Director of Public Services
Oakland University Library
Rochester, Michigan 48063
    Student, Jamestown College, 1957-60.
    B.A., Michigan State University, 1961.
    M.L.S., University of Oklahoma, 1963.
    Photoduplication, University of Oklahoma Library, 1962-63.
    Assistant Reference Librarian, University of Kansas Library,
        1963-64.


Thomas Franklin Grady, Jr.
Dean of Students
Jamestown College
    B.S. Ed., State College, Salem, Massachusetts, 1954.
    M. Ed., Tufts University, 1955.
    Director of Guidance, Malden Public Schools, 1961-64.
    Lecturer in Education, Boston State College, 1964-65.


Colleen Halverson
Junior Student
Jamestown College
    Psychology Major and Top Ranking Student.
    Vice President, Junior Class
    *Who's Who in American Colleges and Universities.*


Steve Hample
Freshman Student
Jamestown College

John Harvey
Dean, Graduate School of Library Science
Drexel Institute of Technology
Philadelphia
  B.S. in L.S., University of Illinois, 1944.
  Ph.D., University of Chicago, 1949.
  Librarian and Professor, Parsons College, Fairfield, Iowa,
    1950-53.
  Head Librarian, Chairman, Department of Library Science,
    and Professor, State College, Pittsburg, Kansas, 1953-58.


Sister Helen (Sheehan) — Sister of Notre Dame de Namur
Librarian and Member Board of Trustees
Trinity College
Washington, D. C.  20017
  A.B., Trinity College, 1924.
  B.S. in L.S., Simmons College, 1926.
  Taught High School and was Librarian, New England Schools,
    1931-34.


*William Emerson Hinchliff
Chief, In-Service Training and Personnel Control
Public Library
Milwaukee, Wisconsin  53233
  A.B., Harvard, 1940.
  M.L.S., UCLA, 1961.
  Representative, Western Oil and Gas Association, 1950-60.
  Chief Librarian, Santa Barbara Public Library, 1961-63.


James F. Holly
Librarian, Macalester College
St. Paul, Minnesota  55101
  B.S. in L.S., Carnegie Library School, 1941.
  M.A., Pennsylvania State College, 1951.
  U.S. Army, 1942-57.
  Associate Librarian, Gene Eppley Library, and Assistant
    Professor, University of Omaha, 1957-59.

B. Lamar Johnson
Professor of Higher Education
UCLA
Los Angeles, California 90024
    M.A., University of Minnesota, 1927.
    Ph.D., University of Minnesota, 1930.
    Dean of Instruction and Librarian, Stephens College, 1931-52.
    Director, California Study of General Education in the Junior
        College, 1950-51.


Robert Thayer Jordan
Senior Staff Member
Council on Library Resources, Inc.
1028 Connecticut Avenue, Northwest
Washington, D. C. 20036
    B.A., Antioch College, 1947.
    M.L.S., University of California, Berkeley, 1957.
    Deputy Auditor, County of Alameda, California, 1955-56.
    Librarian, Taft College, California, 1957-60.


Patricia B. Knapp
Associate Professor of Library Science
Wayne State University
Detroit, Michigan 48202
    M.A., University of Chicago, 1943, Ph.D., 1957.
    Reference Librarian, Wayne State University, 1957-59.
    Executive Secretary and Director, Library Project,
        Monteith College, Wayne State University, 1959-65.


Father Jovian Lang, O.F.M.
Librarian and Associate Professor of Speech
Quincy College
Quincy, Illinois 62301
    M.S. in L.S., Western Reserve University, 1950.
    M.A., Western Reserve University, 1955.
    Assistant Professor of Speech and Assistant Librarian,
        St. Joseph Seminary, Westmont, Illinois, 1955-57.
    Assistant Professor of Speech, Villa St. Joseph, Ferguson,
        Missouri, 1957-60.

C. Bruce Lee
Chief, Office of Foreign Activities
Bureau of Sport Fisheries and Wildlife
U. S. Department of Interior, Washington, D. C. 20240

M.S. and Ph.D., University of Michigan.
Professional Associate, Office of the Foreign Secretary,
National Academy of Science, 1962-64.
Science Specialist in the Life Sciences, Science and Technology
Division, Library of Congress, 1964-65.


Bruce W. Manwaring
Chairman, Art Department
Jamestown College

B.F.A., Rhode Island School of Design, 1962.
M.A., Claremont Graduate School, 1963.
Art Director, Clokey Productions (Film Company),
Glendora, California, 1963-64.
Art Instructor, Webb School, Claremont, California, 1964-65.


Harry Mason
Professor of Physics
Jamestown College

B.S., Pacific University, Oregon.
M.S., Catholic University.
Instructor, Pacific University.
Research Staff and Physicist, Johns Hopkins University.


Thomas L. Minder
Systems Analyst, IBM Corporation
6407 Carolyn Drive
Falls Church, Virginia 22044

B.A., M.A., University of Chicago, 1954, 1963.
Librarian, Curtiss-Wright Research Division, 1956-59.
Librarian, College of Engineering,
Pennsylvania State University, 1959-64.

Theodore Samore
Assistant Professor of Library Science
University of Wisconsin
Milwaukee, Wisconsin

>B.A., University of Missouri.
>M.L.S., University of Michigan.
>Director of Library Services, Livonia Public Schools,
>    Michigan, 1960-63.

College and University Library Specialist
U. S. Office of Education


Paul Schoon
Director of Public Relations
Jamestown College

>B.A., Central College, Iowa, 1960.
>M.A., State University of Iowa, 1963.
>Admissions Counselor, Central College, 1960-61.


Dale Shook
Sophomore Student
Jamestown College

>Physics Major, Class Vice President.
>Hall Counselor, Dean's List.


Louis Shores
Dean, Library School
Florida State University
Tallahassee, Florida 32306
Editor-in-chief, *Collier's Encyclopedia*

>M.S., City College of New York, 1927.
>Ph.D., George Peabody College, 1934.
>Director, Peabody Library School, 1933-46.

Dan J. Sillers
President, Jamestown College

    M.A., University of North Dakota, 1955.

    Ph.D., University of Denver, 1961.

    Director, Counseling Center and Research Consultant, American Institute for Research, Washington, D. C., 1961-62.

    Manager for Professional Development of Engineering and Science Personnel, Martin-Marietta Corporation, Baltimore, Maryland, 1962-63.


*H. Lee Sutton
Librarian, Parsons College
Fairfield, Iowa 52556


John E. Tirrell
President, Oakland Community College
Union Lake, Michigan 48085

    M.A., University of Michigan, 1951.

    Ph.D., Harvard University, 1954.

    General Secretary, University of Michigan Alumni Association, 1958-62.

    Vice-President for Instruction, St. Louis Community College, 1962-64.


Gilmore Warner
Librarian, State College
Lock Haven, Pennsylvania 17745

    A.B., Oberlin College, 1924.

    Ph.D., Cornell University, 1941.

    Head Librarian, Colby College, 1945-48.

    Head Cataloger, Chicago Natural History Museum, 1948-49.

William Morris Westley
Acting Dean, Jamestown College
Mayor, City of Jamestown

B.A., Jamestown College.
M.A., University of Minnesota.
Superintendent, Public Schools, Sacred Heart, Minnesota.
Professor of Political Science, Jamestown College.


R. W. Witt
Librarian, Jamestown College

B.S. in Ed., M.A. in L.S., University of Wisconsin.
Assistant Reference Librarian, Montana State College,
Bozeman.
Librarian, Pontiac, Illinois Public Library.


SECRETARIES

Thelma Brewer, Secretary to the President

Irene Remboldt, Secretary to the Deans


RECORDERS

Alice Holum, Student

Lilly Schubert, Student

Maria Van Brero, Student

# The Term "Library-College," Genealogy of the Idea: Theory, Practice and Publications

ROBERT JORDAN

## PRECURSORS

Alexandrian Library and "University," founded soon after 322 B. C.

Oxford and Cambridge Universities, tutorial system, 14th century

Daniel Georg Morhof, exponent of universal knowledge, author of "Polyhistory," 17th century

Thomas Carlyle, 19th century

George Rainey Harper, early 20th century

Charles W. Eliot and the "Harvard Classics," 1909

Harvard University, tutorial system, 1912

Frank Aydelotte, inaugural address on honors work and independent study October 22, 1921, and instituted 1922 at Swarthmore, soon followed by Harvard, Princeton, and Smith

Harvard University, reading period, 1927

Wittenberg College, independent learning laboratories, 1929

Colgate University, tutorial-preceptorial system, 1934

Black Mountain College, private office for each student, 1943

| | | *Theory* | *Practice* |
|---|---|---|---|
| 1928 | Louis Shores initiates an interest in the library's educational potential after experiencing the "autonomous course" program at Antioch College | quasi | |
| 1932–1952 | Lamar Johnson, books, articles and practice at Stephens College as Dean of Instruction and Librarian | quasi | quasi |
| 1934 | Louis Shores, speech at Chicago Century of Progress Exposition, first use of term "Library-Arts College" | pure | |

| Year | | Theory | Practice |
|---|---|---|---|
| 1940 | Harvie Branscomb, publishes *Teaching with Books* | | quasi |
| 1956 | Patricia Knapp, private proposal | quasi | |
| 1957 | Robert Jordan, private proposal (inspired by Lamar Johnson) | quasi | |
| 1958 | Thomas Minder, private proposal | quasi | |
| | John Harvey, begins teaching "Library-College" theory | pure | |
| 1960–1962 | Patricia Knapp, activities at Monteith College aimed at involving the faculty in instruction in the use of the library as one of the liberal arts | | quasi |
| 1961 | Thomas Minder, initiates a two-year study of the library's role in engineering education at Pennsylvania State University | quasi | |
| | John Harvey, publishes critique of American academic libraries pointing out their failure to follow ideas of Johnson and Branscomb | quasi | |
| | Florida Presbyterian College initiates inter-semester winter term for independent work. | | quasi |
| 1962 | Robert Jordan, proposal, later discovered Shores had preceded in theory; first use of term "Library-College" | pure | |
| | Robert Jordan and Virginia Clark, organize the "College Talkshop" at Kenyon College, on the experimental college and the Library-College | | |
| 1963 | Thomas Minder, initiates a series of faculty colloquia at Pennsylvania State University designed to involve the faculty in instruction in library use | | quasi |
| | Lee Sutton, attempts to organize a Library-College in Iowa | | |
| 1964 | Louis Shores, organizes the Wakulla Springs Conference to introduce plans for a library-centered college at Florida State University | | |

| | | Theory | Practice |
|---|---|---|---|
| Spring 1965 | Stafford North initiates a radical new program at Oklahoma Christian College, Oklahoma City, that includes a carrel for every student | | quasi |
| May 1965 | *Library-College Newsletter* begins publication, edited by Robert Jordan, Patricia Knapp, Daniel Bergen, Louis Shores, Lee and Mildred Sutton, George Bailey, Theodore Samore, John Harvey and Gilmore Warner | | |
| June 1965 | Daniel Bergen, organizes a conference on the Library and the College Climate of Learning at Syracuse University | | |
| September 1965 | John Tirrell, initiates a radical new program at Oakland Community College, Union Lake, Michigan, for 4,000 students | | quasi |
| December 1965 | Jamestown Library-College Workshop organized by Dan Sillers and Robert Jordan, with Louis Shores, Lamar Johnson, and Patricia Knapp, Joint Chairmen | | |
| Spring 1966 | James Nixon (student) initiates the "Special College," a student-staffed unit at San Francisco State College based on "resource coordinators" rather than faculty lecturers. | | quasi |
| December 1966 | Drexel Institute of Technology sponsors Library-College Conference led by Theodore Samore | | |
| 1967 | Florida State University, opening an autonomous library-centered college | | quasi |
| September 1967 | Robert Gaylor, responsible for initiating a program at Oakland University in which the library assumes complete responsibility for the freshman year program of 50 students | | pure |
| 1967 or 1968? | Dan Sillers converts Jamestown to a Library-College | | pure |

# PART ONE

# The Ideal Library-College

# The Library Arts College, A Possibility in 1954?[1]

*LOUIS SHORES*

THE SPONSOR of any untried plan, no matter how worth while, faces at the outset two discouraging types of criticism. There are first those reactionary critics who defend the *status quo* by hurling charges of charlatanism or radicalism at any proponent of change, without pretending to examine the proposal itself. And then, there are those who will listen kindly and tolerantly to the presentation of a reform, and at the conclusion dismiss it as Utopian and fanciful.

To the first group of critics the sponsor of the present plan can merely say solemnly and with all the sincerity at his command that he honestly believes the changes he proposes are vital to the education of young men and women and therefore important to society. It is somewhat easier to tell the second group of critics that the library arts college idea is not new, that it has been predicted for over a half century, and that trends in current college reform point inevitably to the consummation of the plan, possibly before the assigned 1954 date.

Every librarian has used the Carlyle quotation, "The true university is a collection of books." That pioneer historian of pedagogy, Gabriel Compayré, commenting on Abelard's ability as a lecturer, prophesied the downfall of classroom methods over a half century ago, when he wrote in his epochal work:

> Human speech, the living word of the teacher, had then an authority, an importance, which it has lost in part *since books, everywhere distributed, have, to a certain extent, susperseded oral instruction*. At a time when printing did not exist, when manuscript copies were rare, a teacher who combined knowledge with the gift of speech was a phenomenon of incomparable interest. . . .[2]

[1] Reprinted from *School and Society*, Vol. XLI (January 26, 1935), pp. 110-114, first delivered at the Chicago Century of Progress Exposition, 1934.

[2] Gabriel Compayré, *The History of Pedagogy*. Boston: D. C. Heath & Co., 1901, p. 75.

3

How much more strongly Monsieur Compayré would have stated this thought had he lived to witness the replacement of the single-text-book method by the modern reserve book system can only be surmised.

If time permitted, a series of statements by educators and librarians culled from writings and speeches of the last half century and arranged chronologically could be presented here to support the contention that the education of the future will inevitably be a library education, that is, an education which will be centered in the library. A few such quotations may suffice. For example, in the National Education Association proceedings of 1889, the U.S. Commissioner of Education, W. T. Harris, was quoted as declaring, "The school is set at the task of teaching the pupil how to use the library in the best manner—that, I take it, *is the central object toward which our American schools have been unconsciously tending.*"[3]

The president-elect of the American Library Association quoted President Harper, of the University of Chicago, as follows:

> That factor of our college and university work, the library, fifty years ago almost unknown, today already the center of the institutional intellectual activity, half a century hence, with its sister, the laboratory, ... *will by absorbing all else have become the institution itself.*[4]

Nor have these remarks come from educationists alone. In 1916, Librarian Richardson made a startling substitution for Mark Hopkins on his end of the log when he declared:

> It is conceivable that a university should be a university, and a student get a university education if the university consisted only of a library and a student, without a lecturer, tutor, or preceptor, or *research professor,* or librarian—absolutely only a student and a library on a desert island.[5]

We pass by the hosts of criticisms directed against the American college during the two decades following Librarian Richardson's observation, omitting such readable if not absolutely accurate books as Upton Sinclair's *Goose-Step* and Abraham Flexner's *Universities,* for the words of a college professor and a college student.

---

[3] N. E. A., Addresses and proceedings. Washington, National Education Association, 1889, p. 26.

[4] Charles H. Compton, "The Library in Relation to the University," *Library Journal,* Vol. 35 (November, 1910), p. 503.

[5] E. C. Richardson, "The Place of the Library in a University," *A. L. A. Bulletin,* Vol. 10 (January, 1916), p. 8.

4

The professor is Carter Davidson writing on the "University of the Future":

> The faculty and the better students find the lecture and classroom recitation repetitious, boring, and a waste of time; the inferior students feel that lectures are hard to understand, and that classroom recitations are too rapid, failing to make clear the more difficult problems.[6]

The student is Kenneth Roberts' University of Michigan composite who when asked if he could suggest a remedy for the lack of scholarship in the "lit" school shot back:

> I certainly can! I came here to study and if somebody'd tell me what to study, I could do more by myself, in my own room and in a library, than I could by tramping around to a lot of lectures. . . . I don't get much of anything out of classes. . . .[7]

If these few quotations appear to deal harshly with the conventional college and the sacred faculty college librarians humbly serve, look at what current reform has done to American higher education. The 31st yearbook of the National Society for the Study of Education lists 128 reforms which differ only in the degree of instructional responsibility placed on the library. Whether the innovation is styled honors reading, as at Swarthmore, or autonomous courses, as at Antioch, whether the teacher appointed to instruct is called tutor, as at Harvard, or preceptor, as at Princeton, or even professor of books, as at Rollins, whether courses are abolished, as at Chicago or Olivet, and comprehensive examinations instituted, the educational department fundamentally affected is the college library. Current college reformers have at last begun to realize that the material unit of cultural education is the book, and that actually, as well as oratorically, the library is the liberal arts' laboratory. Only the conception of the library as the college and the college as the library remains prerequisite to the birth of the library arts college.

Just how do these trends affect us as college librarians? In the first place, I should like to make a distinction between educational librarianship on the one hand and research librarianship on the other. This is

---

[6] Carter Davidson, "University of the Future," *North American Review,* Vol. 231 (March, 1931), p. 513.

[7] Kenneth Roberts, "Murmuring Michigan," *Saturday Evening Post,* Vol. 206 (1934), pp. 82-83.

fundamental because I believe the two (education and research) are as incompatible in the library as they are in education.

The notion is rapidly gaining ground in college circles that a good researcher is not necessarily a good teacher. Indeed, there are those courageous enough to declare positively that the instructor engaged in research is invariably a poor teacher. No small part of the blame for the inferiority of undergraduate instruction can be traced to the fact that every American college is anxious to become a university engaged in research. The college president is forever exhorting his faculty to produce because he knows he can interest foundations in studies much more easily than he can in that intangible something called "good teaching." As a result, the college neglects its real job—the training of young men and women. If the truth were told, a high positive correlation would be found to exist between the amount of time and energy expended by the college faculty on research and the amount of time and energy devoted by the students to extracurricular activities. Mutually bored by the learning process as carried on in the classroom, the instructor seeks fame and advancement through research, and the student left to his own resources, endeavors to while away the four years as pleasurably as possible in the fraternity houses and stadia.

It is not the purpose of this paper to disparage the recent movement to create research librarianships. So long as American universities continue to produce tons of studies, useful and otherwise, each year, there will be need for research libraries and their staffs, whose duties will include the acquisition and organization of printed material *ad infinitum,* and the provision of even larger quarters for their accommodation.

Far different is the function of the educational library, such as the average undergraduate college should have. Its collection should be highly selective and definitely limited in size and scope. Whereas the research library's book selection problem may be solely one of acquisition, the educational library will be equally concerned with elimination. As protection against the nuisance of research ambitions, the college collection should have a maximum, say 35,000 volumes, imposed upon it, beyond which its collection may *never* expand. Each year the college may undertake to purchase 500 new titles, on condition it weed out 500 old works from its collection for discard or for presentation to some ambitious research university endeavoring each year to report a bigger and better library. In this way only the number will remain static; the

6

educational library's contents will always include the basic books, plus an ever-changing collection of ephemeral material. The result will be a highly serviceable educational library with abundant material to furnish a true culture to young people who want it. Another result of this selectivity will be to eliminate the necessity for providing expansion in college library buildings. Contrary to the Carnegie standard, I see no reason for planning future expansion in a college library building, if those responsible for book selection do a full job.

With the collection definitely limited in size and the actual titles standardized by some such basic list as the Shaw list, the acquisition and organizational duties in the college library will be reduced considerably and rendered largely routine. For example, it is entirely likely that college titles will be purchasable completely classified and cataloged, or that perhaps the H. W. Wilson Company will issue book catalogs cumulatively in which each college will be able to indicate its own holdings. In any event, it is very unlikely that the services of a highly trained cataloger and classifier will ever be needed in an educational library.

The question then arises what, if any, will be the librarian's duties? Primarily, the professional librarian will be instructor. The positions of librarian and professor will merge. Every college instructor will be library trained; every college librarian will be either a professional instructor in some field or a semi-professional housekeeper performing the necessary routines accessory to library education.

With this preliminary interpretation of higher educational trends, it is now possible to look at the library arts college of 1954. A somewhat more detailed description of the plan has been placed in Professor Phelps' hands, and no doubt his comments will elaborate the bare outline given here. The plan resulted from the writer's undergraduate experiences, which, like those of many other college students, convinced him he could learn much more in the library reading than he could by attending most classes. Since then, the plan has gradually developed an ambition to undertake undergraduate instruction to a small group of college men with a selected book collection of not over 1,000 titles, three library-trained instructors, and a small amount of equipment.

At the outset it should be realized that the library arts college is merely the logical culmination of such current trends in American higher education as are exemplified by honors courses, comprehensive examinations and other reforms of the last decade. Unencumbered by outworn appendages, the library arts college benefits from advantages minimized by the transitory experiments of today. It differs from the conventional college in at least five essentials.

In the first place, the library arts college reverses the conventional college's practise of compulsory, regular class attendance supplemented by voluntary and irregular library reading. The library arts college student is definitely scheduled for supervised reading periods and permitted to ask for a class meeting whenever he feels his readings have failed to answer questions. The supervisor of the reading period is a library-trained subject-matter instructor. When the student reports to the history reading room for his history reading period, he finds there a history instructor thoroughly trained in library methods, who, among other things, combines the duties of the history instructor and the reference librarian.

In the second place, all instructional quarters, like classrooms, reading rooms and laboratories, are concentrated in the campus' one educational building—the library. A plan for such a building drawn to scale is available among my notes for anyone who cares to examine it. In general, the drawing calls for four units, one for each of the three subject divisions—humanities, natural sciences, social sciences—and a fourth for administrative and general reading quarters.

In the third place, the instructional scheme employs a principle of the Lancasterian schools which influenced American educational development in the early years of the nineteenth century, and which disappeared only because of improper conditions. Briefly, the principle calls for upper-class students to tutor lower-class students. This practise is mutually beneficial since it insures individual instruction for each lower classman and excellent training for each upper classman. Beginning teachers frequently attest they learned more about their major subject the first year they taught it than they learned in all their undergraduate study. Obviously, when a student has to know his lesson well enough to make it clear to an underclassman, that student not only masters his material, but what is more important, he is able to express himself clearly on the subject. This type of tutoring, reinforced by faculty supervision, supplemented by occasional inspirational lectures, and checked by the requirement of frequent papers, tests and a final comprehensive examination, will do much to restore scholarship to its rightful place on the college campus.

8

As for the faculty members themselves, they will be library-trained, subject-matter experts, but not specialists in the restricted sense which describes our present research professors who teach only incidentally. The chemistry man, for example, will not be so thoroughly consumed by his interest in colloids that he will be unable to supervise a general reading course in science. It is very likely that he will be able to express an intelligent opinion on James Joyce or the Herbartian influence in American education. But above all, he will be vitally interested in the young people he teaches, study their development as zealously as the average researcher does his experiment, and be as proud of the young man or woman he graduates into society as the average scientist is about a notable discovery.

Finally, the curriculum, instead of including a great number of frequently unrelated courses, will represent a carefully planned reading program intended to acquaint the student with man's accomplishments of the past and problems of the present. There is no more direct method of achieving this end than through reading the right books. To the library-trained instructor of the future is assigned the task of selecting intelligently the right book for the right student at the right time. That American Library Association motto might well be adopted as the major aim of library arts college education.

# Vitalizing a College Library Summary and Implications [1]

*LAMAR JOHNSON*

THE ADAPTATIONS of library service to student needs at Stephens College have, of course, developed in terms of a particular college serving a specific student body. It would, therefore, be unfortunate if the administration of another college decided uncritically to adopt in toto the Stephens library program. On the other hand, library developments at Stephens do have a variety of implications for other colleges. For some college, one feature of the program may be significant; for another, a second feature may apply; and possibly a third college may after study find that with few changes the total program can be adopted.

In the pages which follow are suggested possible implications of library developments at Stephens for other colleges interested in increasing the value of their libraries to their students. These implications are presented in broad and general terms; the details of practice at Stephens have been stated in earlier chapters; the details for other colleges would have to be worked out in terms of the situation at a particular college.

1. Books are a constant and natural part of the student's environment. At Stephens books are not confined to the central library but are distributed to division libraries, to classrooms, to the infirmary, to the parlors of residence halls, and to individual student rooms. No matter in what room or hall she may be a student is never more than a few steps from a book collection, for all of the 23 college buildings (with the exception of the heating plant and the auditorium) have libraries.

The administration does not, however, distribute books without discrimination. Rather students and faculty members select books appropriate to the needs of the group using a particular room. If a girl is

[1] Reprinted from *Vitalizing a College Library*. Chicago, American Library Association, 1939, pages 114-122.

in a chemistry laboratory, the books she is most likely to need are either in the laboratory or directly across the hall in the science division library; if she is in the scene shop, the books on stagecraft are there for her to consult; if she is in the office or classroom of her social problems instructor, books to which reference is made will in all probability be in the adjacent social studies division library. On the other hand, if a student is in her residence hall and wants a good book to read (just for fun!) she may turn to a novel, a biography, or a travel book in her dormitory library—or perhaps she turns to a book on her hobby, a collection of plays, or a poetry anthology in the personal library located in her own room.

The purposes of making books a constant part of the student's environment are:

a. To increase the value of books by making them available to students when they are most needed.

b. To make students increasingly aware of the resources of books, both for reference and for pleasure reading

c. To develop in students the "habit" of having books around them.

The administration of any college interested in giving books a more important place in the student's surroundings must make certain that instructors and students select books for each special collection (whether it be in a classroom or in a sorority house, in the infirmary or in an individual student room) in terms of the needs of the individual or group which will be using the collection. If titles for special collections are selected thus, and if the college is willing to duplicate a reasonable number of titles (those needed in two or more libraries), any college can find methods of making books a part of the student's environment.

2. The concept of library materials is expanded to include not only books, periodicals and other printed materials but also pictures, music scores, phonograph records and motion pictures. Since libraries at Stephens aim to help students meet their individual needs and since the libraries are not limited by tradition, it is natural that the staff should consider the use of materials other than books. Loan collections of framed reproductions for use in student rooms, a sizable collection of phonograph records for loan or for use in a soundproof listening room, and extensive provision of motion pictures for class use are among the library facilities and services provided in addition to printed materials.

11

Colleges interested in extending library service to fields other than books, periodicals and bulletins can select from the areas of art, music and motion pictures those materials which will best serve the needs of their students. A considerable number of colleges will wish to consider particularly the use of microfilms.

3. Teachers and librarians merge into a single instructional staff. Instructors examine their objectives and their methods to determine how, in their teaching, the library can contribute to more effective student attainment; instructors work with their students in the presence of books in the central library as well as in classroom and division libraries; and instructors instruct students in the effective use of books and libraries. Librarians not only visit classes and participate in department and faculty conferences, but they also actually teach sections of basic courses. Their interest in and experience with instruction places them in a position to give students particularly effective guidance and aid during their library hours. Because in the college libraries they observe the problems and achievements of students and because they are primarily concerned with learning and teaching (rather than merely with the details of library administration) librarians aid instructors by informing them of the interests and the aversions, the difficulties and the achievements of their students.

If a college administrator were in his own institution interested in recognizing the essential unity of library work and instruction he might raise the question, "What is the situation at Stephens which has resulted in such recognition—not only by the administration and by the library staff, but more particularly by instructors?"

The answer to this question has at least two essential parts:

First, the college administration has given more than lip service to the recognition of the relationship between library work and instruction. By establishing the dual position of librarian and dean of instruction, and by emphasizing the instructional implications of his position, the college administration gave the original impetus to recognition of the place of the library in the instructional program.

Second, the librarian announced to the faculty a new policy of individualizing library administration to the needs of each teacher and of each course. To make this possible instructors were invited to report what the library staff could do to aid them to attain their instructional objectives. Teachers' reports were not only received—

they were acted upon. By its deeds the library staff indicated its desire to abandon traditional practices and to plan library service only in terms of student and teacher needs. This attitude on the part of the library staff, plus the interest of librarians in teaching (as evinced by their visiting classes, taking part in faculty meetings, and actually teaching classes) met the approval of instructors and led them to think of the library in terms of their work.

4. A college in which teachers and librarians merge into a single instructional staff requires a new type of library-instructional building. The library program at Stephens has been limited by a physical plant planned in terms of the usual library-instructional relationships. For example, when it became clear that the faculty wished to work with students in the presence of books, it was impossible to accommodate all instructors in the central library. It was therefore necessary to take books to teachers and students—to classrooms, to offices, and to division libraries. The use, advantages and problems of classroom and division libraries have been discussed. It seems quite clear that with the physical plant available the advantages of these decentralized teaching libraries far outweigh their disadvantages. The faculty has, however, from the first sought a plan which would retain the advantages and eliminate the disadvantages of division and classroom libraries. The chief advantage of such libraries is the opportunity offered instructors to work with their students in the presence of books. This advantage must be retained in any ideal plan.

The chief disadvantages of classroom and division libraries are those associated with a scattering of resources. For example, a student is preparing a paper on "The westward expansion." Most of the materials she needs will be with the American history books in the social studies library. The works of Hamlin Garland, located with the literature books in the general library, are however, valuable for a paper on the subject. The social studies librarian reminds the student of the resources of the general library and advises her to read this author's books. The libraries are, however, two blocks apart, and there is always the danger that because of the inconvenience the student will neglect some materials which she would use if they were more conveniently at hand.

Any ideal library plan must bridge the gap between libraries and at the same time provide opportunity for instructors and students to work

13

together with appropriate books. Relatively early in the library program the staff began thinking in terms of a new type building which would serve these ends. By 1935 the basic idea of a combined library-instructional building was being discussed.[2] In 1937 the administration was sufficiently certain of the need for a completely new type of library- instructional building to invite a committee of distinguished educators and librarians—to work with the staff and an architect on a building specifically designed to meet the needs of a college which recognizes the essential unity of instruction and library work.[3]

The committee began its work by visiting Stephens for several days. During this visit committee members observed classes, studied the physical plant of the college, and conferred with students and instructors, librarians, and administrators. Following this preliminary visit the committee formulated statements of function which must be served by the building.

It was quite clear to the committee that the new building must house instructional activities in all courses which are primarily book laboratory courses.[4] Instructors and students must be given the opportunity of working together with books. When this happens, the classroom actually becomes a book laboratory, a conference room in which emphasis is placed upon learning. This demands a new type of room arrangement and furnishing.

At Stephens the committee found that libraries are functioning work units—not storehouses for books. Books which are not used become mere dust-covered fillers of space; they detract from an active book collection. In any building planned, provision must be made for the storage of little-used titles. Work of the committee has progressed sufficiently to make possible several general descriptive statements:

1. The building will provide space and facilities for instruction in all courses which are primarily book laboratory courses.

---

[2] Johnson, B. Lamar. "Books all around them." *School and Society,* Vol. XLI (May 18, 1935), pp. 676-81.
[3] Paul Packer, Dean of the School of Education at the University of Iowa; W. M. Randall, Professor in the Graduate Library School at the University of Chicago; Joseph L. Wheeler, Librarian at the Enoch Pratt Free Library in Baltimore; and Charles Rush, Librarian at the Cleveland Public Library.
[4] At Stephens all courses are laboratory courses. In art, laboratory materials consist of paper, brush, and paints; in music, of the violin or piano and the score; in science, microscopes and slides. For most courses, however, books are the basic laboratory materials.

14

2. The building will have no classrooms and no offices. It will, however, have conference rooms for all instructors.

3. Conference rooms will be furnished with comfortable chairs (some upholstered), tables, book shelves and reading lamps.

4. Books will be housed in division reading rooms adjacent to the conference rooms of the division.

5. Since conference rooms are adjacent to reading rooms, and since they are equipped for reading or study, they may be used as reading rooms in the evening when they are not being used as conference rooms. This point is important, for it makes possible the efficient use of space: during the day when conference rooms are in use, division reading rooms will accommodate students; in the evening, when instructors are not using conference rooms and when library use is heaviest, conference rooms may be used for reading.

6. Provision will be made for removing from reading rooms books which are seldom used. These books will not be destroyed but will be stored in basement stacks.

Colleges interested in recognizing the essential unity of library work and instruction need not delay such recognition until a new type building is available. In fact, experience at Stephens suggests the advisability of postponing building until experimentation indicates just what type of building is needed for the particular college.

# A Suggested Program of College Instruction in the Use of the Library[1]

*PATRICIA KNAPP*

The fundamental aim is to induce students to use books for many sorts of purposes. The first is for work, for study. When the freshman enters college, he comes for the first time into contact with a library designed primarily for that purpose. The character of his work requires him as never before, seriously to search for the right books, and to use them wisely. Immediately there is a temptation to instruct him in the use of the library directly. That is often done in lectures during Freshman Week, or in a short orientation course. While it is the obvious thing to do, it is really putting the cart before the horse; a student does not learn by being told how to use the library, but by using it. Moreover the responsibility for the use of books should not be centered in the librarian, but in the faculty. All the work of instruction must be so organized that the student will need library books. Once that need is clear to him, he is in a mood to learn how to supply it. His first efforts will be awkward and clumsy, as all first efforts are, but if he is convinced that he is going to use the library frequently in the work in science, in literature and the humanities, as well as in the social studies, he will want to know how to use it effectively. Moreover his use of the library is not merely a phase of some fraction of his course of study; it becomes an inevitable part of his whole college experience.[2]

The statement above serves as the text for this paper. Though it appeared almost twenty years ago, planned instruction in library use at the college level is still limited to one or two orientation lectures and perhaps a "library paper" in Freshman English. The shortcomings

---

[1] Reprinted from the *Library Quarterly,* Vol. XXVI (July 1956) pp. 224-231.

[2] Henry M. Wriston, *The Nature of a Liberal College* (Appleton, Wis. Lawrence College Press, 1937), pp. 64-65.

of this kind of program have long been apparent and are still perfectly obvious.[3] Competence in library use, like competence in reading is clearly not a skill to be acquired once and for all at any one given level in any one given course. It is, rather, a complex of knowledge, skills, and attitudes which must be developed over a period of time through repeated and varied experiences in the use of library resources.

The usual college-level instruction in library use is simply incapable of developing such competence. At the same time, current developments in higher education indicate an increasingly urgent need for good instruction in library use. These developments may be summarized as follows:

First, educators recognize that accelerated social change requires education, particularly general education, be concerned not with solutions for today's problems but with methods of solving tomorrow's. Since the library is an important storehouse of social resources for the solution of problems, the need for training in library use is underlined by the current emphasis on problem-solving in education.

Second, as Lacy points out in a recent article on the role of the college library, the function of scholarship itself has changed: "The acquisition of new knowledge by empirical methods has replaced the preservation and transmission of a heritage as the central function of scholarship. Western learning has become a dynamic force of change."[4] Here, again, the emphasis is on methods rather than on static solutions. And here, again, the library, viewed as the storehouse of the resources for scholarship, has a central role. Furthermore, lest it be assumed that the changing function of scholarship affects only the minority of our college students, Lacy may be cited further:

[One] effect of this penetration of non-academic life by scholarship is that higher learning is no longer the ornament of a small elite. The very operation of our society requires that higher learning be shared by tens of millions who need its skills and technique to participate effectively in the economy or to act intelligently as citizens.[5]

And, finally, the overwhelming increase in the quantity and diver-

---

[3] William Vernon Jackson, "The Interpretation of Public Services," *Library Trends,* Vol. III (October, 1954), pp. 88-94. A few universities offer advanced courses, but the practice does not appear to be widespread.

[4] Dan Lacy, "Tradition and Change: The Role of the College Library Today," *Essential Books,* Vol. I (October, 1955), p. 29.

[5] *Ibid.,* p. 30.

sity of library materials sets an increasingly high premium upon skill in their use.

Because of these developments, we must agree with Stanley Gwynn that the skill required to use a library—that enables the student to select from that portion of society's memory which is represented by his college or university library collection those materials pertinent to his problems—seems to be one of the skills which the college exists to provide. Indeed, I will boldly assert that in these times and in our present state of learning, with the records of knowledge multiplying at an almost uncontrollable rate (bibliographically speaking), the knowledge and skills we have been talking about actually constitute one of the liberal arts.[6]

Why, then, do we still rely on the orientation lecture and the Freshman library paper to provide this necessary skill? Several reasons may be suggested. In spite of the changes in scholarship that Lacy notes, most college instructors are content-oriented rather than method-oriented. In spite of the emphasis upon problem-solving, they tend to teach what they know rather than ways of finding out. For all the lip service they give the library as the "heart of the college," many instructors do not recognize its full potentiality. Those instructors who have themselves acquired competence in library use have acquired it through advanced work in one special field. Not appreciating the fact that higher learning is no longer the ornament of a small elite, they may assume that only those students who go to advanced work will need library skills. Or perhaps they assume that most college students acquire these skills as a natural by-product of their work in content courses.

College librarians know better. College librarians know that many students use only the reserve collection and that very few go beyond the authors and titles specifically recommended by instructors. On the other hand, librarians must share the blame for the fact that after fifteen years the college faculty is still not "teaching with books" in the style proposed by Branscomb.[7] Too often college librarians have squandered their most creative efforts on devices to stimulate extra-curricular use of the library. Those who have given serious attention to the problem have, as a rule, recommended the inclusion of new courses in an already crowded curriculum. They have advocated that the library staff teach

---

[6] Stanley E. Gwynn, "The Liberal Arts Function of the University Library," *Library Quarterly*, Vol. XXIV (October, 1954), p. 316.
[7] Harvie Branscomb, *Teaching with Books* (Chicago: Association of American Colleges, 1940).

18

these courses because "(1) it is competent to explain the library, whereas many faculty members are not themselves sure of library techniques, and (2) the contacts established probably make the students more willing to ask questions subsequently."[8] It is hard to imagine two arguments less likely to convince the faculty that instruction in library use is an essential element of the curriculum. Librarians, then, are to blame for using the wrong reasons.

This paper contends, further, that they are not even arguing for the right things. With Wriston, it maintains that instruction in the use of the library will be really effective only if it is presented by the regular teaching faculty as an integral part of content courses in all subject fields. Only if it is presented in this way will it appear to the student to be functionally related to the real business of higher education. This is the only method which gives proper recognition to the complexity of the competence the student should acquire. This is the only method which meets the criteria for effective organization of learning as noted below.

Clearly, however, the problem of developing such integrated instruction is not a simple one. It requires careful thought in the determination of objectives. It requires the planning of learning experiences in accordance with recognized principles of learning. The co-operative efforts of most of the faculty must be enlisted in working throughout the processes involved, and the whole faculty must be committed to the fundamental value of the project. The librarian's task is most important at this point, for the success of the whole undertaking hinges upon his success in educating the faculty to an appreciation of competence in library use as "one of the liberal arts."

Basically, the job is an individual one, to be done independently in each college. This paper, therefore, will merely offer suggestions. These suggestions will be concerned with (1) the formulation of objectives for instruction; (2) relevant principles of learning and curriculum construction; (3) the development of appropriate learning experiences; and (4) possible procedures for the librarian.

## OBJECTIVES

In the process of formulating objectives for instruction in library use the college should consider the whole range of knowledge and skill desirable for the student to achieve. Some are probably achieved

---

[8] Jackson, *op. cit.*, p. 192.

through present instruction. For instance, students probably acquire understanding of the contribution of the classic works in the major subject fields of general education through presently required general education courses. They presumably acquire elementary skill in the use of card catalog and *Readers' Guide* in their Freshman English course. They understand, interpret, and evaluate whatever reading they are *required* to do.

We are concerned here, however, with suggesting what seem to be important objectives that are probably not now achieved. These may be listed as follows:

1. The student should understand the nature and function of reference materials; that is, the kinds of information available in various kinds of sources in special subject fields.

He is introduced to general reference works in Freshman English, and, if he does advanced work in one field, he may be introduced to the relevant tools. He probably is not made aware of the fact that such sources are an important part of the literature of every subject field.

2. The student should appreciate the value of the library as a source of information.

This objective may be unteachable, and, in any case, is probably a corollary of the first. But, in the light of the findings of the Public Library Inquiry—it is worth stating separately.

3. The student should understand the nature and function of bibliographical apparatus; that is, the way books, periodicals, government documents, etc. are listed, so that (a) the general reader can find his way around in the literature of a field, and (b) the subect specialist can keep up with new developments.

4. The student should understand the function of literature-searching as a necessary step in problem-solving, as simply the use of an important and available resource.

These two objectives echo our introductory comments on the problem-solving skills currently emphasized in general education and on the acquisition of new knowledge currently emphasized in scholarship. It is probable that only graduate students or, at best, honors students at the undergraduate level achieve them.

5. The student should be able to locate and to select various kinds of library materials from the subject approach, such as:

a) General background reading matter
b) Critical and evaluative material, reviews, etc.
c) Opinion, theory—both sides of controversial issues
d) Factual data, information, how-to-do-it material, etc.
e) Materials for illustration, aesthetic enjoyment, etc.

Present undergraduate instruction gives the student very little experience with the subject approach to the library and almost no opportunity to select his reading. Here, again, the objective echoes the recognized importance of providing skills for tomorrow's problems.

The objectives as stated above result from an attempt to indicate the implications for library instruction of current trends in higher education. Much more specific formulations are necessary before the objectives can be used as guides to the planning of learning experiences. For recommended procedures in working out such specific formulations, the reader is referred to Tyler.[9]

## RELEVANT PRINCIPLES OF LEARNING AND CURRICULUM CONSTRUCTION

Tyler's booklet is useful, too, for its brief and lucid presentation of currently accepted principles of learning relevant not only to the formulation of objectives but also to the planning of learning experiences. For example, he says:

> For a given objective to be attained, a student must have experiences that give him an opportunity to practice the kind of behavior implied by the objective. That is to say, if one of the objectives is to develop skill in problem solving, this cannot be attained unless the learning experiences give the student ample opportunity to solve problems. Correspondingly, if another objective is to develop interest in reading a wide variety of books, this objective cannot be attained unless the student has opportunity to read a wide variety of books in a way that gives him satisfaction.[10]

It should be noted that this statement relates to *planned* learning experiences, to curriculum-making. The very existence of the college library on the campus obviously provides "opportunity" of a sort for the student to learn to use it. But the student who is never stimulated to go

---

[9] Ralph W. Tyler, *Basic Principles of Curriculum and Instruction* (Chicago: University of Chicago Press, 1950).
[10] *Ibid.*, p. 42.

beyond the reserve-book collection is not getting a *planned* opportunity really to use the library. The student who is always told what to read is not given the opportunity to develop skill in selecting his own reading. The student who is always given author and title is not given the opportunity to acquire the skill of finding information about a given subject.

Tyler states further that there is

> evidence that learnings which are consistent with each other, which are in that sense integrated and coherent, reinforce each other; whereas, learnings which are compartmentalized or are inconsistent with each other require greater time and may actually interfere with each other in learning.[11]

It is no wonder that the brief experience with the Freshman library paper is forgotten in the flood of textbooks, reserve books, required readings, and optional reading lists. Furthermore, when the library paper is presented, as it so often is, as a kind of busy-work exercise, unrelated to content courses—which seem to the student to be the meaningful aspect of college—its inefficiency may be explained by another of the principles expounded by Tyler: "A second general principle is that the learning experiences must be such that the student obtains satisfactions from carrying on the kind of behavior implied by the objective."[12]

Finally, Tyler describes a theory of learning called generalization which viewed learning as the development of generalized modes of attack upon problems, generalized modes of reaction to generalized types of situations. Judd and Freeman showed that many types of learning could be explained largely in terms of the learner's perceiving general principles that he might use or developing a general attitude towards the situation or method of attack which he could utilize in meeting new situations.[13]

In this instance we want the learner to perceive general principles which are implicit in the nature of the literature and its organization in all subject fields. The general attitude we want him to develop is one of appreciation and interest in making use of this literature. But one cannot generalize from a single experience. The generalization theory of learning, therefore, calls for repeated experiences in which the learner

---

[11] *Ibid.,* p. 27.
[12] *Ibid.,* p. 43.
[13] *Ibid.,* p. 27.

22

can perceive similarities. From this perception he develops general principles and attitudes.

Tyler's application of the generalization theory of learning is revealed in his criteria for effective organization of learning experiences:

> There are three major criteria to be met in building an effectively organized group of learning experiences. These are: continuity, sequence, and integration. Continuity refers to the vertical reiteration of major curriculum elements. . . . Sequence as a criterion emphasizes the importance of having each successive experience build upon the preceding one but to go more broadly and deeply into the matters involved . . . Integration refers to the horizontal relationship of curriculum experiences. The organization of these experiences should be such that they help the student increasingly to get a unified view and to unify his behavior in relation to the elements dealt with.[14]

Here we find the primary justification for presenting instruction in library use as an integrated part of content courses. The student's experiences with the library should have *continuity* throughout the four years of his college education. They should be *integrated* through repetition of unifying principles in more than one course at each horizontal level. And they should provide *sequence* through increasing breadth and depth of the knowledge, skills, and attitudes required.

In summary, relevant principles of learning and curriculum construction indicate that we must plan learning experiences (1) which offer opportunities to *practice* using the library; (2) which are *consistent* with each other and with our desired objectives; (3) which provide *satisfaction* to the student; (4) which enable the student to perceive general principles and develop general attitudes; and (5) which are organized to maximize generalized learning.

## SUGGESTED KINDS OF LEARNING EXPERIENCES

The assignments suggested here are not unusual in the liberal arts college. Typically, however, they are not deliberately planned to provide the student with experiences in the use of the library. They are not deliberately organized to increase the student's library knowledge and skills. It is the library aspect which this paper seeks to emphasize.

Since the first-year college courses are introductory, an appropriate

---

[14] *Ibid.,* p. 55.

objective is that of developing skill in the selection of background reading. In Freshman psychology, for example, the instructor often gives the student an optional reading list to accompany the text. The purpose of this optional reading is not specified, nor is the student guided in selecting from the list. Presumably the instructor hopes that his list will make up for the gaps in the background of some students, stimulate others to pursue special interests, and enrich the learning of others. These several purposes should be specified in class discussion. Individual differences in background, interest, reading skill, and purpose should be identified as criteria which govern selection of appropriate reading. Parallel discussion in Freshman English, identifying individual differences in aesthetic appreciation as well, would produce the desired integration of learning.

Even more important would be assignments designed to provide the student with experiences in locating background reading. A later assignment, again in psychology and in English, might require the student to prepare his own optional reading list. He would be directed in the use of the encyclopedia, yearbooks and annuals, the *Book Review Digest,* and selective bibliographies. He would be expected to understand and defend the criteria used in selecting from these sources.

Other courses usually required in the first year might provide experiences in locating other kinds of materials. In political science, for example, the student could be required to gather references to material on a current political issue. This material would consist not only of general background reading but also of factual information, statistics, and opposing theories and opinions. He would use, with guidance, almanacs and other sources of statistical data, current periodicals and newspapers, the proceedings of legislative bodies, etc.

Integration of learning could again be provided through comparable and concurrent assignments in other Freshman courses. In physics, for instance, the student could be required to locate background readings on a hobby, such as photography, for which physics has relevance. In physiology he might be required to locate factual information and divided opinion on a current health problem such as smoking.

Assignments in the second year should be planned to give continuity and sequence. The humanities course in music appreciation, for example, might require the student to plan his own record library. He would again use the individual criteria for selecting, but this time he would apply them to another kind of material, and he would be introduced to other selection aids, the record guides and the record-reviewing periodicals.

In urban sociology the student might be asked to survey an urban community through the library. He would use census reports and other government publications, newspapers and periodicals, reports of social and civic agencies, and so on. He would identify social and political problems and the forces engaged in dealing with them.

At the upper-class level subject specialization begins. Assignments for all subjects cannot be suggested here, but a few general comments are pertinent. In the first place, the student at this level should be ready to develop understanding of the nature and function of the bibliographical apparatus in special subject areas and of the importance of literature-searching in problem-solving. If his experiences in the Freshman and Sophomore years were properly planned, he would have acquired skill in the location and selection of background reading, factual information, controversial opinion, and theory. He would understand the characteristics of reference sources.

Because of this background, the term paper commonly assigned in upper-class courses can be more meaningful from the library point of view. In the first place, the instructor can use a subject or topic approach and still be confident that the student will be able to locate sound and relevant materials. In the second place, he can justify the requirement that the term paper be supported by a better bibliography than is usually provided.

Another kind of assignment would be equally appropriate to this level of college work and would be even more valuable as a library experience. This is the bibliographical review. It would require the student to locate, select, describe, and evaluate the literature available on a fairly limited topic. He would need to make intensive use of the bibliographical apparatus and organize his findings into a coherent presentation.

Finally, it should be noted that colleges are aware of the danger of over-specialization at the upper-class level and that they guard against this by requiring students to take advanced courses in more than one field. This requirement should provide the opportunity for emphasis upon the general characteristics and function of reference and bibliographical sources. This opportunity should not be lost through haphazard planning of library experiences.

## SUGGESTED IMPLEMENTATION OF THE PROGRAM

At this point the reasoning implicit or stated in the discussion above may be summarized.

Competence in the use of the library is one of the liberal arts. It deserves recognition and acceptance as such in the college curriculum. It is, furthermore, a complex of knowledge, skills, and attitudes not to be acquired in any one course but functionally related to the content of many. It should, therefore, be integrated into the total curriculum. But it cannot be so integrated until the faculty as a whole is ready to recognize the validity of its claim and to implement this recognition through regularly established procedures of curriculum development. Logically, then, the faculty as a body, or through its appropriate committees, must implement the objective. It is probably true, on the other hand, that at present the college librarian is more conscious of the inadequacy of present instruction than is any other member of the faculty. Furthermore, he has the advantage of a broad perspective on the whole curriculum.

For these reasons, the librarian should accept the responsibility of initiating the program, while remaining constantly aware, at the same time, that ultimate implementation must come through the teaching faculty. In other words, the librarian must convince the faculty that library instruction is necessary; he must educate the faculty on the potential role of the library and assist it in planning instruction. And he must do all this with consummate skill and tact. These considerations underlie the suggested steps presented below.

1. The librarian should discuss with sympathetic and library-minded instructors the problem of students' incompetence in the use of the library. He should provide as much objective evidence as is available.

2. If possible, he should persuade some of these instructors to set up experimental assignments which involve library use of the kind desired.

3. He should work with these few instructors individually and as closely as possible in planning learning experiences. He should make the material and personnel resources of the library available as generously as possible.

4. He should use the opportunity afforded in this co-operative work to stress the general values inherent in library competence.

26

5. With the help of instructors thus oriented to the idea, he should draw up an analysis of the problem and a proposed program for its solution.

6. Again with the support of the "educated" instructors, he should present his statement through the library committee, if there is one, to the curriculum committee.

The steps suggested so far are designed to produce a group of faculty members who have become adherents to the cause of library instruction and who, furthermore, understand what library competence is and what learning experiences are effective in helping the student to acquire it. (It should be understood, incidentally, that this process will be a slow one) In the succeeding steps this group may be expected to take over the initiating role of the librarian.

7. The curriculum committee, basing its work on the librarian's presentation, will prepare and present to the faculty a statement which sets forth the basic objectives of library instruction and a proposed program for its implementation in curricular planning.

8. If the faculty as a whole agrees, it will, perhaps, set up a special committee to formulate specific objectives and to indicate specific courses in the curriculum which might provide for them. (Actual units of instruction must be individual, but the faculty as a whole or through its curriculum committee would agree on objectives.)

9. The librarian, or members of the library staff as assigned, will work closely with individual members of the faculty in planning and preparing learning experiences wherever they appear in the curriculum.

## CONCLUSION

This paper has presented an analysis of the objectives of instruction in the use of the library, some examples of possible ways to achieve these objectives, and some suggested steps to implement an over-all program. These are not to be considered as final answers but rather as suggestions regarding the kind of thinking which must be involved in finding answers. Instruction in the use of the library has been described as one of the "persisting problems [which] need vigorous new attack."[15] This paper does not lead the attack, but it may join others in supplying some of the ammunition.

---

[15] Jackson, *op. cit.,* p. 188, quoting K. J. Brough, *Scholar's Workshop* ("Illinois Contributions to Librarianship," No. 5 [Urbana: University of Illinois Press, 1954]), p. 175.

27

# The "Library-College"— A Proposal[1]

*ROBERT JORDAN*

NEVER IN AMERICAN educational history have librarians taken the leadership in designing a liberal arts college, yet librarians often picture themselves as being in the "heart of the institution." Winslow Hatch, of the Clearinghouse of Studies on Higher Education, provocatively states:

> While the library is typically described as the heart of the campus it is often more like the liver for it is often a large structure whose significance lies in the potential it may not be called on to release. What is proposed here is that the library be made the heart of the academic enterprise, in fact, and that it be made to deliver something like its full potential.

Despite this potential, in actuality, college librarians are all too often preoccupied with the mechanical aspects of their responsibilities, to the exclusion of the educational. How many college librarians read the important articles in the leading journals of higher education? Even more ridiculous is to ask how many faculty see the leading journals of librarianship. Yet if we claim to be equals to the faculty, if we claim to share a common educational concern, if we believe the library is as important as we say it is, then there should be some degree of overlap, some common ground in the reading of faculty and librarians. In the words of Arthur McAnally:

> Librarians are not good teachers, nor do we know enough about the effects of reading, research practices, teaching with books, and similar subjects important to successful partnership in the teaching and research process. . . . *We are woefully ignorant of the methods and goals of education.* This is a dangerous condition when education is in such a state of flux. All libraries are basically educational agencies, yet this fact is not dealt with adequately in most library schools. The problem is particularly acute in academic libraries because the librarian must understand higher

---

[1] Excerpts from a working paper prepared for the College Talkshop, Kenyon College, June, 1962.

education as a whole as well as the role of the library in teaching and research.[2]

Only a faculty convinced of the need to adopt the proven methods of academic excellence, and willing to function as a unified team, can create a dynamic and effective educational environment. After all, it is the function of the faculty to produce *change* in the minds of the students, and to educate students who will be capable of meeting a world that knows no constancy except that ever accelerating change is inevitable. If college faculties do not evidence some degree of receptivity to change, instead of resisting any dent in their privileged layers of departmentation, rank, status and traditional methods of lecture-recitation, then the entire edifice of higher education will soon become a complete anachronism, no longer capable of meeting today's challenges.

Administrators are far more receptive to new ideas than the typical faculty, but are far too often "operators," more concerned with detail rules, requirements and administrative authority than the basic need to develop students with the capacity for courageous, critical, and imaginative thinking. Also, administrators are too far separated from the scene of educational activity.

Perhaps the liberal arts college, as traditionally conceived and operated, is beyond patching. The entire history of civilization indicates the persistence of institutions despite the obvious need for drastic change. Yet, it is almost always true that existing institutions do not change rapidly enough to keep up with new requirements. Perhaps a fresh start is needed, preserving the spirit and the philosophy, but not the forms, of existing institutions of liberal education. New solutions are needed, incorporating selections of the best from the past with entirely new techniques and systems. The anachronisms of the past would be rejected.

In recent years an imposing literature has developed around the subject of excellence in the liberal arts college, and the need for implementation of the proven techniques of education. This growing sentiment has become increasingly focused toward the need for fundamental reforms in higher education and particularly for new experimental colleges. Yet, for all the brave words very few old institutions have made any basic reforms, and very few new liberal arts colleges have been founded. And of those few founded in recent years, none (possibly with one or two exceptions) have been thoroughly experimental, not to com-

---

[2] McAnally, Arthur, "Privileges and Obligations of Academic Status" *ALA Bulletin*, XXIV (March, 1963), pp. 102-108.

pare with the group of "far out" colleges founded in the '20's and '30's (Bennington, Goddard, Sarah Lawrence, Black Mountain, Antioch, Reed, St. John's, Bard, etc.). While higher educators continue their dialog, high schools radically removed from the traditions of the past are being constructed. For example, one new high school is essentially and basically a *library*; in other words, there is no library within a school, but rather, the library *is* the school. Surrounding the "resource center" are carrels for each student, with faculty meeting with students either in small discussion groups or very large lecture rooms, and traditional classrooms almost non-existent.

Potentially, librarians have the opportunity to play a unique role, as the most dependable exponents of educational philosophy, because of their broad general interest, and because of their intimate relation to the foundation of the educational process, library use. In contrast to the typical narrow devotion of the faculty member to his subject, the librarian is devoted to the general aims of education and to the students, as individuals. The librarian, in his instinctive appreciation of the value of independent study, of controversial ideas, of self-motivation and outside reading, possesses, potentially, the most dynamic and least parochial concern for the general education of the individual student.

But librarians need courage and self-confidence above all else. They need to end their congenital inferiority complex and assert their unique mission as the guardians of liberal education. Their potentiality needs to be nurtured, intensified, and focused.

Educational authorities would welcome a new quality college. Very, very few completely new independent colleges have been founded in the past few years. Usually new colleges are attached in some way to an existing institution and thus limited in some ways to existing patterns. The new colleges founded in the '20's and '30's are responsible for more lively new experimentation than the colleges founded in recent years. This decade of the '60's is the logical time for such a new quality college. It would be watched with intense interest and would receive much encouragement. Accreditation groups, for example, would probably ease the difficult initial years in their welcome for a new institution which would carry out the practices that accrediting teams have been recommending, often without success, for many years.

There is only one approximately contemporary example of this prediction — Monteith College, which is a subsidiary, but autonomous part of Wayne State University, nonselective in its admissions (admitting

30

an average cross section of Wayne State entrants), but turning out students who are often disturbing to complacent Wayne State faculty members in their enthusiasm and capacity for analytical criticism.

What a shame that 50 years after President Harper's prediction that we do not have hundreds of integrated *Library-Colleges*. Perhaps new ones will spring up soon.

It is my firm conviction that the integrated *Library-College* should be a small institution, not more than 30 faculty and 500 students, to keep all dimensions, architectural and human, on an intimate and comprehending scale.

31

# The College Host Center and the Library-College[1]

*ROBERT JORDAN*

Plan. — The College Host Center is a proposal for a new type of institution that would provide the physical plant for a group of small autonomous colleges. The Library-College would be one of these small autonomous colleges based on complete integration of the library and the faculty.

There are many facilities and services that are provided far more efficiently when organized on a large scale basis; often these are beyond the capability of a completely independent small college. Yet there is increasing evidence that liberal education is facilitated when conducted in small groups, so the entire college can operate as one cohesive unit with each student and faculty member in personal relationship.

How resolve this dilemma? How provide the economy and manifold advantages of centralization and specialization in a large complex university with the educational efficiency of face-to-face relationships in small units?

Actually, this idea is one of the oldest in higher education, being the basic plan at Oxford for many centuries. However, until recently, no university in America has organized more than one undergraduate co-ed liberal arts college on any one campus. It is of course almost universal to have a number of partially autonomous professional and graduate colleges associated together in one large university.

Some recent examples of colleges within colleges are the Associated Colleges of Claremont, the University of the Pacific, and Stephens College. The most promising experimental college, Monteith, at Wayne State, is an autonomous college within a university.

A basic split in responsibility for physical plant and for the aca-

---

[1] Excerpts from College Talkshop, Kenyon College, June, 1962.

32

demic program can be suggested. A College Host Center would provide the buildings, the centralized housekeeping facilities, a centralized major research library, and other complex and large scale services to a group of 20 to 40 small autonomous liberal arts colleges, each entirely independent and free to experiment and devise its own curriculum and academic program. Such a community of colleges would furnish a fertile basis for cooperation, support, and mutual stimulation. Each autonomous college would lease its physical facilities from the Host Center but would be self-sufficient financially, administratively and pedagogically (within a specific contractual framework).

Administration-faculty tension, so fertile a soil for conflict on almost every existing college campus would be drastically reduced. With a maximum limitation on the size of each autonomous college, and with the specialized facilities, services and maintenance provided by the College Host Center, it would become feasible and desirable for the faculties of each autonomous college to undertake the entire operation of the college without the need for a separate full time administration.

The establishment of a College Host Center would make a major contribution towards the revitalization and perpetuation of that distinctly American institution, the liberal arts college. The founding of new autonomous colleges would be easier and more realistic by several orders of magnitude—all that would be required would be 50 students and sufficient tuition or other income to pay the rental fee to the College Host Center and faculty salaries. There would be no problem of raising millions of dollars, finding, and building a campus; these have been such insurmountable problems as to almost completely stifle the founding of new liberal arts colleges.

One of the most inhibiting problems faced by entirely new and independent colleges is that of accreditation, not being recognized by graduate schools until the college has been accredited, and not achieving accreditation until recognition by graduate schools (a simplified description). This vicious circle could be moderated through the strength and influence of the College Host Center.

Not only would it be much easier for a group of inspired faculty to establish and operate their own new college, but it would be equally easy to dissolve a college before institutional rigor mortis has set in. A brief life span would be expected and counted upon by all concerned. Only the College Host Center, essentially a collection of buildings rather than an educational philosophy, would be durable and

33

permanent. Such a brief life span would facilitate correspondence with the ever accelerating requirements of a world that is rapidly changing.

A distinctive advantage of the College Host Center concept would be the provision for a practical base for urgently needed controlled experiments in educational effectiveness. Large scale campus-wide controlled experiments have not hitherto been possible, because of the impossibility of assigning students on a random basis to different colleges. With the concept of the College Host Center it becomes possibile to admit some students to the College Host Center, then assign them randomly to the associated colleges participating in any particular study.

*Autonomous Liberal Arts Colleges.* — Each of the 20 to 40 colleges associated with a College Host Center would vary widely in educational philosophy and technique. It has been conclusively demonstrated that colleges with distinctive institutional cultures are more effective educationally than the completely neutral and colorless. Some possible emphasis might be:

1. Traditional classical studies
2. Inner life, spiritual regeneration
3. Regional planning and development
4. Community development
5. Creative writing
6. World peace
7. Non-commercial TV and radio broadcasting to the community
8. Language and area study
9. A college without a faculty but with highly selected students and an outstanding library
10. Library-College (integration of library and faculty)

*Requirements Established by the College Host Center* — the autonomy of each of the associated liberal arts colleges would be limited only by certain physical, mechanical and programatic paramaters designed to facilitate a common community of colleges. Such requirements might include:

1. Maximum of 500 students on campus at any one autonomous college
2. Minimum of 50 students
3. Maximum of 25 full time professional faculty on campus at any one time
4. Required dissolution of each autonomous college after twenty years (Comparable to the required retirement of individuals at age 65)
5. A uniform calendar
6. Full year operation

34

7. No intercollegiate athletics
8. No fraternities or sororities
9. Minimum size for the basic selected library associated with each college.

*Centralized Facilities Provided by the College Host Center* — These would include:

1. A major research library of 1,000,000 or more volumes, for the use of both faculty and students of the autonomous colleges. The selection for this research library would be made entirely by its own staff of subject specialist—librarians.
2. Testing facilities
3. Counseling: educational, vocational and psychological
4. Exhibition area
5. Museum
6. Art gallery
7. Gymnasium, swimming facilities, etc.
8. Theatre, large auditorium: world renowned lecturers, drama and concerts
9. Large and complex laboratory facilities

*Architecture*. — Emphasis would be placed on simple multi- purpose designs, making minimum use of permanent walls and maximum use of operable soundproof partitions. Since the building shells themselves would not be able to reflect the educational philosophy of each successive college-tenant, every effort would be made to design the buildings in such a way as to make it possible and easily feasible to apply decoration, in the way of fabric, color, sculpture, paintings, etc., so as to completely redesign the environment but using the existing shells of buildings.

*Finance*. — In operation, each College Host Center would be entirely self-supporting, and perhaps self-liquidating, if necessary, from rental fees secured from each of the associated colleges. There is every reasonable prospect that the demand for rentals would be very high. With the source of rental income divided among so many individual colleges, the possible foundering of any one or two colleges at any given moment would not endanger the financial solidity of the College Host Center. With such a sound financial base, it would not be an overwhelming task to secure the initial capital investment. The College Host Center could of course solicit additional contributions, above the level needed for year to year continuation of existing facilities to be used for capital improvements such as increase in the size of the central research library.

35

*Location.* — An ideal location would be a new completely planned community, comparable to Levittown, Greenbelt, Carmel, but of even larger size, on the order of 100,000 to 500,000 people. Such a new completely planned community might include several clusters of colleges, plus varied industries. There is an urgent need for a demonstration or model urban community on a large scale, exemplifying all our present capability for designing beauty in our lives instead of ugliness and vulgarity.

*Summary.* — In a world plagued by conflict and confusion, by loss of personal identity and community, this proposal would restore to the years of higher education the satisfactions and growth-potential of face-to-face relationships of a small tightly knit purposeful group. At the same time there would be unlimited access to all of the facilities and advantages of a large complex institution. The entire structure would be deliberately organized in such a way as to encourage adequate response to the rapidly changing requirements of a dynamic world and avoid the perpetuation of mediocrity or institutional stagnation.

The continuity and stability of the College Host Center would moderate by several degrees of magnitude the present almost unsurmountable obstacles frustrating the founding of new colleges: site, finances, buildings, recognition, recruitment of students, accreditation.

# The True University...

LOUIS SHORES

FIVE SEPTEMBERS after next, nearly every American of Freshman age will be going to college. Most of them will be attending junior college close to home. The next greatest number will overcrowd state and public universities, or what we have smugly begun to exhibit as "multiversities." Those who can, of the rest of the young people, will enroll in private colleges, no longer small. The United States in 1970 will be embarked upon the noble course of providing all of its people with not only an education but with a higher education. History records that no other nation in the world, before or now, has done as much. Those of us who believe universal higher education will bring better understanding between leaders and followers, and thus a more creative society, want this stately commitment to succeed.

But there are hazards ahead. Before another Rickover comes along with a bestselling "What's Wrong with American Higher Education" it behooves us to anticipate such events.

The first of these hazards is numbers. If present organizational patterns persist the total student body will continue to be handled in mass. Every registration period young people line up to be treated like so many ID numbers. The so-called required courses with captive classes rival Oklahoma Sooner conditions as lower classmen scramble to register before the "standing room only" signs appear. For other courses, students shop supermarket fashion, heeding fraternity brothers about reputations. "He's stiff," or if you need an "A" to bring your quality points up, here's a crib. As an effort to counsel is made by the administration, the situation improves, but by the very nature of present campus organization advice tends to be "by the number."

A second hazard is in the present evaluation of learning. The standard measure of higher education is the *classroom contact*. When the student receives a bachelor's degree and has a transcript he has evidence that he has been higher educated.

Class contacts, depending upon the concentration of the student and the consecration of the instructor are expected to stir incentive,

37

flash a bit of inspiration, reinforce some stern reading, perhaps even to point the way for further search and exploration, and with none of these purposes can there be any difference. Only the timing comes into question. Should these contacts precede, follow, or coincide with independent study? Is it necessary to meet precisely at nine every Monday, Wednesday, Friday, or could one of these meetings or all of them be dispensed with and another form and calendar of faculty-study relations be established, one tuned to the individual rhythms of differing human beings?

Evidently, some of these hazards and questions are concerning campuses. In the spring of 1964 at Wakulla Springs, Florida State University invited ten experimenting colleges and universities to share their innovations. From Michigan came representatives of three state universities, Michigan to report on its Dearborn, Michigan State on its Oakland, Wayne State on its Monteith. Here were universities, each with upward of 25,000 students, moving to create innovating campuses and small colleges. From California came two educators, one from the new state university at Santa Cruz planned for 27,500 students to be taught in small colleges; the other from the private University of Pacific, already operating as a cluster of small colleges. All five of these universities, moving toward individualizing instruction, were concurrently replacing classroom contacts with independent study or honors reading.

Five small colleges displayed models of independent study almost completely freed from class contacts. Antioch, long famous for its "autonomous courses" gave evidence of heavy reliance on library reading. Stephens, the junior college for women that for many years centered its learning in a "vitalized" library, had more recently augmented the hard cover with a range of "resources" from tape through long-distance telephone that brought famous voices out of Congress in session into student assembly. There was Parsons in Iowa which had declared any college can educate the gifted; send us the rejects. And then there were two new Florida colleges, one — Florida Presbyterian in St. Petersburg, which in four years had selected a library and proceeded to illustrate the power of library learning by compelling the suspension of classes for one whole month each January to insure uninterrupted reading; and New College in Sarasota, still in the dreaming stage, still to prove that it would turn its back on the "class contact" measure of a student's learning, break with the subject specialist's segmented approach, and probe deeper into the library art by enlisting a faculty of teacher-librarians and librarian-teachers. And finally,

38

host Florida State University revealed a proposal for a prototype college of 500 students which, if demonstrated successful, might, within five years, have 25 replicas on a campus for 15,000 students. The prototype would center its academic life in the library, make reading the central learning activity, offer the heterogeneous student a new breed faculty member, a bibliographically committed counselor.

So at Wakulla Springs, eleven American higher educational institutions offered these solutions: Reorganization, no matter how large the student body, into small manageable college units; abandonment of the teacher-centered class contact as the mode of learning in favor of student-centered library reading as a basis for individual independent study.

It has taken academic librarians a long time to see the opportunity and challenge in this trend. To most of us, independent study means, at the utmost more library money, to buy more books, to hire more staff. It suggests that we must improve our service to faculty and students. But this improvement, primarily, means inducing more faculty attention to book selection and use; to speeding our technical processes so that faculty orders will be shelved and cataloged more promptly.

The faculty members who use the library are our strongest allies in gaining support for library appropriation, material, personnel. But above all they most nearly approach our concept of proper teaching and learning. As long as we contend for our ancillary retriever position the most we can hope to do is encourage as many of our colleagues as possible to rely less on classroom contact and more on library reading in student education.

But let us speculate what would happen where the entire faculty consisted of librarians committed to a primary rather than an ancillary role in education. These librarians could be former classroom instructors who were "library oriented" and had increased their bibliographic competence informally or through a formal program in library science; or they could be librarians who had abandoned their ancillary complex and relegated their housekeeping and retriever duties to the subordinate place of ways and means. Actually, the line between so-called classroom and library faculty would be erased and there would be no artificial basis for establishing status as in many institutions today because one teaches in a classroom rather than in a library.

Let us suppose, further, that in this academic community the only educational building is the library, and that the collection includes all formats of the generic term book — hard cover, paperback, celluloid film, rubber disc, magnetic tape, radio or television wave, computerized or manual learning program. The library annex includes laboratories, studios, shops, conference rooms, seminars, classrooms, auditorium, and gymnasium. This complex of campus learning facilities will be called The Library; that is the true university of these days.

Among these books will be all the good and great ones. The *Harvard Classics,* the *Chicago Great Books* and not over 50,000 titles in hard cover and paperback, newspaper and magazine, serial and government publication, map and globe, picture and object, disc and tape, radio and TV program, in representations of all formats. Only the number of titles will be static, for every new title added an old title must be discarded.

Next to the Good Books in importance is a careful selection of Reference Books. With R books, librarians and library-minded classroom instructors can teach the half of knowledge — where to find it. With R books, too, a beginning can be made in pursuit of the other half — the synthesis and interpretation of knowledge.

Complementary to the Good and to the Reference books will be found a kaleidoscopic selection of other subjects and other forms of material. Music will be represented by phono discs and tapes; art by paintings and photos, sculptures and architectural models, by transparency and opaque projection. Language and literature will be implemented by listening post and audio laboratory, utilizing the latest transmission facilities to convert some student carrels into "stations." Professors' lectures will be canned for transmission only when considered worthy of replacing an older "lecture" already available in hard covers.

Now let us make the biggest supposition of all. There are no subjects, courses, class contacts as we now know them. The basic learning activity is reading. Reading may be broad in overview subjects like history, philosophy, man, the cosmos, communication, or narrow on topics like Napoleon, Existentialism, the nervous system, incunabula, or may cut across several subjects and topics near or far apart, not only as in our integrated courses like physical science where we interrelate chemistry, physics, geology, meteorology and mathematics, but as if there were a real unity to the universe and therefore appropriate to seek for relationships between chemistry and music and among such topics as magnetism, chioroscura, and demography. In short, through library reading the student would be offered the opportunity to synthesize knowledge, to provide for himself a gestalt of the many compartments into which academic man has divided the universe.

What I am doing is amplifying the original Carlyle quotation. Since the library's collection of books represents a significant summary of man's knowledge, it is the only true curriculum for learning. Rather than constructing a curriculum first and then buying books to support it the true university first selects a good library and then lets the curriculum follow it. Instead of scheduling classes regularly in circumscribed subjects and assigning readings in the library irregularly, or not at all, reading is regular, group meetings voluntary, as students feel a need to confer about their library work.

Perhaps the nearest thing to the present regular class contacts will occur in the "Half of Knowledge, knowing where to find it." Rather systematically the librarian will teach by word of mouth, through demonstration, through audio and visual media the use of books and libraries. But this instruction will be done from a perspective far different from that which often renders today's one-hour course in library use impotent. It will be an exciting adventure in searching man's record of thought and deed in order to solve some riddles of the universe.

To bring this "True University" into being we will have to begin with a reconstructed faculty. The individual faculty member will become a cross between today's most educationally-minded librarian and most library-minded classroom instructor. The latter will be one who does not consider his specialty substantive and the library art of knowing where and overviewing knowledge a sort of intellectual slumming. The former will be happy to be relieved of most of the housekeeping and retriever routines of which so many librarians have made a national holiday. He will be challenged to assume the educational role so long denied him. With these two basic teaching functions of "finding where" and overviewing knowledge the new library faculty can achieve what the old classroom faculty could not — a True University.

A look at the experimenting colleges suggests Carlyle's True University has all but arrived. All that is needed is the courage for a university to declare that it is a community of independent study, of reading students under the guidance of a library faculty with a well-selected book collection. This is a True University dedicated to the higher education of all the people. This University commits itself above all to becoming a great library, so that it may communicate individually to its students "the diary of the human race."

# The Library-College—
# A Merging of Library
# and Classroom [1]

*ROBERT JORDAN*

FEW WOULD QUESTION the necessity of liberal library resources to carry out the aims of liberal education. But only a few colleges have highly effective liberal arts programs along with ample library resources per student (the two are almost invariably found together).

Despite lip service and considerable pressure in the post-sputnik baby-boom years to "bear down" on college students, most of them are only slightly exposed to "liberal education" or "libraries." Students involved in "general education" programs still go through the motions of attending a few required courses, memorize lecture notes, read textbooks and cram for exams. The notes and lectures are often not essentially different from those in high school. Libraries are seldom used, or are used in a purely mechanical way, as in picking up a reserve book, or "doing" a required book review.

The world demands, as never before, world citizens, with a sensitivity and responsibility far beyond the narrow boundaries of a profession. In professional training, our times demand more than ever the perspective and balance of individuals who can at least understand how to relate or modify their own often transient specialty in relation to other disciplines, and who know how to use a variety of informational resources to keep up to date. Vocational boundaries shift rapidly and overlap complexly so that increasingly employers are turning to those with sufficient versatility to adapt quickly to any situation on the job, be it computer programming or public relations.

---

[1] Reprinted from Dan Bergen and E. D. Duryea, *The Library and the College Climate of Learning.* Syracuse University, School of Library Science and School of Education, 1966.

Single-tracked specialization, without some of the orientation and critical faculties of the generalist, is insufficient. We might postulate a law as specialization increases, so does it become increasingly necessary that each specialist have the foundation of a general education, else how can he retain any balance and sanity in the increasingly complex world around him, how can he resist bigotry, war hawks, and greed?

The faculty have often lost the vision of an integrated basic education. Teaching undergraduates, especially freshmen, has been relegated to the bottom of the academic status procession, and lags behind research, publication, outside consulting, and intensive subject specialization in glamor and dollar reward.

## Need for New Educational Techniques

Perhaps a fresh start is needed preserving the spirit and philosophy but not the forms of existing institutions of liberal education.

Faculty are resistant to change and to serious interest in educational technique despite increasing evidence that the philosophy and ecology of higher education is of basic importance. Even the word "pedagogy" is in disrepute. In the words of Jerome Wiesner:

> Education has been the most backward field in modern society. It is surprising that scientists and technologists in universities have failed to apply our methods to our own profession. Modern teaching aids have rarely been employed either in general education or in the universities. The process of invention has been ignored.[2]

Francis A. J. Ianni, Director of the Division of Education Research in the U. S. Office of Education said that the

> ... resistance of educators to the product of research is unmatched in other fields ... the average time lag between research and its application is estimated at two years in medicine; in education the process often take 30 years or more.[3]

Only a faculty convinced of the need to adopt the methods of academic excellence and willing to function as a unified team *including the library on the team,* can create a dynamic and effective educational environment.

---

[2] An address to the Federation of American Scientists, April 29, 1965.
[3] *New York Times,* November 17, 1964, p. 48.

## Campus Culture and Peer Pressure

The campus environment or gestalt maintained by faculty and students cannot be allowed to develop by chance. The basic building blocks of the college must be deliberately structured so a sufficiently pressing campus life can come into existence with each new class.

The physical pattern of the campus, the appointments, facilities and relationships between campus areas are all-important. A dreary over-crowded library filled with crotchety over-worked technicians and duplicate copies of old textbooks could in itself undermine any possibility for developing a dynamic campus culture.

If the faculty is structured into discrete departmental entities, jealously expanding little empires of research, then it will be impossible for a liberating general educaton to flourish, or for that matter genuine scholarship. It is quite possible and in practice not unusual to have a lavish faculty-student ratio, and *not* to have a liberating education, if the faculty are largely uninvolved with the students or the teaching process. Many of the faculty caught in the snares of publish-or-perish might as well be in Timbuctoo for all their contribution to the intellectual ferment that must be developed among their own students. Often such faculty fail even to learn the names of their student assistants, and have nothing to do with students on the campus or in community life. The university would be much better off if such faculty were replaced by books and programmed learning, by the lectures of master faculty on videotape, and by faculty whose main interest would be involvement with students in a variety of direct and personal ways, informally and formally, on and off campus.

## Seven Elements of a Liberal and Liberating Education

Seven mutually dependent variables are postulated for the evolution of a liberating education:

1. Library-Independent Study Orientation
2. Constant Innovation
3. Extensive Library Resources
4. Enthusiasm
5. Relevance to the World
6. Student Equality with Faculty
7. Viable Size

44

(1) LIBRARY-INDEPENDENT STUDY ORIENTATION, RATHER THAN LEC-
TURE-RECITATION-TEXT

The basic structure of most colleges is biased towards oral instruction—lecture recitation and faculty control, in contrast to independent
study with the library and faculty functioning as an integrated team. We
are still inhibited by the traditional form of education characteristic of
Western European universities since their founding 800 years ago —
the master and his disciples. In the limited world of Twelfth Century
Europe students came from over the continent to hear the liberating
lectures of such men as Abelard and Bernard. In that age of relatively
few books a few men could store all of the world's accumulated
knowledge in their collective minds.

This is no longer possible, by several orders of magnitude. The set
of faculty experienced by any one student is not sufficiently varied in its
knowledge or enthusiasms to reflect to a satisfactory degree the intricate
relations, variety and changes of the actual world.

Nor are textbooks the answer. Even the *Saturday Evening Post*
devoted an editorial to the mediocre quality endemic to textbooks:

> Many textbooks are strangely dull, lifeless and bear striking
> resemblance to one another. . . . They betray a basic lack of
> confidence in presenting this country full face because some of the
> warts may show. . . . How can our young people understand the
> difficulty and the complexity of the world they live in if we over-
> simplify its problems and water down every controversy to suit
> the popular taste?[4]

A liberal education — the development of knowledge acquiring
skills — is essentially a *liberating* education. It is no coincidence that
the origin of "liberal" and "library" are the same, both derived from the
Latin word "liber" which means "free," "grown," "grown-up," and
"book." Here we have, in a nutshell, a definition of liberal education,
and we find the "liberal" is intimately mingled with "book." A sophisticated knowledge of the method for the exploitation of a good library
can itself form a major part of a definition of "liberal education."

Often in conventional lecture and recitation the instructor is "reaching" or is engaged in a dialog with only a few students. The restricted
parameters of lecture and recitation favor indoctrination rather than
liberation. Instead, a wide variety of educational techniques should be

---

[4] "Our Watered-Down School Books," *Saturday Evening Post* (April 28,
1962), p. 92.

employed to maximize educational effectiveness for each individual student according to his personality and needs. These would include independent study, large and small groups, student-led discussions, programmed learning, tutorial programs, community projects, and preparation of syllabi and reading guides, all with faculty participation as an expert among equals, rather than as a preacher spreading the "word." In such a situation the library would automatically become the focus *in actuality* of a common yet independent search.

Students would be independent of any rigidly prescribed lock-step of classroom, lectures and grades. But this does not mean that students would be locked up by themselves in study cells. Man is a social animal; the mutual stimulation, support and exchange of ideas in groups, large and small, are exceedingly important for perspective, for sanity itself.

The "library-college" with faculty and library losing their separate identity but merging into one integrated team is a logical development from the cooperative search by student, faculty and librarian among the resources of the college and the nation.

In general there should be a drastic decrease in hours spent enduring classroom lectures but an increase in direct faculty involvement with students in all other ways.

(2) CONSTANT INNOVATION AND VARIETY IN PEDAGOGY AND CURRICULUM

The common search made with constant receptivity to innovation should be a basic first principle. Innovation should not be accepted reluctantly or grudgingly. The only constant must be an almost restless change in an effort to provide a microcosm of the world. We have yet to find a satisfactory technique to insure that the institutions of our culture, including schools, do not lag dangerously behind the demands of our times.

It is better to innovate too much than to become ossified. Almost any change is better than no change at all. The very process of making a change is an explicit message to the students of a basic and specific concern. It is human nature to respond positively when attention is paid to us; the recognition itself is more important than the kind of attention.

The faculty must develop a deep-seated concern for the possibilities of pedagogical innovation — the techniques of education. After all, this is their profession. There is a tendency to assume that anyone with a Ph.D. is qualified to teach as we tend to assume that anyone 18 years

46

of age is qualified to make love. Often in both instances this is only technically true.

## (3) EXTENSIVE LIBRARY RESOURCES

To support the common *search* and to explore the possibilities of various educational techniques the library resources must be rich in delight, surprises and variety. The curriculum must be based on exposure to the widest possible variety of ideas, in breadth and depth, primarily from a library collection plus personal libraries assisted by exposure to the community.

In contemporary American colleges and universities there is a striking degree of correlation between size and variety in the library and quality in the institution. The colleges most prominent in educational innovation and quality (two mutually dependent variables) are the very colleges that excel in the variety of their library resources in relation to student size. Jordan ranked a large group of American colleges and universities on the basis of 16 criteria bearing on excellence in the educational process:

1. Faculty influence on students.
2. Lists of "best" colleges as selected by professors and administrators.
3. Proportion of graduates receiving doctoral degrees or other graduate distinctions.
4. Faculty salaries.
5. Strong position in defense of academic freedom.
6. Emphasis on the academic program as contrasted to the social and athletic programs.
7. Receptivity to experimental educational activities.
8. Independent study programs involving freshmen.
9. Intellectual climate.
10. Proportion of faculty in scholarly or professional organizations.
11. De-emphasis or elimination of grades.
12. Elimination of faculty rank.
13. Elimination of faculty departments.
14. Average score of entering freshmen.
15. Proportionate size of scholarship funds.
16. Strength of continuing education program.[5]

Based on the above criteria, the top-ranking colleges and universities in the country were Amherst, Antioch, Bennington, Bryn Mawr,

---

[5] Jordan, Robert. "Library Characteristics of Colleges Ranking High in Academic Excellence." *College and Research Libraries*, Vol. XXIV (September 1963), pp. 369-76.

Carleton, Chicago, Columbia, Dartmouth, Goddard, Goucher, Grinnell, Hamilton, Harvard, Haverford, Mount Holyoke, Oberlin, Princeton, Radcliffe, Reed, St. John's (Md.), Sarah Lawrence, Swarthmore, Vassar, Wellesley, Wesleyan, and Yale.

It is almost precisely these same 25 schools that have the largest library resources per student including per student library salary expenditure.

The library resources should be large enough that students can borrow large quantities of books (or other types of materials)[6] for an entire quarter in order to encourage the life-long habit of maintaining and using a large personal collection in areas of personal interest. Fortunately there is a direct correlation between student loans for non-reserve or non-required reading and books purchased per student. If a student would learn nothing more from his years in college than this, his education would be worth far more than the majority of contemporary B. A.'s. The library should be rich enough that the central collection can easily and freely spill over according to student and project interest into all campus areas — dormitory living quarters, project and faculty offices, etc. Compared to the cost of faculty salaries, this would not be prohibitively expensive. On most contemporary college campuses the conversion of half of all faculty-lecture-hours into books in the library would do the job easily. Instead of 100 books per student typical in the better liberal arts colleges, there might be 500 books per student. Instead of 50,000 books for a college of 500 students, there might be 250,000 books, including extensive duplication. Thus, if each student would withdraw 50 books at one time — there would hardly be room for any more in a dormitory room — only 10% of the collection would be withdrawn.

We should heed the advice of John Ciardi:

> At the heart of every college is one essential and indispensable building—the library . . . . . If our students could use the library without supervision, you'd need only one man to run a college—a janitor to keep the place swept up.

Suppose during the past 100 years at Syracuse that one-third of

---

[6] In the absence of one satisfactory word to define all methods for permanently preserving language and pictures, the word "book" will be used hereafter. Although books are still the most important single means of communication all other media would be used to the limit of their capability. It is bad enough to have a dichotomy between the library and the faculty without having one *within* the library as well between the various media of communication.

48

the money allocated for faculty salaries had instead been spent for the library, and that 3/4 of all faculty classroom lecture-hours had been eliminated. Currently, instead of $15,000,000 yearly for faculty salaries, this would be cut to $10,000,000, with $5,800,000 spent on the library instead of $800,000. The result would have been a collection exceeding that of Harvard in quality and size. Can anyone dispute that Syracuse would be better off today, indeed, would have a reputation as one of the three or five greatest universities in America? Even if no program or curriculum reforms were instituted, the superior efficiency of the faculty attracted would more than make up for the cut in their numbers. Students would hear some extraordinary effective lectures in very large groups, on videotape, but in general would endure far fewer classroom-lecture hours. But would this have been a loss? With an increased proportion of faculty time devoted to a variety of tutorial and student projects, students would have been encouraged to develop individual initiative, resourcefulness and ability to use the library.

A major qualitative improvement of the library at the expense of faculty expansion is a potent and painless way to reform the campus. Money spent for the improvement of the library can be a permanent investment reaping increasing dividends.

(4) ENTHUSIASM

The educational process will remain an exercise impinging on only a fraction of brain power if faculty and students are not enthusiastic and dedicated about what is going on in their minds. Our major life enterprises must combine emotional attachment with the use of reasoning potentialities. Without an emotional commitment, we will learn only a fraction of what we are capable of learning and it will be impossible to imprint, integrate, or absorb what we learn in any lasting or meaningful way. Educational experiences should come at times when the student's mind is receptive and eager. This receptivity and eagerness must be supported by a general campus attitude of serious involvement and excitement. An emotional "engagement" to the learning process should pervade campus life.

It is not unusual for a person from 25 to 30 years of age to have attended school continuously for 22 to 27 years, with 90% of the time spent in the familiar classroom-lecture-textbook-recitation syndrome. His counterpart a hundred years ago might have had half as many years

49

and one-quarter as many days of schooling and usually not in a continuum.

It is a source of amazement to the rest of the world that so large a proportion of the population in the U. S. spends so large a proportion of its time for so many years going to school. Far too often these years merge into one bland repetitious plodding blur. What kind of personality can tolerate and survive such a relentless grind? How many of the restless geniuses of the past would have submitted themselves to such time serving?

Despite the challenge of such men as Robert Hutchins, David Riesman, Paul Goodman, and Fritz Machlup the relentless lock step in junior high school, high school, college and university remains one of the seldom challenged assumptions in education. The result? Commonly children begin to lose interest during junior high school and by high school their sensibilities have already been numbed in the endless plodding of unrelieved mass schooling with curriculums aimed at a low common denominator rather than at the individual. Even if the educational aim is high it is seldom aimed at the individual.

Many are aware of the waste of human talents because of wrong skin color, sex (only one-tenth of doctoral degrees are granted to women), cultural deprivations, poverty. But human talents are also wasted *because* the young person is in school. Far too often the years of school after the first few grades are as much *de-education* as education. Schools should assist in the full and constructive use of human resources, rather than provide a custodial substitute for failure in the economic system. Often the student goes through the motions, gets adequate grades, learns to parrot back what the teacher wants to hear and just as promptly forgets. No person should be encouraged to remain in school when using only 1% to 5% brain power.

Such mass education is spurious economy. Additional expenditures on education of 10% or 20% might double effectiveness by bringing in a wide variety of experiences and materials (including a wealth of library resources) aimed at the individual.

In contrast to lecture and textbook which can aim only at a common denominator the tutor (or bibliographic counselor) and library can match intellectual resources and individual.

(5) RELEVANCE TO THE SURROUNDING WORLD

It is difficult to maintain student interest or for education to be meaningful and lasting without a high degree of relevance to the surrounding world. Social responsibility and constructive creativity cannot flourish in isolation from real life. The typical college curriculum is narrow and time-serving or so broad as to be meaningless.

A library is an essential link between the college and the complexities of the world, to provide the keys to the worlds of the past, present and future. Just as one travels with a guidebook, so the college should always "travel" through time with the guidance of a strong library.

There are many educational techniques for relating the educational process to real life problems and activities. This is a valid principle at any educational level, nursery school through graduate college. One of the most effective medical schools, Western Reserve, is based on a continuing identification of the student through the years in medical school with the personal, social and medical problems of one family. Work-study, travel-study, and internship programs are other techniques. The deliberate commitment of the college to the elimination of such gross social evils as racial segregation is another technique. Perhaps Antioch was first to leap from sanctioning to participation as an institution in social action. In the words of Antioch's President Dixon:

> It is then necessary to live our institutional as well as our private lives in ways that show that colleges know with some specificity what these humane values are . . . . Whenever in the conduct of our affairs as an institution and in the implementation of our educational objectives we see an opportunity to lay siege to bigotry and prejudice we will do so in the name of liberal education.[7]

One of the most effective techniques is a structuring of the college curriculum in terms of real life problems and projects.

## (6) STUDENT EQUALITY WITH FACULTY

Where the faculty is the dominating element on a campus, it is easy for them to assume the role of superior beings, approachable only by formal and respectful rituals. Where the library is the key and focal point in the campus environment it is much more difficult for the faculty to maintain a posture of superiority because the silent phalanxes of information on library shelves stand neutrally waiting for exploitation by faculty and students. Just as we are equals before God so are we equals before the resources of a great library. Perhaps this is the key to understanding why the majority of faculty are so reluctant to exploit the

---

[7] *Antioch Notes,* Vol. XLII (September 1964), p. 1.

library — they secretly or unconsciously avoid having their students "show them up."

There is an enormous reservoir of latent potentiality in human beings when treated with respect and dignity as equals. This is brought out most forcefully in industrial experiments abolishing rigidly rationalized assembly lines and highly structured hierarchies in management and control and in effect saying to workers in a factory, "You're on your own. Organize the work as best you can." As reported by *Business Week:*

> At its core is the assumption that the employee is good, intelligent, and willing to work if work will help fulfill his needs. That's at the opposite pole from the assumption that the worker doesn't want to work. The latter assumption leads to authoritarianism and control.[8]

In this unique example of permissiveness and worker participation in management, production soared. The only group within the factory that resisted such diffusion of responsibility was middle level management which seemed dependent on the emotional reassurance of fixed lines of authority.

Another recent example of an amazing sense of responsibility and maturity is the conduct of Negro children in racial demonstrations in the South reported by a Harvard Child Psychiatrist:

> No matter how hard the lives of those demonstrators, many of them are young indeed to be initiating such responsible, nonviolent protests, to be leaders in social change. Moreover, they are acting in a region that considers them not merely children but, as Negroes, the children of children. They persist in spite of retaliatory arrests, brutalities and jailings, and without discernible psychiatric harm or collapse. Modern psychiatry must certainly ask why children subjected to such strains survive so handily, and modern history has no precedent for children directly involving themselves at their own behest in an attempt to change the social and political structure of the adult. In fact, over our entire Western history only the Children's Crusade compares with what is now happening and priests both prompted and led those children of the thirteenth century.... Many of those youths taking part in racial demonstrations are better integrated psychologically as well as racially than the student rioters at Princeton University and Oxford,

---

[8] "When Workers Manage Themselves," *Business Week* (March 20, 1965), pp. 93-94.

Mississippi. They act out of deep moral convictions and in a spirit of sensitivity and thoughtfulness.[9]

In education we have the example of Monteith College whose students achieve outstanding scholarly distinction in contrast to other closely matched students at Wayne. The one potent characteristic of Monteith is its relation with students — a dialog between equals. There is no coddling, no encouragement of the juvenility of inter-collegiate sports or fraternities. There is no censoring of students' private lives. Social, non-purposive contacts are common between students and faculty, "Around . . . an old converted house, there developed a somewhat Bohemian intellectual and arty group . . . with close personal ties to faculty." [10]

Finally, there is the evidence of Antioch College, a leader for a generation in the extent to which students participate with faculty, administration and trustees in developing and guiding the educational process. We are aware of the Berkeley syndrome and its echoes on campuses across the country by students determined to be recognized as individual human beings instead of numbers and to have faculty pay attention to them. But Antioch has not been afflicted with these troubles; in the words of Antioch's President:

> There is at Antioch no suggestion of the sort of hostile reaction of students to their college that seems to be endemic this spring on many campuses. This situation is a direct outcome of our democratic behavior as a community—and is a test of community in the sense that students know that to attack the College is to attack themselves. We have learned that it is the language of dialogue and not of negotiation that best serves our education purposes.[11]

## (7) VIABLE SIZE

Only in small face-to-face groups can a philosophy of equality between faculty and students be successful. It is anti-human and destructive to the creativity and development of the individual to turn colleges into huge impersonal automated factories. Fifty years ago the faculty knew their undergraduates. Now, it is not uncommon for even doctoral stu-

---

[9] Coles, Robert. "Children and Racial Demonstrations," *American Scholar,* Vol. XXXIV (Winter 1964-65), pp. 78-92.

[10] Gusfield, Joseph and Riesman, David. "Faculty Culture and Academic Careers," *Sociology of Education* Vol. XXXVII (Summer 1964), pp. 281-305.

[11] Dixon, James P. *The President's Newsletter.* Antioch College (April 1965).

dents not to be known by anyone so special counselors are appointed to handle requests for letters of recommendation.

Small groups are essential for keeping important basic dimensions — architectural and educational on a human and comprehending scale, instead of the anonymity, alienation, and impersonality so often typical of large educational factories. The strength of the campus culture seems to be closely correlated with educational effectiveness, but it is difficult to develop a vital campus culture on a mammoth monolithic campus. Vital sub-cultures are sometimes developed in such specialized areas as fraternities, civil rights, football, and beat poetry, but seldom around the central goals of liberal education.

### Potential Influence of the Library

The variety and quality of the library is crucially important in reinforcing each of the seven elements discussed above. It would be difficult to sustain independent study, innovation and enthusiasm without infusions of bibliographic riches. A strong library can provide many windows to the outside world. The better the library, the more obvious that there are options to the faculty and texts as sources of wisdom.

The library is in a peculiarly strategic position. If the library in acquisition policy and size is liberating some of the students will inevitably find their way there and will receive a liberal education on their own initiative even though the campus environment does not contribute or reinforce the "bibliographical way" as the primary objective of college — the preparation for life-long learning.

One man who found his way to the library was John Shaw Billings, founder of the Johns Hopkins Hospital, contributor to the development of punched card calculating machines and founder of the first great international scientific index:

> When I was in college 50 years ago, the library was not recognized as a part of the system of instruction. No professor ever referred the students to it or suggested any use of its books. It contained about 8,000 volumes and was open on Saturday mornings from 9 to 12. Each student could borrow two books; many of them did not borrow any . . . .
>
> During the long summer vacations, I used to make a burglarious entrance into the library where I had long hours of enjoyment. I had no wise librarian to guide me—I simply tried every book on the shelves, skimming and skipping through the majority,

54

and really reading those which interested me, and if there had been a librarian there I should have carefully kept away.[12]

Unfortunately, there is little evidence of any basic change in the past hundred years — it was discovered this year that one-third of the students of a great metropolitan university had made no use of the library or had any knowledge about using it, according to a recent survey of 4,170 college seniors. This study concludes that "current methods are at an impasse," and "the greatest potential source of education for today's youth, the library, is being wasted."[13]

Despite emphasis in recent years on "excellence," this has largely meant a general tightening of traditional methods of teaching, including textbooks, rote memory and regurgitation. Woe to the original and creative undergraduate or graduate student who does not hue to the party-line or "school" of the department chairman. Unfortunately, our whole society is like this, but if a start on change were to be made the colleges would be a logical place to begin.

### Basing the Curriculum on the Library

Contrast this to the liberating influence of a curriculum intimately undergirded by the qualities that define a good library — breadth, depth, controversy, the free delight of fresh discoveries in the full range of man's heritage, without an inhibiting pressure to follow a straight and narrow path.

What conclusions may we draw? That the substance of the curriculum should be based in an integral way on the strength of the library. This is a firmer and more enduring foundation than a curriculum dependent on the vagaries and transient biases of a particular faculty committee or Board of Trustees. For example, it is not conceiveable that any school but a Harvard could, in the past 15 years, have considered hiring a known or secret Communist, no matter what skill and qualification such a person might otherwise possess, but it has been possible for almost all colleges to continue to acquire books by Communist authors. The library should not only be the principal resource of the campus, the "heart of the college," but it should also in a real sense play a central role in generating and operating the curriculum.

[12] Lydenburg, Harry. *John Shaw Billings* (Chicago: American Library Association, 1924), p. 11.
[13] Perkins, Ralph. *The Prospective Teacher's Knowledge of Library Fundamentals* (New York: Scarecrow Press, 1965), p. 202.

It is difficult to conceive of a classroom without a library, or a library without a classroom. But we all know that in actuality there is normally a deep gulf between these two institutions that should be operating in an intimate symbiotic relationship, rather than as two separate polarized entities. This gap is debilitating and destructive. Prejudices and stereotypes are perpetuated. The full potential of the combined faculty-library is inhibited.

We cannot expect faculty "outside" the library to understand or support the "bibliographic way." We cannot expect librarians, trained more as warehousemen and technicians than as bibliographic counselors to interfere with the basic procedures of the faculty.

The answer? Bring the faculty *inside* the library, in one integrated physical facility, combining the best features of classroom, library and independent study. Such dually competent faculty-librarians would have a primary dedication to the education of students, not to research on the one hand, not to library technical problems on the other. Both are equally hazardous to student education in the small undergraduate college (and all undergraduate teaching *should be* in small colleges).

Librarians engulfed in ordering, cataloging, processing and the maintenance of a catalog have little time or energy left for students. But such work can be expertly and efficiently provided centrally, including the preparation of book catalogs. Through the use of new devices and procedures, the computer or the "Jordan plastic book box," it is also possible to design a circulation system that is user operated with minimal circulation or shelving staff that ordinarily absorbs so sizable a proportion of library staff time and administrative attention.

With no outside obligations to publish or perish and with fussy technical distractions removed, the faculty-librarians would be psychologically free to place their entire attention and interest in the educational process, in monitoring and encouraging individual and small group study and creativity.

If the student's attention and work are centered in the library, perhaps with his own private carrel, if the library is physically designed to maximize attraction, if there is no longer any faculty-library conflict because there are no longer any distinct teaching faculty on the one hand and library faculty on the other, then we have developed a distinctive new type of institution, the "library-college."

Instead of giving mere lip service to the library as the heart of the campus, it must *operate* in a central role. This central role should be much more than a physical, storage and dispensing-warehouse kind of centrality, grandly ignored as an organic part of an educational process. Faculty must identify themselves with the library in a complex variety of ways. Students and faculty must learn to turn to the library as automatically as they now turn to their ball point pens, typewriters, eyeglasses, or tomorrow — to their computers.

Although not yet translated into reality, these insights have been seen by many educators throughout history. Recently, Commager wrote:

> Now that students can read for themselves, the English universities have turned more and more from lectures to tutoring or to self-education . . . but in the United States, which has the best facilities in the world . . . professors go on giving courses as blithely as if no printed books were available. One simple way, then, to meet the shortage of teaching talent is to cut down on the lectures and therewith the number of professors that lectures call for. From the point of view of the student, the time spent going to lectures and preparing for course examinations can more profitably be spent in the library.[14]

This insight was perceived in the 17th century by Daniel Georg Morhof, a German disciple of Francis Bacon, exponent of universal knowledge who attempted an all-embracing inventory of human knowledge. Morhof not only discusses library science in his great work — *polyhistory* — but makes it the very foundation stone of his entire edifice. He justifies this procedure in the following manner:

> Information and knowledge are most efficiently acquired through books and learned periodicals: therefore, the mentor must begin by furnishing advice as to which books, or editions, and journals are best in the various fields and why so. Since the well-read scholar needs to know so many books, libraries have become an indispensable tool for him and an acquaintance with their organization and working methods is for that reason fundamental.[15]

The most comprehensive library that the world has ever known, not to be surpassed in size for more than 2000 years was at one and the same time a Library-College, with the world's first great university inte-

---

[14] "The Problem Isn't Bricks—It's Brains," *New York Times Magazine* (January 29, 1956), p. 11.

[15] Bergholz, H. "Daniel Georg Morhof; Overlooked Precursor of Library Science," *Libri,* Vol. XIV (1965), pp. 44-50.

grated with the operation of the library. This was the Alexandrian library, founded by one of Alexander's generals, Ptolemy I soon after 322 B. C., partially destroyed by fire in 47 B. C., and completely destroyed in 391 A. D.

### Physical Design of the Library-College

The actual physical shape of the Library-College is peculiarly crucial, far more so than the relation of the campus design to the philosophy of a conventional college. It would be difficult if not impossible for the Library-College to operate effectively in the bland modular general-purpose series of blocks of office and classroom building common on most campuses. Along with the selection of particularly qualified personnel to staff the Library-College, the shape and space relationships of the building will contribute crucially to the effectiveness with which it carries out its educational philosophy. Unfortunately, no one has yet been bold enough to expand the library to include the entire campus although this has been approached at Blackwater High School in Oklahoma and at Stephens College.

With the library co-extensive in philosophy and program to the entire campus, there are obviously certain limitations. First, there is a limitation on enrollment and physical size. Second, the library collection must be comparatively large to avoid excessive dilution of materials. Third, all of the space in the library-campus structure must be efficiently utilized, to keep the total overall radius and perimeter as compact as possible. With emphasis on independent study in individual carrels and small group work and discussion areas, it is feasible to plan on a relatively high degree of utilization (up to 18 hours a day) in all areas of the Library-College. Fourth, large group facilities (such as cafeteria, auditorium, gymnasium) with the least relation to library resources should be on the outer perimeter.

### Some Possible Versions of the Library-College

There is no reason why a library-oriented college couldn't come in as many shapes and varieties as a classroom-oriented college (the only kind that we have thus far known in America). Brief descriptions follow of four possible versions:

1. Shores College (named after Louis Shores)
2. Student Operated Library-College
3. Combination of Correspondence Study and Library-College
4. Combination of Adult Education and Library-College

58

## (1) SHORES COLLEGE

Shores College would be one of 20 to 40 associated autonomous colleges in the *College Host Center*; perhaps all of these colleges would be variations of the Library-College concept. Although Shores College would be characterized by an absence of any sharp physical or ideational demarcation between the library faculty and the teaching faculty, or between classroom and library, it would be transitional, partway between conventional campus design and philosophy and a pure Library-College.

The key and typical activity in Shores would be independent study. The central resource center (library) closely surrounded by faculty offices, individual carrels and small group discussion rooms, would be the physical focus of educational activity, rather than the classroom. The library would be conceived, planned and operated as an *activity,* a dynamic process, rather than a *place,* or a passive storehouse. Since learning takes place only within the student, he would assume the primary responsibility for learning. Each student would progress at his own pace, as an individual or as a member of a small team.

All professionals in the college would be members of the faculty and would work with students at least one-third of the time. Each member of the faculty would also have another competency or responsibility outside his subject field, requiring from one-sixth to two-thirds of his time, e.g., librarianship, administration, public relations, or athletics. There would be no departments, no faculty rank. Faculty salaries would be equal for all except for moderate adjustment for dependents.

All faculty would share some responsibility in connection with the resource center (library). One-fourth of the faculty would have a special competence in librarianship, plus as much subject training, in a broad subject field or division, as any other of the faculty; one "faculty-librarian" would be assigned to every four or so faculty in each broad subject division to provide specialized bibliographic assistance to both the faculty in the team and to the students studying with this team. The "faculty-librarian" would be responsible for the selection of materials for his team.

The optimum collection would consist of 20,000 titles (the same number as in Antioch's Core Collection which received 80% of the circulation among the 100,000 volumes in the total Antioch collection), plus 20,000 titles in microfilm or micro-opaque. All periodicals would be on microfilm. For the approximately 20% of needed materials not available in this core collection, the students would patronize the two million volume research library maintained by the College Host Center. Half of the bound book collection would be reinforced paperbacks, the remaining half normal case bound. Approximately 2,000 new titles would be acquired yearly at a cost of $5,000. An equal number of titles would be weeded yearly. The list of 55,000 basic undergraduate titles developed at the University of California would replace the conventional card catalog.

There would be five major subject areas: Personal Development and Athletics, Social Sciences, Natural Sciences, Language and Literature, Arts. The materials, facilities, and offices in each of these major areas would be concentrated in one physical area, a pie-shaped wedge radiating from the central library.

The "faculty-librarians" would have their stations at the outer perimeter of the central library and the inner perimeter of the subject divisions. From the central library outwards, the facilities would be graded in order of decreasing density of use and increasing size of area required. Thus, faculty offices, small group viewing and listening rooms and learning resource carrels would be located in the area adjacent to the central library. Next further distant would be individual study carrels. Still further out would be seminar, conference rooms and discussion areas. On the very outside perimeter would be large group facilities, gymnasia, large lecture facilities, cafeteria, etc.

The resultant plan might very well consist of one monolithic single story circular building, without windows, or a similar multistory building. Or, the total structure might be composed of inter-nestled hexagon shaped nuclei. Or, interior courtyards might be introduced. Acoustical treatment and carpets in all areas would facilitate close proximity and eliminate the need for corridors.

Implicit in this design is the philosophy that the college would be built in its final size and limited to a designed optimum size rather than being allowed to expand without conscious limit or control. This single closely integrated complex would function simultaneously as the single intellectual, cultural, social center on the campus.

(2) STUDENT OPERATED LIBRARY-COLLEGE

Just as production soars in industry when directives and controls over workers are removed, so it is likely that student motivation would soar if the responsibility for operating a college was given to them. Students would be given a campus — a Library-College campus — and instructed to organize themselves in whatever way they wished. They would be on their own, except for occasional outside examinations.

(3) COMBINATION OF CORRESPONDENCE-STUDY AND LIBRARY-COLLEGE

It is true that correspondence or home study instruction is one-fifth to one-fifteenth as expensive (excluding living expenses) as conventional college instruction. It is also true that studies on retention of students enrolled in home study courses matched against the same type of students enrolled in conventional college courses indicate that home study is fully equal to college classroom and lecture, perhaps a little superior.[16] It might be possible to raise this retention rate significantly higher than conventional college by adding three ingredients: a large library, bibliographic counselors and community project leaders. Yet the total cost would still be a fraction of ordinary college instruction today.

(4) COMBINATION OF ADULT EDUCATION AND "LIBRARY-COLLEGE"

Here is an area fairly bulging with potentialities. One version of this combination would be expansion of the existing educational responsibilities of public libraries. Some, such as the Louisville Public Library, have almost reached this stage. Already, most public librarians are deeply concerned with the educational aspect of their role, with the content of books, with community problems, and with individual human beings. Public librarians, with their relaxed attitude to "education" often are effective educators. Both public librarians and adult educators are receptive to new ideas in educational methodology.

The average individual should have more educational experiences. But these experiences should come at the time dictated by individual need and motivation, *any time in life*, rather than artificially crowded into the late teens and early twenties. American higher education should consider the lesson of the Danish folk colleges — that adults with formal

---

[16] Parsons, T. S. "A Comparison of Instruction by Kinescope, Correspondence Study and Conventional Classroom Procedure," *Journal of Educational Psychology*, Vol. XLVIII (January 1957), pp. 27-40.

schooling completed in their 14th or 15th years will return voluntarily to a folk college, at a point in their lives when they have an inner desire for a liberal and liberating education, for 5 or 6 months of intensive work, without grades, credits, or any other paraphernalia and will commonly learn more of the liberal arts than the average American student in three years of high school and two to four years of college. Although the traditional Danish folk colleges have no vocational orientation their graduates who immersed themselves in Kierkegaard and Shakespeare returned home to develop the most advanced agricultural, social and economic system in the world, including a highly effective national library network 20 to 30 years in advance of any other country — almost *any* book in *any* Danish library is available quickly and simply to any citizen.[17]

Life-long education experiences with alteration of work, community service and study, might be systematically yet individually organized around a type of public library as the organization center and point of departure. This version of the Library-College might act as a focal point or organizing center for a variety of educational activities now spread throughout the community: part-time and full-time residential adult education, home study, public library, liberal arts college, domestic peace corps, work-study programs, ETV, Great Books, community junior college and educational sit-ins.

## *Initiating the Library-College*

It should be no more difficult to initiate a Library-College than one more conventional. However, in the reorganization of an existing college a proposal to liquidate the faculty as a separate entity is not likely to be warmly received. It is a matter of politics, vested interests, tradition —and mathematics (college librarians are outnumbered 30 to 1 by the faculty). However, librarians are not entirely without friends — there are a few visionary faculty and administrators who see the dynamic potentiality of a situation in which educational leadership emanates from the library itself. The very uniqueness of the Library-College concept would be a positive attraction to some university administrations.

There is certainly nothing to be lost, and everything to be gained in approaching a university administration anxious to develop a "college-within-the-college." A number of such universities would be

---

[17] Larson, Knud. "Danish Library System," *Library Association Record,* Vol. LXII (September 1960), pp. 275-279.

receptive to proposals for variously oriented "colleges-within-the college." At Santa Cruz alone there will eventually be 40 such colleges.

The normal procedure in initiating a new college is to place major emphasis on an "outstanding" faculty, and it is inconceivable that there would be fewer than a standard ratio of faculty to students — the reverse is usually true. Almost as an afterthought in the last frantic few months before the new college is to open someone remembers that the college is expected to have a library in order to be accredited. Since no one has conceived of the library as a primary need, everyone assumes that it must be all right to start with fewer than a standard quantity of books. A major new university began operations this past year with the equivalent of more than 2,000 full-time students, a normal complement of faculty, plus *one* professional librarian and 5,000 old donated books. A major new elite college with every prospect of national recognition opened its campus this past fall with the same paltry number of books.

In founding a Library-College, this traditional procedure would be reversed. An outstanding *liberating* and *attracting* library would be acquired *first,* on the theory that such a library would act as a magnet to attract both students and outstanding faculty-librarians, much as faculty and books attracted students in the Middle Ages.

This would be nothing more (except for the textbooks!) than the prescription for founding a university suggested by Stephen Leacock (quoted by Sir Frank Francis):

> If I were founding a university, I would found first a smoking room, then when I had a little more money in hand I would found a dormitory, then after that, or more probably with it, a decent reading room and a library. After that if I had still more money I couldn't use, I would hire a professor and get some textbooks.[18]

To assist new Library-Colleges in getting started, it would be helpful if a national project could develop package collections that could be shipped on demand. Such "package libraries" would be helpful to new classroom-oriented colleges as well.

### Librarians Must Take Initiative

Librarians have been talking for a long time among themselves about the importance of individual reading and inquiry. Even though

---

[18] *The Cornell Library Conference; Papers Read at the Dedication of the Central Libraries,* October 1962. Ithaca: Cornell University Library, 1964.

administrators are induced to join in the refrain about the library at the heart of the college, it usually becomes nothing more than a cliche, nothing is changed, faculty continue to ignore the library, and all too often librarians are happy enough for being ignored — it allows them to be bigger frogs in their own isolated ponds. Other librarians become cynical and patronizing toward the teaching faculty for failing to use the library creatively.

It is time for librarians to take the initiative and demonstrate their theories about the library potential as an integral and active part of the learning process in a situation in which the "library faculty" will determine overall institutional policy instead of being outnumbered and outpowered. If librarians do not take such initiative, they are not likely to be asked.

### Designing and Staffing the Library-College

The concept of the Library-College is diametrically opposite to almost every morsel of experience in the lives of existing faculty. Thus, it is crucial that only those individuals who believe in the ultimate success of this "radical" new idea should participate in its design or execution. Otherwise, at the first signs of conflict or adversity imperfectly committed faculty will likely revert to the tried and familiar rather than persisting in blazing a new trail.

This does not imply that only librarians can be expected to have such a commitment. There *are* teaching faculty here and there who should play a part, especially those who are inclined to be "generalists," with interest in the boundaries between disciplines or with experience in cross-discipline teams. There are many administrators and adult educators who could provide sympathetic counsel and leadership. Other categories are educational sociologists and psychologists with concern about college effectiveness, reference and reader's service college librarians, public librarians, high school librarians, librarians and faculty from innovating colleges, and bookstore managers. In many instances, individuals with sufficiently deep interest and commitment could be expected to receive library training while on the job with the cost assumed by the Library-College.

### Degrees of Library User-Orientation

There is a natural progression in libraries, in degree of user orientation.

64

First, we have the example of many traditional libraries in Europe and Latin America, *archive oriented,* with the user considered an annoyance.

Second, we have American libraries in general *oriented to the user as a group.* Such libraries provide physical amenities, stack arrangement, indexes to the collection and reference collections oriented to the patron. Such libraries say in effect to the user, "Our collection is well organized to facilitate your use, but we have only a limited interest in how efficiently or usefully you use it."

Third, are most American public and special libraries, *oriented towards providing individualized services for the user* and in the instance of public libraries concerned about the individual independent intellectual and cultural development of the patron.

Fourth, we might project for the future a library that has *incorporated within its structure* both formal and informal educational activities — the Library-College.

### *Summary*

Students are restless and critical and are becoming increasingly receptive to innovations in education enhancing their individuality and dignity. There are trends towards increasing use of the library and independent study. Hopefully students are increasingly dissatisfied with the traditional transmission of material from the notebook of the lecturer to the notebook of the student without any effect on the minds of either.

There are increasing numbers of faculty who do not lecture but instead prepare syllabi and bibliographies and counsel with individual students or small groups. There is little to distinguish such faculty from the more educationally oriented librarians ("bibliographic counselors"). However, as long as faculty and library remain apart physically there will always remain a tendency towards bi-polarization that will keep them apart curricularly and the creative exploitation of the library by faculty and students will be inhibited.

A substantial proportion of courses and faculty lecture-hours can be traded for increased material in the library and increased direct faculty-student relations. Faculty can be incorporated within the library, as faculty-librarians.

The existence of the library as a sharply distinct institution grandly isolated from the rest of the campus should be challenged. The total educational impact would be increased if the library were so completely merged physically and operationally with the discussion rooms, faculty-librarian offices, viewing, listening and programmed learning facilities that it would be difficult for the outside observer to discover where one element left off and the other began.

# The Library as Instructor [1,2]

*MAURICE BROWN*

IF FEW OF US would wish to plan the ideal college around a library with no professors, probably not many more would see Mark Hopkins' log (even with a seminar at one end) as a possible foundation for the ideal college in today's situation. Therefore, it may be desirable to suggest as a workable humanistic educational ideal an "educational log" in which the professor at one end should, like a character in *Alice in Wonderland,* slowly turn into a library during the student's four years in college.

It is probably not necessary to point out that this does not happen for the vast majority of students. Wrestling with this problem over the past few weeks, whatever tack is taken I am constantly driven back to locate the source of the problem in the attitudes and teaching methods of the faculty. Directly and indirectly many instructors work against the student's development of a vital and useful relationship to the library. First of all, there is a small group of instructors who either directly advise the student to stay away from the library or who imply by their teaching that the library is irrelevant to the objectives of a given course. This approach attempts to avoid the danger that the library may divert the unsophisticated or dependent student from his main job by overwhelming him, by becoming a crutch, or by wasting his time. By forcing the student back upon himself, the instructor can work more effectively to develop careful and sensitive reading of a text, critical and sceptical habits of thought, and that attitude which leads the student to find the meaning of *Hamlet* or *The Plague* within himself rather than in the library. Whatever its values, this approach is certainly a limited one for finally sound independence is based, not on ignorance of the ideas and experiences of others, but on sure knowledge of them. Indeed, a situation in which a thousand would-be teachers are sitting on the other end of that log is necessary to freedom of thought.

---

[1] Some of the ideas for specific library-oriented programs draw heavily on discussions with Mrs. Margaret Irwin.

[2] Reprinted from Jordan, Robert, ed. College Talkshop, Kenyon College, *Proceedings.* June 24-29, 1962. Washington, The Editor, 1962, 48 pp. (processed).

There is a second group of us using tried and possibly untrue methods by which we indirectly discourage use of the library in any real sense. All of our familiar structuring devices provide the focus and limitation of topic which are necessary to achievement of knowledge and values. And yet they help produce a college experience which tends to look like a track set up for the hurdles. We define the track, we set the height and number of the hurdles, and the distance. The student is left to do the running and jumping. Too rarely does the student identify the questions, focus and define the issues, or even do much of the sifting so basic to any search for knowledge.

On the basis of this brief critique, we should work toward establishing a dialectic, the terms of which might be the Whiteheadean ones of romance and precision, or those of the introspective and extensive approaches to knowledge, or those of instructor-focussed and student-focussed learning experiences.[3] Instead of attempting to construct a total program which might develop one or more of these dialectics this paper will list some techniques and methods which might profitably be explored to produce the desirable sort of student-library relationship.[4]

I. The Instructor and the Student. We need to experiment with other roles than that of instructor, especially with that of the educated man, curious or disturbed about something, searching for answers. For education generally, this would focus on process rather than on the results of process, and on involvement rather than detached consideration. An important by-product, however, would be to turn the students to the library as it functions in our thinking and scholarly lives. Secondly, we must learn to respect students as human beings, and, with considerably more faith in them than we now manifest, help them explore their concerns instead of setting them to the exploration of our concerns or of artificially-constructed library problems.

II. The Instructor and the Librarian. The instructor and the librarian, especially the reference librarian, should work much more closely together than they do now. Communication is so poor that work here must begin at simple levels of co-operation, mutual understanding of aims, functions, and interests. The reference librarian should have a

---

[3] See Alfred N. Whitehead's "The Rhythm of Education," in *The Aims of Education*. New York: Macmillan, 1929.

[4] It is desirable to point out that I ignore completely an important and thorny question: identification of the nature and extent of the library experience we might expect in an ideal undergraduate program regarded as a preparation for life rather than for graduate study.

co-ordinate degree in a subject-matter area and could function as an instructor, either independently or sharing guidance of work and evaluation in any of a wide range of courses with the professor.

III. TEACHING. Instructors in the small class should explore more fully possibilities of guiding students individually (and therefore almost inevitably to library resources). Large group techniques which deserve much greater experimentation and application might include these: case-method study in which the library is used to compile fact and opinion on a restricted problem; cooperative research and discussion by smaller, self-guided student groups; more experimental use of the "reading period" here and there through the semester; wider use of the annotated bibliography in place of the long paper; and the lecture as a question-raising, problem-defining device, or as a model in methodology.

IV. THE READING COURSE. By the junior year, with library-oriented earlier teaching and some experience in independent work, all students could hopefully embark on independent reading programs in their majors without much of the supervision now needed for superior students in such programs. Instructors and reference librarians could work closely together in guiding the student, and student work could range from "reading around" in areas of interest to narrow concern with a carefully defined problem, depending on the student's interests and abilities. If students have become accustomed to self-directed group discussion, this could supplement or perhaps supplant much of the guidance of a faculty member or reference librarian.

This sort of program could easily be the key to the implementation of many of the aims suggested above: its establishment would lead to necessary change of emphasis and method in introductory courses leading to it; the reading course would be a natural meeting ground for instructor and librarian; and the student would know in the clearest and most direct of ways that his education, from the setting of questions and concerns to the working through to answers, was his responsibility. Perhaps the professor and the reference librarian could eventually disappear, and the student suddenly discover that he didn't need them anyway as long as he had a library.

# The Library-College Faculty[1]

*LOUIS SHORES*

HIGHER EDUCATION faces the greatest challenge and most strategic opportunity world history has ever recorded. The United States has committed itself to higher educate all its people. If the nation meets this commitment perhaps for the first time leaders and followers in a society will be able to communicate with each other in such a way as to preclude violent revolution.

But if the United States is to fulfill this commitment a radically different higher education must evolve. Evidence of changing higher education was dramatically presented in a colloquium at Wakulla Springs, Florida in the spring of 1964.[2]

At the top of the list of reported changes was reorganization to insure numerically small student bodies. Liberal arts colleges are striving for student populations under 1,000. Universities are moving toward the British cluster college pattern. The new University of California at Santa Cruz, for example, announced that its "colleges will vary from 250 to 1,000 students."[3] At the neighboring University of the Pacific President Burns decided:

> Let us grow larger by growing smaller. Let us develop about the University a cluster of colleges which will retain the values we cherish so much and yet will at the same time make it possible for us to accept some responsibility for educating the increasing number of young people seeking to enter institutions of higher learning . . . Let us follow the Oxford and Cambridge system and expand by establishing small, interrelated colleges clustered together to draw strength from each other and from the University as a whole.[4]

---

[1] Read at The Founders Week Faculty Meeting on the Silver Anniversary of the Orlando Junior College, Florida, April 26, 1966.
[2] Stickler, W. Hugh, *Experimental Colleges.* Tallahassee, Florida State University, 1964. 185p.
[3] *Ibid.,* p. 133-44.
[4] *Ibid.,* p. 75.

Michigan State University decided that as new residence dormitories were constructed each would house an experimental liberal arts college

> with a distinctive program which would provide a common educational experience to all students in a single residence hall . . . The first three new halls . . . each houses 1200 students . . . include a total of 14 classrooms, six laboratories, 47 offices, an auditorium, a kiva, a library, and five conference rooms.[5]

Orlando might consider the cluster college idea to accommodate its gratifying enrollment increase, and at the same time, protect its personal attention to the student's education.[6] If the University of Orlando is activated there will be even more reason to establish several small colleges rather than attempt to handle the student body *en masse*.

But even more exciting than the cluster college movement were reports of variations on the independent study trend. Antioch has experimented with autonomous courses in which the student, after a preliminary lecture introducing the broad outlines of the subject and the sources, spends the term reading independently in the library. From time to time he confers with the instructor. When several students feel a need to discuss their readings, the instructor calls a class meeting.

At Florida Presbyterian College:

> The winter term is a special four to five week period of independent study . . . Designed to develop qualities of self-discipline in pursuits requiring the student to be the prime explorer, the winter term asks him to work without customary routine of classroom and lecture hall . . .[7]

Individualized student learning in the library is steadily replacing group teaching in the classroom as the educational mode. This is demanded by the national commitment to higher educate all people, for as college approaches the compulsory status, the range of student individual differences becomes ever wider. This widening range makes a classroom focused education ever more untenable. By the nature of the group approach in the classroom the teacher's activity must be greatest. And he is confronted by the necessity of preparing a class plan which aims at the mythical average. Furthermore, as he

---

[5] *Ibid.,* pp. 127-28.

[6] Shores, Louis. "The Library Junior College" *Junior College Journal* (March 1966), pp. 6-9.

[7] Stickler, *op. cit.,* pp. 96ff.

lectures or leads the discussion, the most he can hope for is an intellectual passivity by the majority.

The classroom as a mode of learning is a persistent holdover from ancient and medieval days when the principal medium of communication was the master's oral communication of information to his pupils. Even after the invention of the printing press, books were so limited that the best the individual could hope for was a single textbook to supplement the teacher's lecture. It was not until this century that libraries began to develop in strength sufficiently to enable faculty to adopt reserve readings as a classroom assignment form. But the classroom contact as a measure of education persisted beyond World War I, despite frequent rebellions by both students and faculty.

Independent study has grown in popularity in undergraduate colleges. Even some high schools, like that at Ridgefield, Illinois, have moved to independent study, and an elementary school in Shaker Heights, Ohio, with a subsidy from the Ford Foundation, is experimenting in independent study.

Evidence is mounting of the passing of the classroom contact as the measure of learning. As libraries reach high standards of quality and quantity they can match individual differences in students with individual differences in instructional materials. The universe of library media is now so nearly universal in subject, format and level that it is entirely possible to customize learning so each learner can begin at his individual point of readiness.

What then is the role of the faculty? With enthusiasm I exclaim, more exciting than ever before. The college instructor can now do creative teaching that the outmoded lockstep of the medieval classroom precluded. He can begin to develop the individual mind, talent, and spirit of his students. The coming of the Library-College frees both the professor and student to undertake liberal education together.

In his new role the Library-College faculty member is a counsellor to the individual student. He maintains daily office hours not in excess of the time required presently by combined class meetings and student appointments. Less frequently, but as the situation demands, there are seminar or small group meetings. Once or twice a term each faculty member presents a lecture, open to any one in the college. The content should represent original investigation and contain information not readily available in library material. Because the lecture is not routinely delivered at a fixed hour three times a week it reflects the incentive and inspiration harnessed for the event. The essay may even be prepared for publication.

The Library-College faculty member is also a bibliographer extraordinary. He knows the literature of his subject so well that he can prescribe for the individual differences of his students as adroitly as the skilled physician diagnoses and treats his individual patients. To do this the faculty member must know each of his students individually. The instructor should be able to sense the young person's talents and limitations, to determine the point of readiness to learn. And then out of his intimate knowledge of the literature of his subject prescribe medium or media which will best start the youngster off toward the common goal.

Today there are many highly bibliographic faculty. Although no stereotype for this new breed of faculty member can possibly exist, here are some examples of library teaching.

In an Antioch Economics class the group came together for one hour on the opening day of the fall term. The professor talked briefly and informally about Economics as a subject. Then he handed out an overview which defined some of the terminology. A second handout was a basic bibliography of sources, classics, journals, learned societies, key publications, federal and state government agencies, movements and problems current in the subject, famous economists, and Dewey Decimal numbers among which to browse in the library. The third handout was a syllabus of a standard course in beginning Economics.

Said the professor:

Now, you are on your own. The next time I see you will be when you want to see me. My office hours are at the bottom of your third stencil. There is also a calendar of minimum events. You owe me three written reports of progress at the times indicated. The forms for these reports are indicated on the reverse side of the third page. And there is a final day of reckoning. What will be required for that is also indicated. So long, and happy reading in the library.

There are many variations of independent study. For instance a professor may take his class to the library the first day and browse with them in the stacks. Another interesting approach has been to assign overview articles on the course subject from the major encyclopedias. Another way has been to open the subject with a controversial motion picture. Another exciting opening has been entirely bibliographic, with annotations and displays of the basic reference sources for the subject.

Soon individuals begin to raise questions which arise from their reading. Here a concept may be unclear, so the Library-College faculty member begins his diagnosis by prescribing from his rich knowledge of the literature a precise format and level that will exactly match the

73

individual's readiness. There a conflict may develop between two accents, or points of view, or even sets of facts. A subtle diagnosis is called for, related to the maturity as well as foundations the students bring to the situation. Perhaps the issue warrants a seminar or even a major essay-lecture by the professor.

It is apparent that the Library-College faculty must be extraordinarily equipped in bibliography. The library sophistication of this new breed professor must be beyond that of most of college faculty. The professor who library teaches is known and revered by the librarian. In countless ways he who teaches with books reveals himself by the nature of his assignments, the library sophistication of his students, his current awareness of the literature output in his subject, and his orders for new materials.

As for library sophistication, a number of graduate schools are now offering courses in literature searching that go beyond undergraduate library orientation.[8] I recommend increased exploration of the library learning idea.

---

[8] Shores, Louis. "Library Research and Reporting" *Collier's Encyclopedia.* 1965. Volume XIV, pp. 601-7.

# The Caravan Library-College

*ROBERT JORDAN*

*Need* — The most characteristic feature of the Library-College is its emphasis on investigation, inquiry and search rather than on a master-disciple relationship limited by the capability of one set of faculty or texts. But it is not sufficient to confine the "search" to one campus or one library. Yet, how can the college, solidly rooted in its buildings and campus be uprooted and taken to the point of investigation or need? The answer—place the campus and its library on wheels so it can move out into the world. This can be called the Caravan Library-College or CLC.

Just as we have been bound by an oral and authoritarian tradition that has inhibited the development of the Library-College so have we also been bound (psychologically) by the stability and permanence of the campus and its buildings. Undoubtedly the most brilliant years in the history of the university were the earliest, in the twelfth and thirteenth century, when the university was not rooted in one location, sometimes hounded out of a community, vigorous, initiatory, a hot-bed of controversy and disputation, before rigid ecclesiastical and lay control, and buildings, were imposed. This was a "community of scholars" responsible primarily to itself, not inhibited by rigid association with one set of buildings and authorities.

True, in the past few years we have seen an increasing interest in "field work," in community service and work-study. But these activities lean too much in the opposite direction, of disassociation from the community of scholars, of remoteness from library resources, of impermanence. The answer — establish a new kind of institution that deliberately exploits the mobility so characteristic of our age.

In a fixed campus, with a fixed library, the pressure is almost irresistible towards an attitude of withdrawal, rather than initiative. A closely knit community, working and living together, inspired by useful work among people and continual close association with books and other resources, might conceivably be able to reach new levels of self-

75

awareness and common concern in the human condition. Of all the aims of education, moral instruction is most desperately needed today. Yet it is the most elusive—it certainly cannot be achieved by a frontal attack. As Milton Mayer has pointed out, "It is going on two and a half millennia since the first discussion of education opened with the question, 'Can you tell me, Socrates, whether virtue is acquired by teaching or by practice . . . or in what other way?' We are not able to answer the question . . . But perhaps another two and a half millennia of unrelenting inquiry will produce the answer; all the more reason for getting started at once." Here is the key, *combine teaching and practice in a new and meaningful way.* It is not inconceivable that this combination together with the more modern third essential, the *Library,* might enable us to reach the goal of educating men to be good far before the year 4500 AD. However, we must start soon, before we blow ourselves to smithereens.

*Role of the Caravan Library-College (CLC)*—The CLC would be a semi-autonomous unit attached to a permanent campus. Its facilities would be based on a fleet of self-contained trailers. There are severe restrictions as to the optimum size of a mobile unit; this, and the limitations of field work indicate that CLC would be best adapted to concentration on one project, problem or area by a fairly compact and cohesive group of staff and students. The educational approach would be multi-disciplinary. The CLC would study various ramifications of life in a given community, or concentrate on one problem or project in one geographic area or series of areas. At the same time, the staff would provide leadership in various kinds of educational activities based on both the resources of a mobile library and on the resources of the community being visited, including its library resources.

Trailers have the twin features of easy transportability and self containment. Hence, the CLC could be easily transported overseas as deck cargo on ships to all parts of the world at comparatively low cost. The CLC could function in primitive areas as well as in trailer parks.

*Prototypes* — Possibly the closest approach to this educational technique is exemplified in the work of the Lisle Fellowship which conducts six week travel programs and camps during the summer which combine community work and education. The effect on the participants in terms of moral education and change in personal philosophy is often profound.

The University of the Seven Seas is an even closer prototype.

76

However, the economics here are difficult; at best, a mobile college on a ship will always be a fairly expensive undertaking. Because of minimal crew requirements it is essential in such a college that there be several hundred students, but this becomes too many for all to work as one unit on one project.

In developing further the concept and program of the CLC the following types of activities will furnish experience and insight:

1. Work camps, such as those conducted by AFSC
2. Civil rights projects, such as those conducted by SCLC, SNCC, and CORE
3. Various non-violent and peace training camps
4. Work-study programs such as at Antioch
5. Educational camps such as those conducted by Lisle Fellowship and the Ethical Culture Society
6. Hosteling
7. Junior year abroad programs
8. Community service periods such as at Goddard
9. The annual trailer caravans conducted each year by a major trailer manufacturer
10. The folk school movement in the South especially Highlander and Berea
11. Religious orders and communities.

*Suggested Projects:*

1. Community survey
2. Community history: oral, language, songs, etc.
3. Demonstration schools in deprived areas
   adult
   supplementary—for high school students
   nursery
4. Voter registration
5. Literacy training
6. Search for effective educational techniques
7. Recruiting of staff and students for the Library-College
8. Stand-by for emergency service at point of need, such as natural disasters—floods, forest fires, etc.
   demonstrations
   strikes
   archaeological salvage—protection of new discoveries
   political campaigns
9. Community redevelopment (as in TVA but on a small scale in a small watershed)
   contour farming
   check dams

fertilizer
cooperatives
adult education
writing proposals to secure state and federal money
library service

10. Pool of mobile labor force for seasonal or temporary needs
national parks
resort areas
agriculture
mining
archaeological and ethnological surveys
jails, hospitals and other institutions with fluctuating population
public opinion surveys
census taking

*Areas of Activity:*

1. Geographic
South Carolina Sea Islands
National parks
Resort areas
Suburbs
Planned communities: Reston, Columbia City
Inner city

2. Types of people
Amish
Indians: Mexico, Eskimo, Navajo, Hopi
Intentional communities: Bruderhof, Hutterite, Doukobors,
Quaker, etc.
Urban minorities: Negro, Jew, Chinese, American Indians
Rural poor

3. Types of occupations
Lumber camps
Coal mines
Textile mills
Massversities
Tenant farmers
Migratory workers
Poor homeless aged single men
Institutions: jails, insane, alcoholic, narcotic

*Optimum Size* — Some of the factors involved in the optimum
size would be:

1. Sufficient staff to cover major disciplines
2. Sufficient students to justify the library resources capable of being
housed in one trailer

3. Small enough for mobility
4. Small enough to be housed easily in most trailer parks
5. Small enough to participate in a maximum number of projects.

Such factors as these suggest that not less than 40 students and 5 staff nor more than 150 students and 15 staff are indicated. If there are no more than 40 students, the entire group can meet for large group sessions in one trailer. But 40 students and 5 staff are minimal in other respects. Closed circuit TV between trailers could be used for large group sessions involving more than 40 students at a time; alternately, one trailer could include an expandable side, or two trailers might be joined together, side by side.

*Equipment and Cost* — A minimal size CLC would require twelve vehicles including five all-purpose trailers (staff office-dormitory-classroom) and one library trailer, plus six heavy duty truck type station wagons for pulling the trailers. Where maximum mobility is important, a maximum trailer length of 30 feet and width of 8 feet is indicated. (The trailers could be 10 or 12 feet in width and from 35 to 70 feet in length, but would require special permits, obtainable at a fee of from $10 to $25 in each state for each transit, and would also require heavier trucks than are available with a station wagon body.)

In CLCs designed for dependence on trailer parks, it would not be necessary to provide any more than emergency toilet, shower and cooking facilities, since all of the larger trailer parks provide these facilities centrally. However, a toilet and shower for all people living in one 30 foot trailer (8 students and one project-coordinator-librarian) would not take up much space; practically all modern trailer parks provide ready connection to water, sewers, telephone and electricity.

In some types of CLCs, the sleeping facilities in the trailers might be considered an emergency provision; the students would normally live in homes or other facilities in the community.

A new 30 foot empty trailer costs from $2,500 to $3,500. (A 40 foot furniture van, with 123 inches of clear inside height between axles costs $4,900 from Fruehoff. In such a trailer two decks could be provided.) It might cost triple these amounts to completely equip each trailer or a total of $14,000 for each trailer, plus $70,000 for a completely equipped and stocked library trailer ($20,000 for the trailer and $50,000 for books and other materials). Add to these figures $3,000 each for six heavy duty nine passenger station wagons for pulling the trailers and providing personal transportation in the field.

79

The total is $158,000 for a CLC for 40 students (8 students to a 30 foot trailer) or $4,000 capital investment per student. We might guess the investment per student for equipment would range from $2,500 to $5,000, depending on number of students, amount of equipment and size of library. The investment per student in a normal college campus ranges up to several times this figure. An expansion of 50 or 100 students would be far less expensive in the form of a CLC than in the form of fixed campus facilities.

The operating costs of a CLC are also significantly low. The only full time paid staff are the project coordinator-librarians, who double in performing various professional roles (such as advising, counseling, discipline, administration, lecturing, evaluation, etc.) typically assigned to separate individuals on the large campus (at a heavy cost in student alienation and resentment). The numerous clerical and sub-professional tasks, including many instructional assignments found on the fixed college campus are assigned to the students in the CLC (some volunteer, some paid), contributing to a sense of identity, purpose and community.

The cost for meals should be no higher than on a fixed campus. The cost of space in a trailer park is low, typically $3 to $4 a night for a trailer or $25 to $45 a month plus 15% of these amounts for each person beyond the first two.

Instead of expensive special facilities, such as gyms, the CLC makes use of community facilities and the outdoors. The CLC provides a low cost method for handling temporary peaks in enrollment. For example, the availability of a CLC can help to insure that the relatively more expensive facilities on a fixed campus are used to capacity; a CLC can be used during the early part of the school year, before the decline in enrollment due to drop-outs.

The interior design of the CLC offers a challenge to the architect; a multitude of fascinating arrangements come quickly to mind. One principle is clear—the avoidance of any interior hallways. Access to all areas should be from the exterior. Each trailer should be quickly convertible for multiple uses, such as discussion areas, work and lab areas, AV & TV viewing and listening, demonstration classrooms etc.

*Library-Trailer* — With moderately narrow aisles and six 8″ high shelves (for pocket-books or PBs), except for the bottom two shelves (12″ high), up to 2,500 feet of shelving can be housed in a double deck converted 40 foot moving van (about 550 square feet of floor space). The top six shelves would be 5″ wide, aisle width 30″; the bottom two shelves 8″ wide, aisle width 24″. Reducing the shelves by one-third to allow for office space and working area, it should still be possible to house 15,000 PBs and 2,500 ordinary books in the library trailer. Half this number could be housed in a trailer at the size that could be pulled by a heavy duty station wagon. PBs would be emphasized, for their light weight, compact size, and amenability to simple low cost indexing by use of "Pocket Books in Print." With the increasing availability of books and journals in microform or ultramicroform, there is hardly any limit to the potential size of the collection that can be housed in a library-trailer.

There would be few study tables or carrels—the students would use built-in facilities in their own all-purpose trailers. The floor of the library-trailer would be carpeted for insulation and for sitting on the floor while browsing, etc.

Ordinarily, about two-thirds of the collection in the library-trailer would be basic materials and one-third would be reserved for special materials accumulated in connection with each major project embarked upon by the CLC.

In many applications it would be desirable to use a minimum of physical processing for the books so the collection could double as a bookstore in locations where this would be desirable (for sale to both students and local residents). Books could be arranged by large subject area, corresponding to the subject divisions in PBIP, with a simple removable label constituting the only physical processing.

*Use of Libraries in the Field* — In "real" life the student will be faced with a bewildering array of potential resources. The best possible training for the "real" life of the typically urban and mobile American is practice and training in the critical and efficient use of all community resources, including libraries.

These include:
1. University, college, public, state, federal, and special libraries
2. Museums
3. Science information centers
4. Newspapers
5. Governmental records and archives
6. Computer centers
7. Instructional materials, AV and TV centers
8. Research institutes and laboratories

81

9. Trade and professional associations
10. Government offices
11. Testing Laboratories

In some instances for work in a remote area away from any of the typically urban resources listed above, the CLC would stop off in a major urban center for a period of time for materials and background, before embarking for the remote area. Major universities would constitute an especially potent resource. Fortunately, trailer parks can usually be found not far distant.

*The Small Compact College as a Community* — The CLC offers an excellent environment for the development of the values associated with a compact face-to-face community engaged in socially relevant activities. The matching of theory with social practice and experience should help develop sophistication, maturity and responsibility. The infinite variety of activities in the "wide world" offers opportunities of many kinds to that majority of students who are not "intellectuals" and are often ill adapted to the chill academic pressure of so many campuses today; such students are likely to find many more opportunities to develop self confidence and moral values in the CLC. The small compact college, out "on its own" in the world, will almost automatically involve and mobilize the latest talents of the students on a basis of equality, in matters of administration, organization and planning.

Counseling in a group in constant intimate daily relationship is a far different matter than the typical counseling offered today. There is no danger that the student in the small compact college will complain of being impersonally "processed"; everything will be brought down to a human and concerned scale.

*Particular Values to Jamestown* — The CLC would be valid for any college, but would have particular attractions for a college so isolated as Jamestown. The students at Jamestown need the development of new personal resources that can come with experiences in traveling and living in different parts of the world. Jamestown needs a dramatic attraction in order to recruit faculty and students to so isolated a location. By developing the CLC concept, the isolation of Jamestown can become a counter-posing attraction, as periods of comparative repose, retreat and meditation, to help in the assimilation of the rich experiences associated with the periods in the CLC.

Jamestown is in need of a sudden and rich infusion of lavish library resources. But the acquisition of such resources is a slow and painful process, at best. A simple way to expose the students to rich library resources is to physically transport them to the vicinity of some of the nation's major libraries. In the long run, as the number of CLCs multiply, this might become more difficult—the welcome might wear off. But there would likely be few major university or state libraries that would not welcome students from a North Dakota college if arrangements were made in advance, especially if the CLC scheduled its visits during slack periods. A letter from the Governor of North Dakota to the Governor of the state being visited would help to insure hospitality.

A library-college albeit unconventional is in some ways a subtle and difficult concept; it might not have qualities of immediate drama and appeal for the average citizen. After all, many educators and librarians have had difficulty in understanding the concept! But the CLC would be marvelously dramatic — a perfect subject for public relations and an attractive project for fund raising. It would be difficult to think of any project more certain to attract national attention for Jamestown. Whereas the development of a fixed library college will require years of time, a CLC could be developed and in operation within a few months. The concept of the CLC offers a unique opportunity to Jamestown to develop a national base for a regional college, while the library-college at Jamestown is being developed.

Finally, Jamestown needs faculty and students. One goal of the CLC field trips each year can be a deliberate effort by students and staff alike in recruiting.

*Conclusion* — Because of its emphasis on the "search" and "inquiry", the library-college concept is peculiarly adaptable to mobility. The college itself and its library goes with the student in the field, and furnishes a "home base" for continual reinspiration, reinforcement and education. A kind of mutual feedback or dialog can ensue between the student's experiences in the field and his "home base" in the field— the trailers, staff and mobile library of the CLC.

# North American Library-College

*WILLIAM HINCHLIFF*

*Philosophy.* North American Library-College construes education as an internal self-sustaining process which is synonymous with the art of good living. The essence of Library-College's philosophy is active student involvement; thorough commitment by the student to the principle of full personal responsibility for his own education, goal-selection, self-evaluation, and character development. At Library-College everything is done to make wide-ranging reading and thinking natural, comfortable, exhilarating, and successful for the individual student.

Library-College's unique design and continuous year-round operation are predicated upon unwavering recognition that a student's time is provably worth over three dollars per hour. This economic fact completely reverses the whole approach to higher education as taken at conventional hierarchial colleges which place the student at the bottom of the status structure and which ignore the needless waste of students' time resulting from inadequate curriculum design and facilities.

Library-College students' time is not wasted for any cause which is within the College's power to prevent. Examples which prevail at conventional colleges and which have largely been overcome at Library-College are:

1. Costs of slower group learning paced according to the lowest common denominator,
2. Costs of noise, interruptions, and other adverse environmental factors which disturb or destroy the processes of thought,
3. Costs of travelling to the library and waiting for books and other materials,
4. Costs of quasi-professional athletic spectacles,
5. Costs of diverting students' time into drudge jobs solely for money earning.

84

*What Happens at Library-College?* Throughout his career every student reads, discusses, practices, and experiments with library science and immerses himself in the history and philosophy of education in addition to work in his major and elective disciplines. He works in the Central Library, does some teaching, tutoring, and coaching, and performs voluntary social service in the community. Religion, morals, and ethics are fostered. Every student reads, compares, writes, and discusses man's highest and best thoughts and practices in these spheres, and in his daily life deliberately attempts to apply the basic tenets of the world's great religious thinkers and exemplars. The same comprehensive policy extends to reading, discussion, and creative work in the fine arts. Physical health and hygiene are promoted through universal participation—on a perfectly amateur basis—in team and individual sports. The College does not raise money by engaging in the sports entertainment business. There are no "athlete-ships."

Library-College maintains lively communication with other experimental colleges and with research in progress on all aspects of the improvement of education.

*Instructors, Librarians, Students.* Instructors—the title "professor" is rarely used—are fewer in number but are paid twice as much as their counterparts in conventional colleges. Librarians, relatively more numerous than are found on traditional campuses, are paid within the same salary scale. Both instructors and librarians are selected on the basis of love of books, ideas, and people; library science knowledge; teaching skill; ability to write; and enthusiasm and capacity for educational experimentation and innovation. All instructors and librarians work year round. Vacations and research leaves are spread flexibly throughout the year.

Instructors, librarians, and students exchange roles at various times and places, in varying proportions, at various levels of difficulty. For example, the student applies rigorous criteria as he selects his own books and systematically catalogs and classifies them. Organized intramural debating is nearly universal. Students debate major issues in world affairs, race relations, politics, religion, economics, birth control, and other vital spheres. Instructors, librarians, and students frequently conceive, present, debate, and defend ideas for improving the College. Ideas adopted bring appropriate recognition and rewards such as cash, travel grants, and book purchase credits.

85

*Campus Design and Architecture.*   Campus design and architecture are of paramount importance. The master plan and the new College Center were developed by eminent architects after several surveys and a well publicized continental design competition. The entire College is under one roof. Enclosed, insulated, air conditioned walkways lined with book displays and art and science exhibits connect the older buildings to the new College Center.

The College Center includes the Central Library, cooperative bookstore, lecture halls, seminar rooms, apartments for faculty and married students, and separate wings for women and men students. It also contains a cafeteria, snack bar, geodesic domed solaria, gym, pool, steam rooms, round theater, art studios, galleries, and music rooms.

A key factor in the College's extraordinary academic success is that each student has his own private living room-study, a place of peace, privacy, beauty, and utility. The student's own room provides an optimal environment for study and reflection. Approximately one-hundred thirty square feet in size, carpeted and draped, the room is acoustically engineered to be noise-proof. It contains sixty linear feet of built-in shelving, an oversize desk, file cabinet, TV, film viewing, and phonograph listening equipment, a studio bed, large bolsters and well-aimed recessed lighting for comfortable reading, viewing, and listening in bed. The student's room, containing approximately one thousand books, is a small special library, almost an extension of the student's brain. It has an entire wall of solar heat and glare resistant glass affording a soaring, inspiring view of the countryside. The bond between book learning and life is always visible.

The student in his own private room has a basic core collection of one hundred reference books selected by the student himself and borrowed, rented, or owned by him. A book-type catalog, including a classified shelf list section describing the Central Library's holdings, is in every student's room. This annual catalog is composed cooperatively by all members of the college community and is printed in the student-manned College Print Shop and Bindery. Every student receives each year his own personal copy of the current edition of the Bowker *Annual PB Book Guide for Colleges* which lists 11,000 titles by broad discipline.

*Book-Rich Faculty and Students.*   Library-College's goal is a magnificent Central Library collection containing no less than one thousand books per student, including many rare books and manu-

86

scripts, or Xerox copies, which represent original sources and historic milestones in the evolution of civilization. Other resources are in similarly generous ratio. Each student enters the College with a personal library of at least fifty books. He leaves it with approximately one thousand, including up to nine hundred paperbacks. While building his personal library he also helps build the College Library. Each student contributes one hundred dollars worth of carefully selected books and other library materials to the College each year. His donor plate goes into each book. Selections are made by the student chiefly from lists prepared by librarians and instructors. Alumni are "Friends of the College Library."

*The Central Library and Bookstore.* The one million volume open-stack Central Library, fully carpeted and draped, and acoustically perfect, is in the College Center, reachable by any student in less than two minutes in any weather without an overcoat. The architects and librarians have made it a warm, friendly, informal and inviting place with the hospitable atmosphere of a farm or ranch home, not an institutional atmosphere. The Library, largely student-staffed, is open 168 hours per week. It operates on an honor system, with minimal restrictions supplemented by effective mechanical security devices and annual campus-wide inventories in which the entire College community participates.

Library-College students operate a cooperative bookstore carrying a vast range of high quality books—paperback, hardcover, and used—and other valuable permanent records and learning apparatus.

*Courses of Study.* Half as many courses are offered as at traditional colleges. Each course is broad and flexible and is described in honest and extensive detail in the course catalog which is cooperatively composed and published by faculty and students. The descriptive notes contain pro and con criticisms by students who took the course the previous year. Before the oral part of the course begins each student selects from approved bibliographies and reads from five to fifteen paperbound books and library hard-cover volumes. He makes evaluative written notes about each book. In most cases, because he owns it, he underlines and marginally annotates his book as he reads it.

*Independent Inquiry.* In his largely self-chosen blend of reading the student strikes his preferred balance among the Great Books of the past and the most influential books of the present. This reading is supplemented and enriched by "consuming" taped lectures by distinguished scholars, viewing filmed demonstrations, drama, opera, poetry readings, spoken foreign languages, pictures, microdata etc. obtained from the Central Library. The student uses a Xerox copier to obtain copies of pages from books, journals, newspapers, and documents. He keeps a brief written critical account of his viewing-listening-experimenting-speaking-writing. Largely because of his wide freedom of choice and his nearly ideal reading-thinking environment, each student reads, sees, hears, speaks, or writes the equivalent of fifty thousand words per day.

It can only be briefly alluded to here but the students not only "consume and digest" books, articles, pamphlets, documents, films, discs, and tapes ("Consume and digest" includes lectures, seminars, panel discussions, debates, and tutorials about the principles, concepts, and ideas involved); they also produce and distribute all these tools of scholarship!

*Community Involvement.* The College is co-extensive with the surrounding community. The Library, Bookstore, and other central facilities are open to qualified local citizens, particularly to present and potential community leaders. College exhibits and conferences are held throughout the community; many community conferences and exhibits are conducted in the College Center. There is extremely close and constructive cooperation with the community's schools, public library, and other important cultural development agencies of the region.

*The Mobile Year* (Jordan's Idea). During his second year each student joins the Library-College Caravan which visits and studies at first hand the strengths, weaknesses, progress, and decay of several distinctive North American cities and rural areas. Legislatures, colleges, schools, libraries, bookstores, publishing houses, book factories, museums, zoos, botanical gardens, and mass media agencies are visited and studied. Notable persons, teachers, librarians, and students in every area meet frankly and informally with the members of the mobile community.

*The Community of the Future.* Because the College affords a superior yet eminently practical mode of living for civilized men and women it represents the advanced community of the future. Its graduates, having established personal patterns of satisfying intellectual growth, will never be content with complacent culturally barren communities.

# Oakland Community College: A Case Study in Independent Study

*JOHN TIRRELL*

*Introduction.*—When Oakland Community College (OCC), Oakland County, Michigan, opened in the fall of 1965, it became one of the 500 to 1,000 similar new institutions which will open their doors in the 1965-75 decade. Fifteen months from the date it was approved, Oakland Community College accepted on two separate campuses a record community college initial enrollment of over 4,000 students. Upon becoming its first employee, the President immediately started recruiting key management personnel and assigned them to work on specific problems of designing and planning the campuses and the development of the functional requirements for the instructional program.

*The Need for Change.*—The need for innovation in instruction generally and in higher education in particular has been widely accepted and any demonstrated achievements can be utilized beyond this institution. Jerrold R. Zacharias, Chairman, Panel on Education Research and Development of the President's Science Advisory Committee in the Committee's report stated: "The task of educational research and development is to learn how to provide for all students the education an exceptional teacher provides for a few." This is the crucial requirement for educational technology and certainly must occur if the independent and continuing study needs of society are to be met. Unfortunately, the Zacharias panel did not produce a significant plan for translating the goal of educational research and development into reality. At OCC we have taken a significant step forward in implementing educational innovation.

*Design and Planning.*—The College staff reviewed virtually all recent literature on learning theory and the application of that theory to teaching. Research on class size, space and time utilization and instructional innovations at colleges and universities were carefully studied. Design specifications for the OCC instructional methodology were derived from the information assembled. The success throughout the country of learning techniques based on individual study was convincing. It was this research and design effort which established OCC as a unique institution.

*Instructional Methods: Conventional and Tutorial.*—The tutorial laboratory model employed at OCC presents a striking contrast between the methods and techniques of conventional instruction and those of the individual learning proposed by the instructional systems approach. Conventional methods of teaching are basically teacher oriented or "open-loop" instructional systems. The teacher plans and organizes his subject matter presentation in terms of material coverage in specified units of time; he tells groups of students what he considers to be relevant based on his best "guesstimate" of what is important and to what degree of understanding he wishes to achieve in his students. Little if any provision is made for directed and continued student response and correct answer confirmation as the prime criterion for the design and pacing of instruction. The student usually plays a passive role, being neither required nor able to respond and receive correct answer confirmation at every step in the learning process. Usually there is no finite pre-statement of final or terminal performance objectives specifying exactly what the individual student must be able "to know" and "to do" to achieve acceptably. With conventional "open loop" instructional models, the student is evaluated by means of tests which sample the material covered during the instructional sequences. The test questions may or may not be relevant to points of significance required for the concise understanding of principle, concept or application involved.

The instructional systems approach applied at OCC is a learner-centered or a "closed-loop" model of instruction. It is a self-adjustive performance system based specifically on the pre-definition of (1) what is to be learned, (2) the required levels of terminal or final proficiency to be achieved by learners and (3) the most appropriate sequence of instructional steps for learners to insure their success on each progressive step leading to the attainment of the pre-stated terminal performance specifications.

Of critical importance in designing the "closed-loop" instructional model as applied in the tutorial laboratory is the pre-specification of

90

the "critical or optimal learning path." This learning path is limited to "need to know" instructional requirements; to the use of only relevant demonstrations, exercises, etc.; to the reinforcement of concepts to be learned; the sequence and order of presentation of instructional components to be included as integral parts of the instructional sequences; the prescribed role of instructor and student in each instructional setting; and, of great significance, the means of controlling pacing of instruction based on the measured understanding of individual students.

The real measure of validity of such a system lies in its capability to produce the predictable learning achievements designed for the learners in question.

*Instructional Methods.*—In contrast to conventional methods of curriculum planning and instruction the Oakland Community College designed and implemented instructional methods which are primarily student or learner oriented. Courses of instruction have minimized traditional group teaching applications. Instead, students are provided carefully designed instructional sequences which stress supervised self-directed instruction. Learning is controlled and placed by the individual student, consistent with his abilities to perform successfully.

This model of self-directed learning is based on the work of Professor Samuel Postlethwaite of the Botany Department, Purdue University. With the audio-tutorial or tutorial-laboratory model of instruction developed by Postlethwaite the responsibility for learner achievements rests primarily in the learner himself. Instructional materials, equipment and all other resources required for successful terminal achievements are provided each student in a specially designed study carrel. Self-directed instructional sequences include audio-tapes, visual displays, books, periodicals, laboratory experimental set-ups, programmed materials and manuals among others. Faculty members are always available during self-directed study activities to assist students as required in achieving pre-defined knowledge and skill objectives. This "tutorial laboratory" environment enables the student and instructor alike to utilize their respective abilities at maximum capacity. In essence, the method places the responsibility for learning and the mechanics for study time on the student while permitting the instructor to have maximum personal contact with the student on a "need to know" basis. The instructor can direct his skills more efficiently toward orientation and guidance.

Students are provided large group assemblies on a scheduled basis. A skilled "master teacher" uses this time to discuss course objectives, present new developments in the field, point out applications of the subject matter and integrate subject matter with other areas in the pre-designed educational program. Student performance is frequently evaluated by written, performance or oral exams as the basis for advancement and to furnish feedback information to the learner.

*Implementation and Field Test.* — In order to insure a properly functioning system it is most critical for implementing personnel to be fully oriented to their task. At OCC an in-service program covering the following areas was conducted:

1. System design applications
2. Roles of instructors, students and administration
3. Student performance evaluation criterion and techniques
4. Teaching strategies to meet individual student needs
5. Operational conditions required by the field-test program

As with any system it can be expected that individual components will undergo a series of design modifications. In an instructional system the means for determining design change requirements will be based on how well specific instructional materials, sequences, etc., produce the desired terminal learning achievements which they were designed to produce. Normal practice requires several minor modifications in materials in order to insure the highest level of performance predictability. A fair test of all system components for individual courses of instruction will require a minimum of two years field-testing with a third year required for full scale implementation.

A System Model must be followed indicating the design, development and system evaluation steps which must occur in the achievement of the operational stage of a "closed-loop" instructional system. On completion of these steps the system designer provides a learning system which will perform with the highest degree of predictability in the achievement of the pre-stated learning objectives. It is the "closed-loop" model of instruction which has been implemented at OCC for all courses of instruction applying the audio-tutorial or independent study concept.

*System Management Methods and Procedures.* — Critical to a learner-centered systems approach is the design and implementation of management organizational principles which can accommodate the functions to be performed in the achievement of its objectives. At OCC

92

a significant departure from conventional system management principles and organization was implemented.

The underlying design principle of the OCC management model places major emphasis on instructional management requirements which are consistent with the learner-centered approach. Major divisions of management responsibility are placed with the offices of Vice President for Curriculum and Vice President for Campus Administration. The former office is charged with total responsibility for the design and selection of instructional systems components (materials, people, facilities) which are required to produce the desired learner achievements. The latter office is charged with the responsibility of achieving stated student terminal performance specifications by providing independent control for the implementation of the instructional system design completed by the office of Vice President for Curriculum. These activities are of equal significance for achieving stated system objectives and as such represent by a process of checks and balances the necessary controls to assure system integrity.

On completion of the design of an instructional system by the Vice President for Curriculum it must be approved by and accepted for implementation by the Vice President for Campus Administration. Once accepted for implementation total responsibility for system and student performance evaluation will rest with the Vice President for Campus Administration. Requested modifications in the instructional system, insertions and deletions will be based solely on performance criteria derived in the actual process of operation. Quality assurance in the achievements of learner products becomes the central theme of this systems management model. The student is paramount in the definition of policies and procedures for total system operation. In turn, the functions performed by system support groups under the Vice President for Business, including the offices of Finance, Personnel, Systems, New Facilities and Purchasing are in every case defined in terms of the achievement of the student terminal performance specifications.

*OCC Development Commitments (1964-66).* — The Board of Trustees has committed over $20 million for developing four campuses to be in operation in Oakland County by 1970. When fully operational these sites will serve the needs of over 15,000 junior college students. All campuses will be elements of a single integrated junior college system under one administrative director. The Board has further authorized interim plans for the integration of computer techniques for

93

administrative functions and computer-assisted instructional applications. Integrated television programming in the four campus complex is also under consideration. Each of the campuses will be modeled after the tutorial laboratory approach in operation at the two existing campuses.

*System Planning, Design and Implementation Phases.*—Under the direction of the President an extensive planning, design and implementation program was initiated to achieve the present operational posture. The five major functional requirements to be completed between January, 1965, and June, 1966, are:

1. An Instructional Systems Approach which would coordinate the management efforts of administrators and faculty members.
2. A plan for orientation and training of new faculty members in the use of the Independent Study approach, since no experienced staff existed.
3. Development of instructional materials to meet the exacting specifications written by the faculty.
4. Design of an inexpensive student study carrel which would have the necessary flexibility for using all modern media.
5. Design and selection of reliable equipment to be used in the carrels.

OCC contracted with Litton Instructional Materials, Inc., Anaheim, California for the following system management services:

1. Provide a management model allowing the tutorial laboratory method to be designed and implemented using the instructional systems approach.
2. Conduct an orientation and training workshop to provide key faculty members with knowledge and skills in planning and developing instructional course designs using the systems approach.
3. Develop Programmed Instructional Packages which meet faculty developed OCC specifications.

*Phase 1 (January, 1965-June, 1968)*

1. Evidence on the success and failure of students using various approaches to learning, media, teacher and learner time, etc., and other implications for equipment and architecture would be available for dissemination to existing institutions.
2. Validated programs would be available for the use of other educational groups. There are significant costs of designing, writing, testing, revising and evaluating various media and it seems unnecessary for others to duplicate this effort—even if they have the desire and financial resources.

94

3. A large group of faculty in the many academic disciplines and numerous technical fields would be trained to develop effective learning materials using a multi-media approach. This could provide the basis for the immediate development of Phase II materials for national junior college curricula.

4. Computer-Assisted Instruction. CAI is possible and awaits the training of a large group of subject matter specialists and the availability of a substantial number of programs. OCC provides the first opportunity to implement CAI where extensive software was developed prior to computer purchase.

## Phase II (1968-1970)

By July 1, 1968, Oakland Community College will be able to demonstrate objectively the effectiveness of the tutorial-laboratory approach in a fully operational junior college. Beginning September, 1967, a third campus especially designed for the tutorial-laboratory self-directed approach will be opened for operation at a cost of $13.7 million. During 1968, therefore, instructional systems field tested during 1966-67 will be implemented in a physical facility especially designed for their applications. Validated instructional system course designs and instructional components integral to these designs will be available for dissemination to other junior colleges in academic and technology courses. Cost effectiveness criteria will be derived in all operational phases. A validated system management process specific to a learner-centered systems approach will be available for dissemination to other junior colleges. A variety of student performance indices will be provided relating to the effectiveness of alternate method-media combinations for academic and technical training objectives.

These accomplishments will provide the empirical criteria and necessary resources to extend the OCC operation to a computer-assisted instructional environment. Recent recommendations for the development of this computer capability were postulated at the U. S. Office of Education Symposium held at the University of California, Irvine, November, 1965. It was specified that the OCC type of facility would be best suited to long-range community needs. The development of extensive learner-centered instructional materials in Phase I in conjunction with the large faculty capability to produce further materials will provide a unique operational testing capability for computer-assisted instructional applications in the junior college setting.

# Schools Without Teachers: An Existential Pragmatic Possibility

*BLAKE FISHBURNE*

TRADITIONALLY the task of education was the teaching of knowledge. From studying old absolutist philosophies such as Platonism many educators drew the assumption that educating someone required only recognizing the absolute truth about something and then teaching it to youngsters.

Modern epistemologies such as those of pragmatism and existentialism dispute man's claim to absolute knowledge, but pragmatism has sought to reconstruct the word "knowledge" so we might define it as that which is congruent with our funded beliefs. Pragmatism suggests that we should always be prepared to revise our beliefs or our knowledge but that we may call it knowledge only as long as it does not conflict with our overall system of beliefs.

The effect of pragmatism on progressive education is generally recognized. Progressive educators, perhaps due to the reconstructed definition of knowledge proposed by the pragmatists chose to retain the word *knowledge* and the general impression of tested beliefs which the reconstructed word implied. By retaining this word both pragmatists and progressive educators were able to enjoy a degree of popularity. Charles Stevenson has suggested that we consider the effect of certain words upon the public and the ways by which they can be led along simply by retaining these words and changing the definitions. Words such as "god," "knowledge," and "truth" are good examples.

But by retaining these words and reconstructing the definitions there is a danger of also retaining the undesirable emotional attitudes which the public has attached to the words. It may be desirable to have enthusiastic followers carrying signs reading "God," "knowledge" and "truth" (or Veritas) — but are we prepared to consider also the effects of the simplification and prejudice which retention of the old terminology allows?

One of the major criticisms of pragmatism is that there always appears to be an infinity of the effects of action. Therefore, an instructor who tells his students that he is teaching them truth or knowledge (even by the reconstructed definition) is misleading them somewhat, it appears. For considering the infinity of possible effects the teacher is only qualified to say, "I am deciding subjectively which effects are noteworthy and agree with my own funded beliefs and am presenting them to you as pragmatic truth — when in honesty I should be careful to note that this is *my* pragmatic truth or knowledge (or *meaning* which I choose to call truth and knowledge in order to impress you). You, however, may further consider the infinity of effects and draw quite different meanings. If you prefer, I will allow you to call your meanings 'truth' and 'knowledge' also, so that you may impress me in turn and I will also become more accustomed to the continued use of the terms and so be more delightfully satisfied when I myself choose to use the terms again."

At any rate there seems to be an ample amount of deception in teaching what is purported to be truth and knowledge even in the best progressive schools. This conclusion depends on one's epistemology, but it also depends on one's recognition of the emotions as biologically somewhat prejudicial to logical thinking for human beings.

My own hypothesis—I have no truth or knowledge to offer—is that education might profit from the epistemological angst of existentialism — that those who have heretofore called themselves instructors might appropriate a little more hope and fear over their hypotheses and meanings and rather than saying, "Let me teach you truth and knowledge," say instead, "Let us study the possibilities for common meanings from our perspectives and let us try to do so tentatively and with respect for infinite complexity. I do not call myself an instructor —not even an instructor of meanings or probabilities, but like you I am still a student."

Existential epistemology and possibly an existential pragmatic epistemology with a pragmatic hope-nexus on the hope side of its balanced hope and fear, may lead to such radical changes in educational philosophy as to abolish "instructors" in favor of "senior students" (older students who *may* have valuable resources to offer). Additionally, this radical philosophical position may bring some searching lights on such terms as "curriculum" and may lead to the abandonment of subject areas in favor of unlimited interdisciplinary questioning with only phenomenological nexus-areas as anxious reference points.

Perhaps those who have heretofore called themselves "instructors" and espoused "truth" and "knowledge" will get a feeling that a more thoughtful way to walk a posited line across an abyss is on tiptoe.

The position of radical reflection on *meaning* and intentional continuous reconstruction of hypotheses presented in this paper indicates that we will need more data on which to form our constantly changing hypotheses. We will need all the library communications we can muster for our shared meanings to anticipate as many points of view as possible. The shared or cultural meanings usually *given* or *taught* by instructors, however, will be *presented* by "senior students" as a *resource* for new meanings and hypotheses. Etymologically, *re*-search will be the continuing process of creating new hypotheses out of old and new data for changing actions. Although the word "research" has come to mean trivial technical tedium in some academic circles this need not be so. An important emphasis would be to find, and to help students find, significant and challenging issues which make the process of *researching* interesting and exciting. *Possibilities* might be presented by the senior students as stimulation, but the student should then be allowed to *re-search* according to his own interests, as forced searching seems unlikely to offer the creative excitement and interest found in a project agreeable to the student. Forced or slanted searching (searching which is slanted beyond the presentation of *possibilities)* would also be in opposition to the philosophy of an intentionally continual reconstruction of anxious hypotheses. But the presentation of *possibilities* in voluntarily attended lectures (preferably exciting "talks"), in group discussions or brain-storming sessions, or by other means of voluntarily accepted communications are resources for additional data and alternatives in the construction of working hypotheses.

The Library-College concept may meet several problems in attempting to mediate between society's demands and what is otherwise thought to be the best hypothetical Library-College. Accreditation associations, for example, exercise much influence for faculties of M.A.'s and Ph.D.'s. While we may consider the possibility that a person with an M.A. or a Ph.D. may have been exposed to a greater range of experiences and may have more meanings to share as a "senior student" this is not necessarily the case. The Library-College might exercise influence with accreditation associations and bring about re-evaluation of existing policies. Another approach would be to meet the present accreditation requirements but allow some flexibility by having a limited number of "senior students" elected from the undergraduate student body and other sources after review of submitted "communication proposals" to the Library-College community. If a person's "communication proposal" were accepted he would then become a "senior student" on a grant. These elected "senior students" should have equal status with the regular faculty, and every effort should be made to impress the M.A.'s and Ph.D.'s with their own *exciting* status as unpretentious but important "senior students."

Lastly, the Caravan Library-College presents a flexible Library-College well designed for our changing world. The existentialists and pragmatists agree that mobility can increase freedom, and it seems quite important that a Library-College emphasizing reconstruction of hypotheses have its own flexible hypotheses concerning location and ability to facilitate maximum social and educational aid.

# Hanky Panky

*REV. GILBERT M. ARMSTRONG*

LET THE PROPOSED College be named by any name; its epithet will be "sabotage" for the Moderns and "Hanky Panky" for the Victorians. Since the former has a connotation of war and destruction, and the latter a more subtle suggestion of underhand but not malicious scheming against the Establishment, a somewhat picaresque tone, it is my name for my Liberal Arts College. In effect the appelative indicates my attitude, for in this matter one must adopt a tone of lightness, a sense of humor in order to avoid pretentiousness, *hubris,* and to preserve a sense of humility. Nevertheless the proposal is made in all seriousness with an awareness of the danger to the personality of the proposer and the far-reaching effects of the proposal.

The first radical proposal is that the College be a real community: a community in fact rather than in catalog description. Of this, more later. The purpose of the community is the first concern.

Its purpose shall be to help men and women engage in life for themselves in the existentialist sense of the word "for." In Hanky Panky students will become men; in learning to become men they will of necessity become better citizens of the local community. The College should have no interest in making well-adjusted citizens; therefore, the community will exist for its members who will make themselves. After they leave it they will, being free men who accept themselves, be fit to accept and to a great extent control their environment rather than be controlled by it. This search for humaneness shall be the primary purpose of the College.

Its secondary purpose shall be to prepare students for graduate schools, people who will perpetuate learning by acquiring facts, by inquiring further and more deeply, by developing more skills in the art of contemplation, of reflection. These people will not only perpetuate, they will propagate the ideal and its practice.

How is all this to be done? By two steps within the community. Every entering student will be required to learn through expository lectures and specialized dictionaries basic factual data and a scholarly vocabulary adequate for the discipline in which he is to engage. In this first step use will be made of all the technological tools by which factual knowledge may be acquired. This step is absolutely necessary if there is to be communication: in a world new to him and which he is to inhabit for only four years, there is no time for the student to spend in empirical learning of that world's language.

Then, having been prepared, having prepared himself, he will take the second step. Let us say he comes of age in the community. Now in a small group he reads, and here I use the word to include the practice of arts, laboratory work in the natural sciences and so on, as well as the actual reading of books, under the leadership of a faculty person whose function is to guide not dictate, to inspire rather than require, and it might well be, to learn along with him.

In the small group he will be engaged with his subject, his peer group, his guide and himself. Person will be superior to subject so he will learn, not in order to pass examinations but to become more human. However, as guides and indicators of his development he will take two comprehensive examinations during his academic career, one at the end of the sophomore and one at the end of the senior year.

Now all of this is not practical. I rather think it is. Be that as it may, let us be practical. Let us face realities.

The first practical necessity is for faculty people who are so broadly educated as to be able to range far and wide, experts in their own fields but aware of the philosophy and major concepts of other disciplines. They must be aware of source materials on a broad scale in many areas and in fact they ought to be librarians to a great degree. As persons each must be secure in his own self, must learn to laugh at himself and be laughed at without rancor or fear. As each of us needs somehow to be superior so he must resist his own response to the pressure of students that he be superior except in excellence, experience, and humility. No faculty person at Hanky Panky will dwell on Olympus as the companion of Zeus nor will he come down from Zion as the messenger of God. The seminar will replace to great degree the lecture and the student will discover truth for himself rather than accepting it from on high. The guide will suggest approaches, not dictate opinions. This seems like an overt suggestion that many faculty people do *lecture* with that approach. We do. It suggests that students demand that faculty *tell* them. They do.

But people who are secure in their own persons, openly knowing their strengths and happy in them, openly knowing their weaknesses and seeking to overcome them in humility, attempting a little more than they can do and working at being more than they are, can resist the internal and external pressures to seek security in an assumed role of superiority. Faculty in Hanky Panky will, because of their quality, and because of their personal security, be secure in their positions.

Of course, people of this calibre will be hard to find, and harder still to attract to a small college. Perhaps those of us who are eager to engage in such a Herculean task have nominated ourselves; those who will approach the task with some misgivings will find in the community the strength and support to develop; those who see it as impossible or faulty will disqualify themselves.

Far greater is the problem of students. Some will come prepared to coast for four years in a glorified bull session. Some will come with strong opinions founded only on strong opinions. These will have but short terms — of their own choice. By far the greatest number are those who, because they have not tried, are afraid to think, and those ill prepared to confront reality. These, if they can and will think, with the few (and they are not so few as we imagine) who are prepared for the confrontation, and in our schools and colleges now, stifled by conformity, hardly aware of what a college can do. These will be our students.

Now this sounds Aristocratic. Is education for the few? It is, if we mean only the brilliant. It is, if we think in terms of the democratic view that education is for those in the first two groups. But if we remember our first purpose — to help men and women engage in life that they may become for themselves — to become truly human to the best of their ability — then the College will be truly humane, truly a community, truly democratic. Our problem may well be one of effecting a complete change in attitude of both faculty and students.

As for the community's organization: Hanky Panky will be a liberal arts college, without professional schools because their specialized training processes make demands upon faculty and students preventing the development of the college ideal. Neither will there be an Athletic Department as we now know it. Games and contests will be intramural, inter-house. All who are physically able will take part. In a small town or suburban setting the College will have a maximum enrollment of 1,000 with a faculty of 90 to 100. Freshmen, being so

102

to speak in their nonage, will have no active part in the management of community affairs. All others, both faculty and students, will be voting community members. They will elect faculty, administration, Trustees, and ultimately the President, who will be a member of the Trustees. The Trustees will be responsible only for the care of endowment and College business affairs. The administration will care for discipline and housekeeping. The faculty will be responsible for leadership, for guidance, and for their own academic and personal growth. Every member of the community, as citizens, will be taxed to pay for community services.[1]

But this matter of building the community and the administration of it can safely be left in the hands of those now skilled in the field who can pass on their skills to others. Basic to the community are the sense of belonging, the knowledge of interdependence and the practice of it, together with a love of persons and of learning.

The Library? It must be *The* building — the house of all the tools, the museum, the display place of the arts, the community cultural center. More than this it shall be the place of thought, of reflection, the place where thinkers can share insights gained from reading, from the hard work of thought. Let the architect and the artist, sensitive to its purpose and possibilities, design it. Let the faculty and the students use it.

---

[1] For this section the author is indebted to Dan Sillers whose ideas it summarizes.

# The Shores Library-College: An Outline[1]

LOUIS SHORES

## LEARNING MODE

I. *"Passing" of the classroom as a mode of learning.*

L. C. (Library-College) reverses present relationship between library and classroom. Instead of a *class meeting* in U. S. History on Monday, Wednesday, and Friday from 9-10 A.M. and *Library Reading* when the student can get to it, L. C. schedules *Library Reading in U. S. History,* Monday, Wednesday, Friday from 10-12 and class meeting when the students feel the need for one, or not at all if individual conference, small seminar, inspired lecture is preferred.

II. *Library Reading.*

This is the learning mode. Tough, hard struggle with the printed word is the regimen. Education is a struggle. Suffering is a prelude to learning. This is not to say medicine must be bitter to be good. On the contrary, "creative understanding" affords a sweet triumph. Library Reading underwrites *viability*. But it does much more than provide power to maintain existence; it arms the young mind to contend with the riddle of the universe, to ask "Who am I?", "Why should I exist at all?", "Is there any point to maintaining existence, to viability?".

III. *Library Viewing, Auding, Tasting, Smelling, Feeling are also part of the learning mode.*

And for that reason the L. C. library includes all formats. Each format has a peculiar pertinence to the individual learning situation occurring at various points in the student's college life.

---

[1] This outline and miniature essay is based on a book-length manuscript currently being written titled *U. S. U. (United States University); Idea for an American University,* which includes a cluster of Library-Colleges.

The unique strengths and weaknesses of each of the 100 or more classes of educational media, from textbook through television including programmed, manual and computerized devices should be part of the equipment used by the new generation of college faculty, a cross between the best qualities for the present classroom instructor and librarian-teacher.

IV. *"Each One Teach One."*

Under this system as they advance in their work students become, under faculty direction, instructors, tutors, or monitors of students not as far along. This method provides a natural complement for the Library Learning Mode, benefiting not only the student but the tutor. All of us learned more about our subject by teaching it.

## CURRICULUM

### Generalia Areas

Reading Area A Information Retrieval
Reading Area B Knowledge

### Knowledge

Reading Area C Humanities
Reading Area D Social Sciences
Reading Area E Sciences
Reading Area F Physical Culture
Reading Area G Useful Arts

### Specialty Units

Reading Unit C1 Philosophy
C2 Religion
C3 Music
C4 Visual Art
C5 Language-Literature

Reading Unit D1 Sociology
D2 Political Science
D3 Economics
D4 Anthropology
D5 Psychology

| Reading Unit | E1 | Mathematics |
| | E2 | Astronomy-Space |
| | E3 | Physics |
| | E4 | Chemistry |
| | E5 | Biology (Life Sciences) |
| Activity Unit | F1 | Athletics |
| | F2 | Dance |
| | F3 | Self-Defense |
| | F4 | Gymnastics |
| | F5 | Swimming |
| Activity Unit | G1 | Agriculture |
| | G2 | Health |
| | G3 | Food |
| | G4 | Clothing |
| | G5 | Shelter |
| | G6 | Etiquette |
| | G7 | Marriage and the Family |

V. *"The Half of Knowledge is Knowing Where to Find It."*

Current Freshman orientation in library use, whether a half-hour "Cook's tour" during the opening days, a one-semester hour separate course, or a six-clock hour unit in Freshman English, is at best only a beginning. Ignorance of basic reference books, the components of this "half," is daily demonstrated by the inept handling of these tools. For 105 years, *Statesman's Yearbook* has appeared annually with the most compact and authoritative data on the governments of the world. Yet, even majors and faculty in government neglect this source. *Information Retrieval* earns a curriculum place, therefore, that it has never had before.

VI. *"The Other Half"* is much more *inter*-disciplinary than subject areas. It is now "old hat" to point to an "integrated" curriculum that consists of "phy sci" in place of separate courses in chemistry, physics, geology; humanities in place of isolated offerings in philosophy, literature, and music. The time has come for beginning and capstone syntheses. Along with the generalist *Information Retrieval* offering must come a "generalia" course in knowledge which interrelates science, social science and humanities and confirms the unity of the universe.

106

VII.  *The Five Major Areas* complement the two generalia and are somewhat like the components of post-World War II general education. Each reading area consists of Reading Units which resemble and provide a transition from present courses. But the word "reading" is emphasized, based on the precedent in England where a student "reads" in history, philosophy, physics, and even mathematics. It is further confirmation that evaluating a student's achievement shall not be measured in terms of class contacts.

Areas C, D, E comprise five reading units designated by subjects which currently name our academic departments. They are areas in which reading (including auding, viewing, and other sensory and extra-sensory media of communication) predominates, and in which activities (principally laboratory, field trip) are secondary. However, performance (writing and oral) is considerable.

Areas F and G are predominantly activity and performance; reading is enlisted but is secondary. These areas aim to prepare men to *do,* just as Area A-E aims to prepare students to *think, know, feel, appreciate,* and *believe.*

Self-defense is a vital part of every boy's and girl's life. Instruction and practice in boxing, wrestling, judo and other aspects of the manly art deserve a place. The dance as an art or as a social grace is in demand. Inter-collegiate football deserves a place not only as a more colorful spectacle than the late Ernest Hemingway's bull fight, but as a much more creative release of those forces which promote demonstration and rebellion in less mature nations. There is educational, esthetic, ethical and physical development in playing games to win according to well defined rules. All of the current collegiate sports including circus should be encouraged.

Area G is intended to equip every college graduate to assume responsibilities in home and community. It includes handyman skills for the man and homemaking proficiency for the woman. The range of units comprehends such prosaic but necessary talents as fixing leaking faucets, repairing torn screens, painting neglected exteriors, preparing balanced and delectable meals, knitting, sewing, child care, first aid, gardening, and etiquette.

Overall, the curriculum is a continuous interplay between the broad general and the minute special with all the degrees in between. A student's broad reading, at first, and concurrently

107

later, in the two "Generalia" and five "Knowledge" areas leads to increasing concentrations in specialist units and specialized topics. As he approaches the senior months he is recalled by the "capstone" period in his knowledge area which seeks to interrelate the many particles with which he has been concerned.

## STUDENTS

The Jamestown College Catalog statement of interest in "extending admission consideration to academically capable students of good character, emotional stability, high morale, and seriousness of purpose" is fundamental. The particular interest in "those who demonstrate special abilities in extra-curricular areas" adds a bit of insurance for a well-rounded student community. Especially comforting is the absence of the vindictive and often flaunting declaration of interest "only in the superior student." Such colleges are cowards. Nor should an independent study, library-centered college be for the "superior student" only. Rather, I believe the "class contact" college has been even more difficult for the "average" than for the "superior" student, and impossible for the below average student. Consequently, a heterogeneous student body is recommended for the L. C.: all ranges of intellectual ability, skill, talent, physical perfection, wide representation geographically, including people from other nations and non-Christian faiths.

Only the limitations of the Jamestown statement are desirable. To evaluate, the standard tests and secondary school performance, letters of reference and interview, health certification, and comment from a religious affiliation should be included in the admission folder.

Quantitatively, 400 to 800 students should constitute one L. C. As the upper figure is approached a second L. C. should be activated and then a third, so no matter how large the campus, impersonality is prevented by this organizational cluster of small colleges, Oxford, Cambridge—like.

## FACULTY

Ultimately the new breed will be a cross of the best found among those who today teach predominately by classroom lecture, discussion-recitation, and those who guide through library reading, auding, viewing.

Presently there are enough classroom instructors and library counsellors in both ranks (classroom and library) to provide a nucleus faculty for the L. C. There are also some graduate students who because they are less committed to the classroom contact "lock-step" can be more easily re-oriented. Under this direction, student monitors, tutors, fellows will herald the next generation of college faculty.

## LIBRARY

For an undergraduate L. C. 20,000 titles are basic. This will represent many more volumes and items.

Qualitatively, the parts of the selection are (1) Reference (basic lists); (2) General Reading (books every educated man should read) The *Harvard Classics, The Great Books* and by innumerable other lists; (3) *Hard Cover and Paperback Books* (divided by faculty decision with such assistance as library aids and reviews offer); (4) *Serials,* including a selection of newspapers, periodicals, scholarly journals, government publications; (5) *Graphics* largely library and faculty produced instructional materials; (6) *Projections* (still, opaque and transparent, motion, micro); (7) *Transmission* (disc, tape, radio, tv, computer); (8) *Programmed* media, manual, mechanical, electronic; (9) *Community resources* (compilations, guides, contacts, reports relating to natural, institutional, human resources).

Library organization should take advantage of central technical processing wherever possible to release librarian-teachers from housekeeping duties. Broad classification, preferably by D. C. third summary in most instances, because of that system's greater nmemonic and instructional potential, and now with the 17th edition more up-to-date than Library of Congress. However, if the latter is adopted, copy classification exactly, without tampering.

Plan for print-out book catalogs instead of central card catalog. Provide copies of total catalog for all faculty regularly kept up-to-date by computerized supplements and cumulations.

## FACILITY

Since the Library is the College, academically, it is the main building of every campus. Thus a university consists of a cluster of Library-Colleges, somewhat after the Cambridge, Oxford pattern and reflected in U. S. trends at Santa Cruz, Pacific, Michigan State, and elsewhere.

The Library-College may be planned as a quadrangle—with four major building units: (1) Library-College; (2) Dormitory and recreation; (3) Laboratory, shop, gymnasium, for activity, performance; (4) Chapel for meditation, worship, quiet forces of music, art.

The Library-College building may be octagonal or circular. At the core is a traditional (not a modular) stack, two to eight tiers high to correlate with circumference reading—study-conference of one to four stories high. Circumference areas will relate with the Dewey stack segments approximately.

| Curriculum Area | Dewey |
|---|---|
| A & B | 000-099. |
| C | 100-149; 179-199; 200-299; 390-399; 400-499; 700-789; 800-899; 920-29. |
| D | 300-389; 900-919; 930-999. |
| E | 500-599. |
| F | 790-99. |
| G | 600-699. |

Reader accommodation is 100%, individual carrel or station. Table accommodations are available in conference rooms, seminars, near index, catalog, viewing, auding, and certain other group facilities. Carrels are located in the inner circumference contiguous with stacks. Faculty office-studies, large enough for faculty research, preparation, and conference with up to three persons at one time are located in the inner-outer circumference along with work rooms. Seminars, listening and viewing rooms, each accommodating 10 to 20 are located in the outer circumference.

Lighting, darkening, acoustics, outlets provide for newer media including "listening posts" in reading areas and eschew modular construction for the L. C. building. Campus lawn esthetically landscaped and possibly a center fountain. Outside of central area place athletic fields and "where the action is" equipment.

## FINANCE

Parsons College has shown the way to independence. Many parents share the quest for a college opportunity for young people. If a $2,000 to $3,000 annual cost for college is now within the pocketbook of the nation then a 500-student college underwrites, independently, a million to a million and a half dollar program. This should cover food, shelter, recreation, health protection and academics.

110

Approximately (for 500 students)

Housing ................................$100,000
Food ..................................  250,000
Health, recreation, etc. ...............   50,000
Library materials and maintenance (clerical) ....   50,000
Faculty salaries
    Distinguished visiting lecturers (20 @ $1,000)   20,000
    Distinguished resident scholars (5 @ $20,000)  100,000
    Library Professors (40 @ average $8,000) ..  320,000
    Administration ......................  100,000
    Contingent  .........................  210,000

## EVALUATION

Most difficult of all is the measure of education, for the L. C. evaluation must be eclectic in the transition period utilizing all conventional instruments and devices for the sake of comparability and transfer. Qualitatively, writing, speaking, performing tests must be utilized. In preparation for these, students undertake:

*Writing* of weekly, term, comprehensive essays, quizzes, examinations. Standardized tests are used wherever possible with stimulation to achieve without apology, for best national averages, for preeminence.

*Speaking,* dialogue, debate, forum, tape, assembly, at scheduled, frequent opportunities.

*Oral* examinations of both information finding and concept exposition. For the former, a type of competitive "college bowl" or tournament device should be constructed. Despite criticism of the "walking encyclopedia" kind of learning, L. C. can demonstrate that it is more effective even in this kind of learning. And since most national tests are heavily slanted in this direction, L. C. cannot afford to disdain.

*Performing* should strive not only for excellence but for record breaking. Perhaps the Russian method of keeping constantly in front of their athletes existing performance records in their specialties has advantages over Big Ten Conference restraints against winning.

# The Library-College, A Merging of the Identity of the Faculty with That of the Library[1]

*ROBERT JORDAN*

### Current Crisis in Liberal Education

Practically all colleges in America, including junior colleges and universities, subscribe to the philosophy of a liberal or general education, for at least a significant portion, if not all, of the college years of their undergraduates. The independent liberal arts college, unique to America, is still the guide and model for this philosophy and presumably the locus of this practice in its purest form.

Unfortunately there is an alarming gap between profession and practice on the 2,000 plus undergraduate campuses. Far too many liberal arts or general education programs consist of little more than slightly warmed over texts and lectures from high school or even *junior* high school. Far too large a proportion of faculty and students have an entirely minimal interest or enthusiasm about any education beyond the purely professional or technical, in the face of the fact that the world has become so complex as to require citizens with world or solar perspective.

.   .   .   .   .

Paradoxically, despite a recent interest by employers in the "generalist," the entire conception of liberal education is under severe attack today, even at the colleges most clearly identified with all that a humanistic or liberal education has meant. The generalist is in ill repute, the

---

[1] Excerpts from a paper delivered at the School of Library Science, Syracuse University, November, 1964.

term "general education" often arouses a slight smirk or knowing glance of ill restrained intolerance.

. . . . .

### Basing the Curriculum on the Variety in the Library

In many contemporary colleges, it might well be observed that the quality of the library exceeds the quality of the faculty. Expressed in another way, we might say that the library is under-exploited, under-appreciated, or that the variety and depth of the library exceeds the variety and depth of the faculty. Typically, the faculty is limited in vision; textbooks are watered down to a common innocuous denominator. But still, one can find controversial books in the library. It is much easier to defend and maintain a variety of materials and viewpoint in a library than in a faculty. A faculty is more subject to the winds of doctrine and fashion than the library.

. . . . .

### The Library as the Key to Educational Reform

The reform or re-organization of a campus is a somewhat hopeless job, one that only a person with a streak of martyrdom would ordinarily care to get involved in, with the prospect of prolonged and bitter internecine battles between the various intrenched interests. No person in America so jealously preserves and defends his ancient (and often completely antiquated and outmoded) vested rights as the faculty member giving battle to the forces of evil that might abolish his department.

The educational reformer should look more often to the more painless reform possible by gradually increasing the proportion of total campus money spent for the library. Imagine the following typical situation. A college is spending 3 or 4% of its budget for the library. As the college expands, let the existing faculty remain undisturbed. Instead of hiring additional faculty for existing departments, simply add librarians and materials to the library. Establish the library as an autonomous college-within-the-college. In five or ten years, we can anticipate the following result. It will be evident to all that the only dynamic educational activity is taking place *in* the library. The quality of the library will be drastically improved, resulting in the attraction of increasingly effective faculty-librarians. By this time the traditional faculty will either have resigned, joined the bandwagon, or retired, all without a fight and without the need to attack their situation frontally.

113

## The "Library-College"

The *Library-College,* deliberately extrapolated and enlarged as a concept from the singular importance of the library and the book-centered campus, is the logical development from the idea that the library is "the heart of the campus." The Library-College with the faculty and library losing their separate identity but merging into one integrated team is not perhaps essential for a liberating education, but will help insure that it becomes a reality.

### Example of the Public Library

We might not be ill-advised to take our cue in professional orientation from children's and public librarians who seem to be much concerned with the educational aspect of their role, with the content of books and with the individual human being. In contrast to many university librarians it is seldom that a public librarian sees himself as a technician, a gadgeteer, an information scientist, a manipulator of things or paper or catalogs as ends in themselves.

And yet it is the college librarian who is working in a deliberately formalized educational environment. As a result of this very process of over-organization and formalization we have become so specialized in our educational behemoths that we have lost an appreciation of our true calling as educators. Public librarians, with their far more relaxed attitude to "education" (they do not fuss around with such evils as grades and credit hours that defeat the development of initiative and responsibility which should be the goal of the entire educational process) are sometimes more effective as educators.

Public librarians have learned how to cooperate, to reduce the amount of technical drudgery in any individual branch library. Full use is made of centralized selection of basic books, centralized ordering, processing, etc. With their technical needs supplied automatically, branch librarians are left with the most professional work possible, counseling with people as individuals and groups.

Suppose a college library of 100,000 volumes receiving 5,000 volumes a year were to receive 3,000 of these automatically and were relieved of all processing and maintenance of a catalog. This would all be done centrally by far better qualified experts than the individual library could afford including the preparation — centrally — of book catalogs. And further supposing that it would be possible to circulate books without conventional circulation records and without any paid

114

circulation or shelving staff. In other words, the entire circulation department ordinarily absorbing a sizeable proportion of the library staff and administrative attention would be eliminated. This goal can be approached with on-line computer self-charging or in a non-automated system.

What activity would be left for the library staff in the hypothetical library described above with all technical details and all clerical and semi-professional activity supplied centrally? As in the branch public library the library staff would be freed from fussy distractions in reality and psychologically. They could for the first time place their entire attention and interest in the educational process, in monitoring and encouraging individual and group independent study, growth and development. It would be much easier for the college library staff to see themselves for what they really are — faculty rather than technicians ... faculty with special training in "the bibliographical way," stationed permanently *within* the library, the logical home base for *all* college faculty.

## APPENDIX A

### Accelerated College and Elimination of High School

No doubt we will soon begin to question the validity of expecting every young person in high school and junior college to be enrolled in formal educational activity. The educational system cannot function positively if its main purpose is custodial, a kind of gigantic and camouflaged baby-sitting operation. School should not substitute for a failure in our economic system to utilize human resources fully and constructively. The interest of the federal government and the NEA in enforced free education at the junior college level is perhaps suspicious rather than auspicious.

It would be desirable to experiment with a drastically reduced minimum average age for college entrance. The general education program should be considerably accelerated and completed at an earlier age than is now common. There is now a vast amount of wasted time and duplicate effort between high school and college.

Isn't it possible or even desirable that the experimental college of the future avoid, in a variety of ways, the rigidity of 15 to 25 class-hours a week, nine or twelve months a year? The future experimental college will expand in both directions from the 18 to 22 age level, replacing or being absorbed by the high school in one direction and

115

standing ready to receive anyone who has arrived at the proper state of psychological readiness in the other direction.

The world is not simple — but complex — so school should likewise be complex and should include a variety of experiences. A rich and non-rigid mixture of work camps, citizenship camps, community service, living in a home in a foreign country, hosteling, work, language camp, independent study, and college could be introduced for 14 to 19 year olds eliminating the present wasteful duplication between high school and college. Motivation and morale could be maintained at a far higher level increasing the efficiency of the educational process. A long period of residence in a foreign country could come at an age when the desire for new experience, a break from home, and perspective for examination of one's own culture is highest.

The most deadening aspect of present teenage education is the endless plodding of year after year of unrelieved and uninterrupted school. There is too little recognition in the educational structure of the increasingly common practice of early marriage. The years of high school and undergraduate college are too often unrelated to life with consequent slight lasting impression from the years of custody. The "custodial" or "WPA" function is all too common in an economy with a perpetual unemployment crisis.

The following proposed program calendar is based on each school year commencing October 1 and the typical student's birthday also being October 1:

|  |  | *Formal Study* |
|---|---|---|
| 14 2/3 years of age June 1 | | |
| Work-camp | 2 months | |
| Citizenship camp (similar to the Encampment for Citizenship or Lisle Fellowship) | 2 ” | |
| 15 years of age October 1 | | |
| College—full-time | 9 ” | X |
| Free time | 1 ” | |
| Language camp (in a foreign country) | 2 ” | X |
| 16 years of age October 1 | | |
| Study in a European secondary school, living in-home | 10 ” | X |
| Youth hosteling or work-camp in Europe | 2 ” | |
| 17 years of age October 1 | | |
| College—full-time | 9 ” | X |
| Job or community service | 3 ” | |

116

18 years of age October 1
    College—full-time                      6     "        X
    Job or community service         3     "
    College—full-time                      3     "        X

19 years of age October 1
    College—full-time                      3     "        X
    Job or community service         3     "
    College—full-time                      6     "        X

20 years of age October 1             Graduation from
                                         College

Ages 14 2/3 through 19            48 months of formal study

Conventional high school and college program ages
15 through 21 years 8 months:

| High school | 3 years | @ 9 months per year | 27 mos. schooling |
|---|---|---|---|
| College | 4 years | @ "    "    "    " | 32   "     " |

           College A. B. at age 21 years 8 months    59 mos. schooling

As justification for the 11 fewer months of school the following factors
may be cited:

1. One integrated program for the later teen years with elimination of
   present wasteful duplication between high school and college.
2. Capability of considerably greater educational load (per school day
   or month) through increased morale and motivation.
3. Maintenance of interest by the great variation of techniques implied
   in the above program.
4. Educational value of the citizenship camp, work camp, hosteling,
   foreign travel, job experience and community service can legitimately
   be added to the 48 months of formal schooling.

Some of the features of this proposed 5 1/3 years combined high school
and college program:

1. Granting of college degree 1 2/3 years sooner, ready for professional
   training that much sooner.
2. Elimination of high school—generally considered the weakest element in the educational structure.
3. Fourteen months total time spent in residence in a foreign country
   at the precise age (16) when the desire for new experience, a break
   from home, and perspective for examination of one's own culture is
   highest.
4. Six months total experience in citizenship camps, work camps and
   hosteling.

5. Intensive language training, resulting in native speaker fluency.
6. Nine months job and community service experience.
7. Forty-eight months formal schooling compared with normal 56 months.

## APPENDIX B

### Suggestions For a Relevant and Meaningful College Curriculum

Instead of lectures, courses, and formal subjects the college curriculum would be structured in terms of real life problems and projects. This would guarantee relevance and enthusiasm which in turn would guarantee the motivation for a sufficient amount of discipline-centered background reading and study under the guidance of a multi-disciplinary team of faculty-librarians in charge of each project. Only when we are "involved" in a real life situation does our background and basic study "take."

A variety of such projects and programs would be pursued simultaneously at a given college to insure that every student would find projects in which he would have a high order of interest. The faculty-librarians would be involved in such activities as committee activity, personal counseling, group counseling, project leadership, field trips, preparation of bibliography and syllabi, evaluation of reports, instead of lecturing and recitation. As part of their background work, the students would be better off reading the lectures and essays of the great leaders, past and present, on a particular problem or background than listening to the lectures of a local instructor. Each project would partake of some of the qualities of a social movement in the commitment and enthusiasm of its participants. For many projects, it would be desirable to develop several sub-units, each pursuing different paths or alternate and controversial approaches toward the solution of a common problem. All artificial "exercises" would be eliminated — it would be recognized that by age 18 a person is fully adult and capable of significant and meaningful achievement. These projects would be conceived as a means of triggering the release of the hidden talent that is present and usually buried in all of us.

The headquarters for each project or faculty-librarian team would be in the library building close to and integrated with the material resources needed in pursuing and understanding the ramifications of each problem. Location of the project offices in the library and requiring that each active faculty leader also be a librarian would insure that the project would remain content-full, bibliographically. According to the

118

subject background and specialization of each faculty member all written work would be evaluated in terms of quality of language, historical understanding, sociological and psychological understanding, etc.

Some examples are suggested projects:

1. Air pollution or pesticide survey
2. Voter registration
3. Development of community centers and community activities
4. Wild life survey
5. Construction of a telescope
6. Registration of historic buildings
7. Oral history
8. Archaelogical field survey
9. Learning a foreign language
10. Murals and other art works for public buildings
11. Operation of a radio or television station
12. Design and operation of a playground
13. Work in hospitals, jails
14. Model of a regional plan
15. Design of a rapid transit system
16. Design of a model city.

# An Experimental Library-College at Jamestown

*DAN SILLERS*

*Background.*—For the past two years faculty, students, and administration have been considering possible changes to improve the quality of education at Jamestown College. These investigations have been carried out in a number of ways: (1) Conferences, symposia, and self-study committees which have analyzed the College's present programs and student needs, and searched for ways in which the faculty could be more effective in guiding students; (2) Faculty visits to other small colleges with experimental programs (Reed, St. Olaf, Macalester, Franconia, Sarah Lawrence, Bennington, Goddard, and Marlboro);[1] (3) Interviews with persons from such colleges as Florida Presbyterian, Monteith and Parsons which are doing experimental work; (4) A visit by Winslow Hatch, Director of the Clearinghouse of Studies on Higher Education, U. S. Office of Education who gave invaluable information on "new dimensions" in higher education, means to improve the climate of learning, and on mental health and the student; (5) The services of a Visiting Professor in Education and Philosophy who worked with students and faculty to break down resistance to change and improve College learning atmosphere; and (6) During this same period the Board of Trustees appointed a national committee to study the College which was chaired by J. L. Zwingle, Executive Director for the American Governing Board of Colleges and Universities. This group examined the College's role and value to its geographic region, financial resources and educational needs, and then estimated college prospects. Their major recommendation was to raise $1 million to build and equip a new library.

The Zwingle recommendation and the preparation of faculty, students and administration not only to accept change but move toward greater experimentation give Jamestown a remarkable opportunity to

---

[1] Made possible by using $1,500 of a grant by the Esso Foundation in 1964-65.

improve its educational program and perhaps even to develop a new dimension in American higher education.

With this concept in mind a number of steps have been taken. First, Edmund Bullis, mental health consultant, spent a week on the campus counseling with trustees, administrators, faculty, students, and educators in the area. His main objective was to assist in evaluating the potential for a mental health climate favorable to change from within the college community. Bullis found the morale, trust in each other among the parties involved, and mental health climate not only conductive to change but such that emotional support was forthcoming when new ideas were expressed or tried. This evaluation was substantiated when the faculty voted unanimously two months later to design an academic calendar permitting greater experimentation and evaluation of learning theories. The faculty also approved the re-evaluation of all curricular offerings and are now wholeheartedly involved in this project. Simultaneously, administration, faculty, and students were searching for ways in which learning and teaching could be improved when they came upon the concept described by Robert Jordan and Louis Shores of a Library-College. Thus, a workshop was planned to bring 20 national educators and librarians to the campus during the Christmas vacation period to evaluate and crystalize the concept.[2]

The workshop consensus indicated that great steps had been made and others were yet to be made. Recommendations were made by B. Lamar Johnson for consideration by the participants, and further recommendations have been received from all members of the workshop. After evaluating them the following proposal is submitted to develop detailed program, curriculum, and facilities for establishing an experimental Library-College at Jamestown by the Fall Term, 1967.

## Proposal

I. Establishing an eight man "idea" team

A. Purpose.

This team would devote its efforts to forming goals and principles; curriculum; instructional program, procedures, and resources needed; facilities; special problems; and the organization and administration of the Library-College concept in practice. Additional responsibilities would include testing and evaluation of

---

[2] Made possible through partial support of a $2,500 grant from the Esso Foundation.

ideas through research in the academic setting. A major responsibility would be preparing faculty, administration, students, trustees, and staff to understand and apply the concept. The team would also work with Admissions, Development, and Public Relations to prepare prospective students and the general public.

## B. Personnel

The "idea" team would consist of

1. The College Dean or the Director of Institutional Research.
2. A psychologist whose academic interests are broad, has interest and background in learning theory and educational goals, and is capable of designing educational action research (member of the Jamestown faculty).
3. A scholar with educational background and experience in the humanities who is aware of the library's impact upon this discipline (member of Jamestown faculty).
4. A scholar from the sciences familiar with new learning techniques, the library, and the importance of liberal education in a technical society (member of Jamestown faculty).
5. A librarian on one year leave of absence with ideas on using the library more effectively in the educational process and who is familiar with the new communications media.
6. A systems analyst on leave of absence who is familiar with and interested in educational problem-solving.
7. An expert on leave of absence who is known for his ideas and experience in developing effective college educational programs.
8. A College trustee interested in the institution's educational aspects.

## Advisory Council

The "idea" team should be assisted by a National Advisory Council of twelve members:

a. Two experts on developing effective college educational programs.
b. Two outstanding librarians interested in the educational process.
c. Two experts in supporting media (A-V, microfilm, computers, tapes, etc.).
d. An expert who has been involved in initiating a new experimental college.
e. Two outstanding institutional architects.
f. An expert active in institutional accreditation.
g. Two outstanding college administrators known for their administrative skills.

This Council should have a two-day conference to be instructed and establish their objectives. Each individual Council member would meet with the "idea" team from time to time to assist in areas where his expertise would be helpful.

Project Secretary

A Secretary to assist the "idea" team and record the results of their discussions and experiments and conduct necessary correspondence.

II. Procedure

The areas to be studied by the "idea" team will be: (The amount of time spent on each area will vary with the problems arising and the experimentation necessary before conclusions and procedures can be developed. A three-day conference will bring in the Advisory Council to assist in establishing the general objectives, procedures, and guidelines which the "idea" team will research.)

1. Formulation of goals and principles
   a. Participants
      1. "Idea" team.
      2. Two members of the Advisory Council most experienced in such formulation.
   b. Work of the conference
      1. Specify the student changes, qualities, and developments which the new educational experience is to affect.
         a. Intellectual objectives
         b. Moral objectives
         c. Other objectives
      2. Initial discussion concerning the nature of the new program as it will evolve from the search for the most effective means of reaching the goals.

2. Curriculum
   a. Participants
      1. The "idea" team.
      2. The members of the Advisory Council selected for their ideas and experience in developing effective educational programs.
   b. Work of the conference
      1. Specify the curriculum to meet the goals of the new college.
      2. Formulate the instructional means utilized to implement the curriculum.
         a. Types of educational activities
            (1) Individual study
            (2) Discussion

           (3) Lecture
           (4) Laboratory and studio
           (5) Field study
     b. Student-staff relationships

3. College resources   (library)
   a. Participants
     1. "Idea" team
     2. Two experts
       a. Librarian
       b. New media
   b. Work of the conference
     1. Specify the resources needed by the instructional program.
     2. Organizing the resources so they will be more effective.
     3. State the principles and means of selecting college resources.

4. Special problems
   a. Participants
     1. The "idea" team.
     2. Two experts who have been involved in initiating new experimental colleges.
   b. Work of the conference
     1. Student problems
       a. Recruiting
       b. Orienting
       c. Evaluating
       d. Transferring
     2. Faculty problems
     3. Facility requirements
     4. Developing a time schedule for establishing the new college.

5. Facilities
   a. Participants
     1. The "idea" team
     2. Two outstanding architects
   b. Work of the conference
     1. Formulate building needs in relation to existing facilities and the present college.
     2. Draw up architectural specifications.
     3. Discuss possible architects

6. Administration
   a. Participants
     1. The "idea" team
     2. Two presidents of experimental colleges

b. Work of the conference
   1. Personnel requirements
   2. Public relations
   3. Finance
   4. Unresolved problems

III. Time

One year.

IV. Rationale

The rationale for this proposal follows:

1. The small, private college must become experimental, be adaptable to change based on sound psychological, sociological, and educational principles, and be concerned with each individual student and his intellectual and social development (The Danforth Foundation's Preliminary Report *Eight Hundred Colleges Face the Future* makes this same recommendation).
2. The Board of Trustees has decided a new library is an important addition and the structure must be designed to assist learning as effectively as possible. The Board is interested not only in bricks and mortar but during the last three years has authorized substantial increases in book and periodical expenditures. And the Alumni Association has made library improvement and financial support its project for the year.
3. The Library-College plan will upgrade the quality of education by providing new opportunities for creative teaching and new stimuli to motivate students. It will bring together the three most important ingredients in higher education: men with ideas, those eager to learn, and books!
4. More effective teaching and learning will be accomplished in a Library-College by using the latest techniques and inventions in the communication sciences. For example, study carrels with built-in television receivers enabling students to play back video-taped lectures; the use of programmed learning and teaching machines, microfilm cameras and readers; various kinds of audio equipment; and computers to simulate real life situations for test purposes in the social sciences.
5. By having a number of Jamestown faculty on the "idea" team, the team's concepts, ideas, and practices will be more easily accepted and practiced by faculty and students.
6. The team will use as resource persons students. The students' assistance will give the team perspectives which might otherwise be ignored and will also be helpful in preparing students for new concepts.
7. In view of the library interest, the desire for experimentation and the plan to build a new library soon, it is necessary to study the Library-College concept carefully. Such a team could accomplish this.

125

*Cost*

The total cost of the "idea" team will be $138,700 plus office space and research costs which cannot be estimated until the team and Advisory Council establish the specific research projects required. Beyond the $74,700 requested Jamestown will match other costs of approximately $64,000 plus office space, furniture, heat, light, and the additional costs of research, whatever they may be.

|  | Total Cost | Amount Requested In This Proposal |
|---|---|---|
| Eight members of "idea" team including fringe benefits (retirement, living allowance for those on leave, Social Security, etc.). | $108,000 | |
| Three members of "idea" team @ $16,000 including living allowance and fringe benefits. | | $48,000 |
| "Idea" team member travel to see present programs and attend a professional meeting. | 3,800 | |
| Faculty travel to visit experimental programs | 1,500 | |
| National Advisory Committee (12 members and honoraria). | 10,000 | 10,000 |
| Secretary | 5,400 | 3,600 |
| Supplies, printing and expenses | 8,000 | 6,000 |
| Special equipment | 2,000 | 1,000 |
| Indirect costs 5% | | 3,300 |
|  | $138,700 | $74,700 |

126

# PART TWO

# Elements of the
# Library-College

# Vitalizing a College Library: A Quarter of a Century Later[1]

*B. LAMAR JOHNSON*

UPON OCCASION, the library is referred to as the "heart of the college," and yet anyone who has studied use of junior college libraries can well raise the question, "Has the library yet achieved the dignity of becoming even the little finger in most of our two-year colleges?"

Archibald MacLeish once asserted, "The librarian must be more than a hat check girl in the halls of learning." At the recent Conference on the Junior College Library, Lee Sutton voiced a somewhat similar view when he expressed concern lest librarians simply be "a corps of ribbon clerks, . . . highly trained storekeepers of information."

The emphasis at the July Conference was, of course, entirely away from the hat check, ribbon clerk concept of librarianship. Rather, stress was given to the expanding role of the library and to its essential unity with the educational program. Recognition was given to the library as a learning resource center and to the fact that automation is coming to the library.

The Conference materials can be grouped under three headings:

> An Expanded Concept of Library Materials
> Electronics, Automation and the Library
> The Library and Instruction

### An Expanded Concept of Library Materials

Reported in this section, for example, was the development of learninig resource centers at Cazenovia College, Columbia Basin College, the Junior College District of St. Louis, and Miami-Dade Junior College.

---

[1] From the National Conference on the Junior College Library Held at UCLA July 12-14, 1965.

129

Although Dean Ewing from Foothill College asserted ". . . we operate a basically traditional library," he did make clear the fact that library materials at Foothill are by no means limited to books, magazines, and other printed matter:

We maintain a single union catalog of instructional materials which lists and classifies each item on the campus except the approximately 6,000 individual art and science slides which are listed only as sets. All printed materials, except standardized tests and desk copies of textbooks, are ordered through Library Services for the entire college, and all instructional films, recordings, and audio-visual equipment are ordered through Audio-Visual Services. There are no separate collections that are the property of the instructional divisions, although portions of the general collection, such as sets of slides, maps, dictionaries, or definite pieces of audio-visual equipment are often checked out to a division for an extended period of time . . . .

Audio-Visual Services expends much effort to remain alert to new materials and devices and to inform instructors about them. Decisions to purchase materials and equipment are made in terms of the probability of effective use for instructions, with a conscientious attempt not to succumb to the lure of the merely fashionable. The selection, purchase, control, and maintenance of all audio-visual equipment rests ultimately with Library Services which also assists instructors in their more effective use. In cooperation with the Office of Community Services, Audio-Visual Services maintains the equipment in the theater and other lecture halls used for public events, and in the instructional program it is responsible for providing classroom screens and darkening curtains, training student projectionists, scheduling and maintaining equipment assigned to the instructional divisions, supervising technicians and equipment in the forum building and the language laboratory, maintaining the multiple response system and the video-tape reorders—and even the underwater sound system in the swimming pool. All of these devices which serve the instructional program and the technicians who operate and maintain them, as well as the graphic artist and the photographer who execute faculty requests for visual materials, the 12-channel 200-station listening facility, and the small listening and preview rooms in the library building itself are under the central control and guidance of the experts in Audio-Visual Services; the use of these materials and equipment are detemined by the instructional staff with the counsel of Audio-Visual Services. As with the single collection of materials, this single administration of all audio-visual materials, equipment, and services seems to us eminently efficient and reasonable. It also seems logical that Audio-Visual Services should be a subdivision of the total Library Services.

130

## Electronics, Automation, and the Library

Some would say that the coming of electronics to the library is signalized by the introduction of the Sentronic System of checking out books at Miami-Dade Junior College. Under this plan a metal insert in the book is demagnetized when it is properly charged out. If a book has not been charged out a buzzer or gong is sounded when it is taken through the library turnstile.

Others would suggest that the dialogue-learning labs at St. Louis— as described by Robert C. Jones — represent the arrival of electronics in the junior college library.

Libraries on two campuses contain an advanced version of the language lab. The Dialog system can be used in the conventional lab sense with the instructor playing tapes or records or talking and listening to the students. But each station in the lab or in the library contains a head set and a dial so the student simply consults a listing of programs and dials the desired lesson, which may be Spanish, French, German, Russian, humanities, music, art, shorthand at various speeds, composition, sentence structure, etc. The remote tape deck cabinet stores 88 simultaneous programs, any of which can be changed in seconds. One program last semester included a work book in sentence structure which was checked out from the library and a taped lecture which the student dialed. When the lesson was completed the student was given a test after which he dialed another number and got the answers with explanations. This program has been very effective in bringing students up to an acceptable level of performance. When suitable video tape recorders are available the carrels will be wired for video and TV programs; it is interesting to note that 5 years ago a video tape recorder cost $60,000; 2 years ago the price dropped to $12,000; in March Ampex introduced a $6,000 model, and last month Sony hit the market at $1,000. The next step will be to run all audio and video programs through the computer and have hundreds of listening and viewing stations throughout the libraries. Numerous experiments are being conducted by faculty on released time to develop Dialog programs, audio-tutorial programs, video-tape and TV programs. The Instructional Resources staff is assisting these efforts by continuous research and demonstration of latest AV equipment and its uses, and by producing color slides and transparencies and making taped programs. From a situation of wondering how faculty would take to all of the innovations, we have come to a point where they are cooperating us to death. We have produced 8,000 color slides and have requests for 1,500 transparencies this summer alone. To the question of replacing teachers with teaching machines, any teacher who can be replaced by a machine, should be.

131

Also developed at St. Louis is a plan for doing away with the library card catalogue:

To avoid having to hire numerous catalogers requiring desks, typewriters, supervision, etc., all books are ordered through Alanar Book Processing Center, with which I had been dealing while at American River Junior College. Alanar will procure books from nearly all publishers, out of print and foreign, and deliver them fully catalogued and processed with plastic covers, cards and pockets ready for circulation. This service costs only $1.70 per title (additional copies 75 cents) as compared to a national average processing cost of $5.50; it also provides a more consistent product, and relieves the problems of maintaining a full cataloguing staff. Upon receipt, books and L. C. cards (which are also included) are checked to avoid duplication of numbers, the books are sent daily to the campuses which ordered them. Alanar also allows the same discount as other jobbers, and pays shipping charges. It is far better service than do-it-yourself production.

As librarians know one of the biggest library headaches is the care and feeding of the card catalog. The cabinets themselves are costly and cumbersome, seldom if ever up to date and difficult for students and faculty to use. Consequently, we never bought any cabinets and we do not have card files; this again was an advantage of not having precedents or established routines to follow. Several libraries, mainly special collections, had produced book catalogs by some form of IBM print out. This required key punching all entries, much hand filing, and the purchase or lease of some hellishly expensive equipment; further, the print out was hard to read in teletype lines across the page, and much needed information was omitted. Since the L. C. card contained all necessary information in familiar form, it was decided to photograph the cards individually with a high speed camera (8,000 cards per hour) and print out the pages from the negative. This produced a nice looking index, easy to read and use, but did require hand filing of all the cards by author and title, and by subject, before photography. Further, to bring the indexes up-to-date required interfiling of all additions, and re-photographing the entire set. So with the camera produced indexes available for student and faculty use in the libraries and in faculty offices, we continued research on ways to develop a better process. What was needed was a way of combining the accuracy of the camera with the speed of the computer, and it was by this process that we produced our first total cumulative indexes.

After lengthy planning with Alanar Book Processing Center, we developed the following procedure: Alanar was sent one L. C. card for each book in the Junior College District collection. These cards were laid out in sheet form, each sheet having a page number and space designation for each card. Thus a code number "7OR,"

132

would mean page "70," space "R," which would be a photograph of the entire L. C. card. From these sheets, key punching was done and then transferred to 1401 computer tape for print out by author-title and by subjects. The print out was photo-reduced for clarity, and the pages hard bound into book indexes. Each entry in the indexes contains the author, title, subjects, editor, edition and date, and the classification number for locating the book on shelves. And each entry also includes the code number mentioned above for reference to the full L.C. entry if needed. Campus locations are also given if the book is not in all three libraries. Since the full L.C. entry can be located only by getting a code number from one of the indexes, new sheets of entries are filed at the back of this full entry volume. The indexes are kept up to date by cumulative supplements, issued at intervals depending upon acquisitions, and each year a total cumulation will be produced. Each campus now has 15 sets of 3 volumes each (Author-Title Index, Subject Index and the L.C. card catalog) for faculty offices; they find the indexes as easy to use as a telephone directory requiring little or no instruction from the librarian.

Cost comparisons are difficult to make because one bulky card file cannot be compared to multiple sets of the book indexes. The 50 sets of 3 vols. each which the District now has cost less than the card file cabinet for one campus would have cost. Once the tape is made any number of the indexes can be produced at little extra cost, and for reruns the cost is mainly that of punching the new acquisitions.

Further developments of this process are already evident. When the Junior College District and Alanar both acquire a full complement of computer equipment, we can tape book orders here, connect our computer to theirs by Data Phone to place the order, have their computer call ours back with billing information and print out the new catalogs. Another built-in advantage is that we have all of our titles on tape and if we wish to convert to some form of computer circulation, we can simply call Alanar for a run-off of the author entries on IBM cards and change circulation systems over the weekend.

A somewhat similar plan — though operationally different — was reported by Edward Heiliger from Florida Atlantic University:

Each cataloger and each reference librarian has a catalog on his desk. Catalogs can be found throughout the campus, as well. Each faculty department has at least one set, one has as many as six. Many professors using the library a great deal have their own sets. We find that a faculty member will now check a nearby catalog before sending in a book order. When he does not find it listed, he sometimes decides on an alternate

133

that we do have. This saves time, effort, and money. The professor also uses the computer-produced book catalog that he has at hand to counsel students on additional reading, prepare reserve lists, plan new courses, and write research papers. The student also finds the availability of the new catalog very convenient. Copies are available with which he can make a sit-down use of or borrow for home use, and Xerox pages of shelf-search or bibliographic reference in writing papers. Copies of the catalog are also sent to nearby junior colleges and public libraries, to the other state university libraries, and to the Library of Congress.

The absence of a card catalog always causes comments from visitors. It is our conviction that the book form is much more familiar to people than the card catalog. People use telephone books, merchandising catalogs, and book indexes, but they seldom use a card file. The scanability feature of a book catalog seems to make it easier to search and appraise, also.

## *The Library and Instruction*

Regardless of how adequate a book collection may be, of the extent to which electronic and other materials are included in the library, of the quality of library furnishings and equipment, of seating capacity — regardless of all of these, the use of a junior college library ultimately depends upon the kind and quality of teaching. All other library plans and developments are mere "window-dressing" if teaching is not library-oriented. Papers at the Conference particularly highlighted library-instructional relationships.

Harriet Genung — the only California junior college librarian ranked as a dean — reported a plan at Mt. San Antonio College in which each department has a librarian assigned to work with it — to help establish and maintain effective library and instructional relationships:

> To each of the subject libraries a reference librarian has been delegated to work personally with faculty and students. It is hoped that under conditions similar to the early years of our development when it was possible to work with individuals in small numbers that we can maintain good rapport. By confining his efforts to four or five departments with a total of fifty instructors, with the responsibility for the supervision of 200 student readers within the reading areas, the reference librarian is better able to maintain the rapport which stimulates active student-library-faculty relationships. Book selection is still possible as a faculty-librarian activity. It is possible for the librarian assigned to this segment of the curriculum to adequately explore new publications, notify the faculty of them, and evaluate the strengths and weaknesses of the

134

library collection within the subject areas for which he is responsible. It is possible to maintain an active lower division library collection with frequent, systematic evaluation and culling of obsolescent materials.

At Florida Atlantic University one member of the library staff devotes his entire time to conferring with professors about their teaching, particularly as this relates to the library.

Under the title "The Library as an Agency of Instructional Importance" Arthur Cohen reported a survey in which 34 California junior college presidents and 29 deans of instruction — representing 45 junior colleges — spent three or more hours in libraries and reported their observations regarding instruction on an open end inquiry form. The purpose of Cohen's survey was (1) to determine whether presidents and deans could gain new insights regarding instruction by spending time in their college libraries and (2) to identify suggestions for increasing the use of the library.

In general, it can be said that the participating administrators did identify strengths and needs in their instructional programs as a result of their library observations.

When one president responded to the invitation to participate in the survey he wrote, "Taking this much time away from other needs scares me to death." Nevertheless he did participate and when he returned his inquiry form he wrote a letter in which he asserted, "I suppose you realized when you made this assignment that a college administrator is not likely to spend an extended length of time in the library unless forced to do so. Without your requirement I would never have made it."

Twenty of the presidents and nine of the deans of instruction reported that the time they spent in their libraries was sufficiently valuable to warrant more frequent visits.

Patricia B. Knapp reported a systematic plan for achieving library coordinated instruction at Monteith College:

> Library competence is acquired only through actually using the library. It cannot be transmitted in a one-shot fashion in a unit of freshman English nor even in a full semester course of instruction in library use.
>
> Because we believe that all undergraduates, not just the elite few, should have the opportunity to develop library competence, all assignments in our model program are coordinated with the basic courses required of all students at Monteith. And because we conceive of library competence as consisting not of a specific body of information about the library but rather as a kind of general

135

preception and certain general skills, we are concerned in each assignment with process rather than content, with principle rather than fact. Our model program consists of a sequence of ten library assignments coordinated with a four-year program in liberal, general education. Seven of the assignments were specifically designed for the first two years of the Monteith curriculum.

The sequence as a whole is unified in terms of the idea of "the way." Each assignment is expected to contribute to the student's understanding and skill in the choice of a way, or path, from where he is to where he wants to go and to his understanding and skill in the way, or method, to use the bibliographical tools of the library and the scholarly world.

At the July Conference I reported library developments at Stephens College in the '30's under the title: "Vitalizing a College Library: A Quarter Century Later."

The most important library developments at Stephens were those which emerged from changes in teaching. In some cases—as, for example, in world literature—the library became the locale, the text, and the entire focus of study for a course. In other courses—in communications and in social problems, for example— the library became an increasingly important adjunct to a course syllabus or text. Instructors in science increasingly assigned papers which required study in varied books and periodicals. Books were also increasingly used for reference purposes during science laboratory periods.

The fact that something was happening to teaching at Stephens during those days is suggested by data regarding the book circulation. During the five years preceding these developments the average Stephens student borrowed nine books per year, excluding overnight reserves. During the thirties circulation quadrupled to more than thirty-six books per student. Such a change would be impressive even in today's post-Sputnik period. It was particularly notable in the thirties—and at Stephens where the plan of library administration (open shelves, dormitory and classroom libraries, for example) made books unusually accessible and therefore made book borrowing less essential than in an environment in which formal circulation was the sole means of accessibility.

Increased use of the Stephens library can be attributed to changes in the instructional program. Changes in library administration were significant only to the extent that they influenced the kind and quality of teaching.

I am, of course, aware of problems associated with putting into operation plans developed at Stephens—particularly in colleges markedly different and should like to identify and discuss four of these difficulties.

136

1. Having a single staff member serve as both dean of instruction and librarian may be possible in few junior colleges. The responsibilities of a dean of instruction may preclude his also serving as librarian. Likewise there may be few people qualified—or interested in becoming qualified—in both librarianship and the administration of instruction. Nevertheless Harvie Branscomb, former Chancellor of Vanderbilt University, in commenting on the Stephens plan, asserted, "It may not be wise in other situations to place the librarian in charge of instruction, but college administrators who turn from this solution will find it incumbent upon themselves to seek by other means the integration of effort which this solution achieved."[2]

I do not today urge junior colleges to combine the position of librarian with that of the dean of instruction. I do venture, however, to suggest that such a plan may prove workable in some colleges. Regardless of what plan may be adopted, however, I suggest that the position of librarian—with or without joint tenure in a second position—be such in the hierarchical structure of a college that he has a role of central importance in the development of the curriculum and in the improvement of instruction.

2. A plan of decentralized libraries—division libraries, for example—is expensive. Such a plan makes it necessary to employ more librarians than are required in a single central library. Also under a decentralized plan it is often necessary to duplicate holdings for use in different libraries. In addition, under a decentralized plan students and faculty members upon occasion waste time in locating books because they do not know in which library to seek a particular title that may be relevant to two or more fields.

Division, department, or classroom libraries may be practical in few colleges. Nevertheless, means should be sought to make books and other library materials conveniently available to instructors and students at those times when they may be most useful. Methods for doing this may include—to the extent that this is possible—providing faculty offices, classrooms, and conference rooms in the library building. Mention should also be made of the value of having classes come to the library for laboratory periods.

3. There are problems associated with channeling to instructors the observations of librarians which can be useful in improving instruction. All too often there is locked up in the heart, soul, and mind of a librarian unused information about the problems and successes of teaching. How to make this available where it can be useful may be a problem. Having a specific librarian assigned to work with a particular division can be helpful, for such a plan aids in establishing lines of communication and in develop-

---

[2] Harvie Branscomb. *Teaching with Books.* Chicago. American Library Association, 1940, p. 101.

137

ing mutual confidence among librarians and instructors. In no sense, of course, can librarians be evaluators of the work of individual teachers. This would destroy the entire basis for cooperative work together—instructors and librarians—on common problems of teaching.

4. A junior college library of the type developed at Stephens is expensive. At Stephens the library budget was generous but not extravagant. As a matter of fact, when costs were computed on the basis of the cost per book circulated, Stephens fared remarkably well when compared with other colleges.

Nevertheless, any administration which aims to provide library service of the type that I am advocating must recognize that such service does not come cheaply. It costs money.

The late W. W. Charters once asserted, "If I were an educational administrator, the first charge against the budget, after faculty salaries, would be the library." Such a policy can be justified, for through the library we are able to add to our faculty the greatest minds of all ages—in the library we have the recorded thoughts of our greatest scholars.

There are seven implications which library developments at Stephens in the thirties may have for junior colleges in the sixties.

1. Use of the library is ultimately dependent upon the character of the teaching done in the classrooms and laboratories. The single most important contribution at Stephens was to demonstrate that library developments must emerge from changes in teaching. Instruction inevitably affects the library and its use. Book collections, buildings, budgets—these are all essential. But if we have all of these and teaching is textbook and lecture centered, little happens in the library.

A library program which simply starts off with buildings, library staff, and library collections is doomed to failure. On the other hand, a library program which takes off from the "launching pad" of teaching—and a recognition of the mutual effect of teaching on the library and of the library on teaching—has done much to assure success. Book collections, buildings and budgets will inevitably follow.

2. The unqualified support and encouragement which the college administration gave to the library at Stephens is a *sine qua non* in any college which wishes effectively to utilize the library in its instructional program. This includes financial support but more important than this, it includes a recognition of the importance of the library accompanied by an awareness of its relevance to many aspects of college operation.

In passing I should mention that the physical facilities of the Stephens libraries were underprivileged. The general library was located in a low ceiling dormitory basement, the decor of which was disturbed by unsightly heating pipes crossing the ceiling. Division libraries were typically reconstructed classrooms.

Nevertheless the college administration was committed to unqualified support for the library.

3. The librarian must have a position of central importance in the college organizational structure. Regardless of the method, means must be found to assign the librarian an important role in the instructional program of any college committed to making optimium use of its library.

4. If a librarian with the qualifications envisaged in this paper cannot be found, a person with the intellectual and other personal characteristics required for the position might be selected and sent to a school of librarianship for a year. At Stephens a man with a doctorate in another field studied at a library school and worked on plans for library-instructional developments. I could conceive of a group of successful junior college faculty members—most of them already having their doctorates—being selected for a year's study at library schools. They could then go to positions of library-instructional leadership.

Similarly highly qualified librarians might be assigned to universities for a year's study of the curriculum and instruction in the junior college—and also of junior college administration. They could then go to positions of central library-instructional leadership.

Plans of the type I have suggested might be made possible by the generous sabbatical leave policies now in effect in many junior colleges—supplemented perhaps by foundation or other grants.

Regardless of the method, a highly qualified librarian-educator must be found if a college is committed to vitalizing its library.

5. It is desirable—to the greatest extent possible—for instructors and librarians to merge into a single unified instructional staff. To a degree this can happen as librarians serve as members of departments and divisions, participate in curriculum planning, and in teaching, not only in the library but also as they visit classes and even teach sections of basic courses. This merger can further be extended as librarians share with their faculty colleagues insights regarding instruction—including both the problems and achievements of students—which come inevitably to the librarian serving at a circulation or reference desk.

6. The library can serve as a center for all instructional resources including those which emerge from recent developments in electronics. Varied audio-visual materials were included in the Stephens library of twenty-five years ago. An amplification and extension of this concept is exemplified in the learning resource centers recently developed in colleges and universities, including Stephens.

139

7. It is desirable to plan the buildings in such a way that instruction in courses—including faculty offices—in which books are the basic laboratory materials will be located as close as possible to appropriate library materials.

It is clear that making library materials conveniently accessible to students and faculty can encourage the effective use of such materials in teaching. Planning buildings and teaching in such a way that instruction can be brought to the library will contribute to this end.

The implications which I have discussed are suggestive only. The staff of every college must examine its own objectives, program and facilities and in the light of such examination project plans for the effective utilization of library resources. In such a projection administrative support is essential; an expanded concept of library resources to include all types of instructional materials is desirable; and the cooperative awareness of librarians and faculty to library instructional opportunities is necessary. Above all, lirary use is ultimately dependent upon the character of the teaching done in the classrooms and laboratories of a college.[3]

[3] See also B. Lamar Johnson. *Vitalizing a College Library*. Chicago: American Library Association, 1939; and B. Lamar Johnson, Eloise Lindstrom, and others. *The Librarian and the Teacher in General Education*. Chicago: American Library Association, 1945.

# Some Few to Be Chewed and Digested:

# Library Teaching — Humanities Model

*GILMORE WARNER*

IF THESE REMARKS were to have a text it would probably be that oft-quoted apothegm of Francis Bacon:

"Reading marketh a full man; Conference a ready man;
and Writing an exact man."

Certain things happen, we know, through the dialectic process, the give and take of conversation — the conference — where statement is followed by "yes, but . . ." from the listener and then a new statement, and this with another modification, until by a regular chain of dialogue a new truth is revealed. A good seminar presupposes well-filled minds, so that we have represented here at last the first two parts of Bacon's triad.

But the third part also has its values, which we recognize in the customary requirements of the freshman "library" paper, the term paper, the senior and master's essays, and finally the doctoral dissertation. In these, as Patricia Knapp remarks 'the student is increasingly expected to engage in a critical dialogue with sources of information, though, to be sure,' she adds, 'his "feedback" is almost always an unpublished communication to his professor.'[1]

My own experience includes not only that of working as a teacher with his student, but also as a librarian advising the floundering student who has simply been sent to the library to find a topic. What are some of the ends to be sought in these 'research' papers? To what part of the

---

[1] *Library College Newsletter* no. 4 (Dec. 1965), p. 3.

stream of knowledge can we direct our beginning fisherman, with a reasonable expectation that he will find the fish he seeks?

Exactly what skills are we hoping he will develop in the process, and how may we keep that delicate balance between frustration and the sense of discovery which ideally should motivate his work?

First of all much of our unsuccess — and there is admittedly considerable — is the result of our failure to narrow our aims sufficiently, then to select carefully such projects as will accomplish these aims, and to pursue a methodology in keeping with them. Certainly one of the aims of research is thoroughness and no one — student or teacher — can be thorough or reasonably exhaustive with too wide a subject. Incidentally, it is customary to put this word 'research' into quotations, as though only the advanced professional were able to do real research. My own use of the word would define the process by which any student at whatever level systematically discovers things not known to him before — perhaps not known to his teacher. There will always be limitations within which any researcher must work, whether at an elementary or very advanced level.

Secondly, if discovery is to take place we must set the stage for it. We must be careful to relate our subjects to our resources, and to make sure that essential resources are available. And in the interests of efficiency it is almost essential that the students of a particular class work together on different but related or similar subjects, so common methods and problems can be discussed by the group, both at the onset and along the way.

The following example of a library project is limited enough in scope to produce reasonably thorough treatment, is closely defined in objectives, and worthwhile in the knowledge which the student is expected to gain. The student has considerable latitude for original treatment. It is offered as an illustration of the sort of work needed in schools and colleges and with no suggestion that it is the only one nor that it cannot be improved.

## THE SONNET

*Aims:* To interpret as exhaustively as possible a concentrated artistic literary document, using first of all the student's own eyes and then a systematic body of reference materials. The sonnets are to be chosen, one to a student, from a carefully compiled list.

*Inclusion:* Sonnets are selected not primarily for literary greatness, but because they do contain the elements of an elementary bit of search-

142

ing. For instance, each must contain at least one literary, mythological, or literary allusion. Each must be by a poet about whom some biographical material *is* available. For example, Wordsworth's 'The world is too much with us' is often included because of its allusion to Triton, but Keats' 'On first looking into Chapman's Homer' is usually excluded because of the ample treatment it receives in Amy Lowell's biography.

*Method:* First the student is expected to find the best available edition of his author, locate the poem, and make a careful copy of the text with proper citation. He is expected to master all available information about variants and the verbal development of the poem. Next, he is held responsible for an understanding in depth of every word in the poem, such as he may gain from a careful study of the *Oxford English Dictionary,* and other comprehensive linguistic tools, including concordances, lexicons, etc. He is also expected to acquire the historical background of the period in which the poem was produced (e.g. London, 1802) and likewise of the poet's own life and thinking at that time. Finally, we shall expect him to learn something about the form or type of poem he is dealing with, such, for instance, as he might find in the article "Sonnet" in the *Encyclopaedia Britannica.* Along with this information, carefully cited on note cards, and a carefully compiled list, also on cards, of the works consulted, the student also begins to work up an outline and to consider *how* he can most interestingly present his findings. Statements such as "Wordsworth was born in 1770" are ruthlessly deleted as irrelevant, but interpretative statements of the type "Wordsworth was 28 when he set out for Germany with his friend Coleridge," are encouraged. All along the way the class is discussing Louis Agassiz's laboratory practices, until 'Look at your fish!' has become the by-word which it was for his students.[1] And also along the way, the challenge is held out to the student that he is to become an 'authority' on his one poem, so that he knows more about it than anyone he knows (including his instructor).

The final product is to be a *small* but completely relevant paper in order like a book, with title-page, contents, text of the poem, interpretation (not more than five or six double-spaced pages for this), citations and notes, and 'List of Works Consulted.'

Sometimes a final outcome comes a month or so later — the production by the student himself of an original sonnet.

---

[1] As outlined in *Louis Agassiz as a Teacher,* [compiled] by Lane Cooper (Ithaca, 1945).

143

# Library Teaching—
# Engineering Model

*THOMAS MINDER*

THIS IS A REPORT on a program in the College of Engineering at Pennsylvania State University to (1) develop in the graduate an awareness of the proper role of recorded information in the practice of his profession and (2) develop a closer working relationship between the library and teaching activities so recorded information can be efficiently coordinated with personal contact and experimentation in the practice and teaching of engineering.

The program began with a two year informal study of the library's role in engineering. The major areas of observation were:

1. The statistical record of library use was poor.

2. A sample of course outlines showed no reference to literature as a source of information except reserved book assignments used to fill in for inadequacies in the text.

3. A study of the curriculum showed the entire teaching program to use only lecture and laboratory as information sources and teaching tools.

4. The students who used the library, even Ph.D. candidates, were not aware of its resources and mechanics.

5. An analysis of engineering school accreditation procedures showed:

    a.   Evaluation criteria were limited to quantity of volumes, budget, and hours open;

    b.   No librarians were assigned to evaluation teams or consulted by the accreditation organization.

6. A survey of the faculty concerning library and literature showed considerable prejudice, ignorance, and lethargy.

144

7. The engineers' method of problem-solving demonstrated that recorded information could play a significant role in their traditional methodology.

8. All the seniors were formally quizzed on their awareness of information tools and were found poorly prepared to use them.

About the time these studies were completed, the President's Science Advisory Committee published a study of information in science and technology. The engineering profession was singled out for its almost complete ignorance of literature. A major cause of this deficiency was the inbreeding practice of teaching as they were taught.

Armed with the studies and "White House" support, the administration backed a study to correct the situation. The only limitation was that no time could be taken from the already overloaded curriculum (no library courses).

Since it was obvious that the fault lay with the education system, a decision was made to hold a series of courses for the faculty. The Dean supported the program financially and required each department to send at least two faculty members to each program.

Emphasis in the three day program was on the nature of information, its role in the education and practice of engineering, and the problems of integrating recorded information into the education process. The library was not mentioned except as one of the principal recorded information tools. The last day was devoted to faculty discussion especially ways of integrating recorded information into courses.

As a result of these programs a number of agreements were reached. The principal ones were:

1. The freshman should have a formal library introduction as part of a particular course. A design problem in Engineering Graphics was selected as the medium.

2. There exist many non-term paper methods of integrating literature into courses such as:

    a. Look up "quickly" questions;

    b. Assign controversial topics;

    c. Require students to go through the problem-solving routine, not just find the solutions to well defined problems at the ends of chapters;

    d. Simulate real life projects;

    e. Do term projects.

3. Present text books are completely inadequate. However, they are the skeleton of the course and must not be abandoned.

145

4. Today the library cannot compete well with the laboratory and lecture. It is too slow and the tools (indexes, card catalogues, etc.) are too ambiguous.

5. Introduction of recorded information into engineering practice and teaching requires changes at all levels including the classroom, curriculae, department, college, profession, continuing education, and engineering practice.

6. The librarian must be included as a dynamic integral element (not just a service) at each level.

7. The problems are too complicated to be resolved in a series of three day programs. Effort should be made to conduct a long-range profession-wide program.

The implications of the faculty consensus at Penn State for the Jamestown College Workshop are obvious.

# Curriculum and Instruction

*FR. JOVIAN LANG, O.F.M.*

## INTRODUCTION

By education we want to draw out or mature the intellectual powers of man. We are not thinking of pouring in information although information is a by-product of any system of mental development.

We need liberal education because in freeing or liberalizing the mind it prepares the individual to discharge the duties of his citizenship intelligently and is thus a safeguard in our national democracy. With a liberal education man can choose his ultimate objective and the numerous preliminary choices directed to that goal. To achieve this, man must possess a mature mind. He must have knowledge, not a superficial knowledge of isolated facts, not merely a penetrating acquaintance with one area of knowledge which would be narrow and grotesquely lopsided, but a comprehensive view of all that concerns human living. He must also have a disciplined will which implies strength to keep his appetites in check and to conquer opposing forces of environment. He must possess a trained body, not necessarily a robust body or the type of trained body sought by athletic coaches, but one which can support the intellectual dictates and moral imperatives of the soul.

Liberal education is designed to develop individual ability to attain truth, choose the good, appreciate the beautiful, strengthen bodily and mental health, and maintain a temporal well-being by economic preparedness.

## THE CURRICULUM OF A LIBERAL EDUCATION

For the ideal college we are pointing out those areas of liberal study necessary for the curriculum. They are all requisite but perhaps not to the same degree to produce the effect at which liberal education aims. They are Philosophy, Theology, Language, History, Mathematics, Natural Science, Social Science, Literature, and Fine Arts. Since the entire field of liberal study is so vast in attempting to secure breadth the program may become shallow and in attempting to secure depth the program may become narrow, there must be a workable mean between these two extremes — a compromise.

Another factor — student aptitude — must be considered. Different as we all are, we know that every individual can best develop by centering his attention on one topic rather than another. But each one must nevertheless profit from study in the other areas too, if any effect of breadth is to be secured. Each person must be thoroughly grounded in the fundamentals of human knowledge (nine fields) even though he may not be professionally skilled in one.

Because of the advantages of perspective, breadth and depth and the free play which should be afforded to individual aptitude the following classification of fields of knowledge is set up:

A. THE CORE CURRICULUM

Three subjects: Philosophy, Theology, and Language are proposed as the core of the curriculum.

1. *Philosophy*. The objective of Philosophy is to test, evaluate, and synthesize. Every department of learning leans heavily on Philosophy for its own accurate appraisal. Philosophy scrutinizes all reality. Man himself, all the marvels of nature, even God himself, lie in Philosophy. Philosophy studies diversity in the unity of all being and arranges that diversity in a rational, harmonious and beautiful pattern. As the student's mental processes increase he becomes intellectually self-reliant and therefore needs the sharpness of vision, balance of judgement, and tolerance in disagreement which Philosophy alone can bring to the individual's intellectual life.

2. *Theology*. The rational and intellectual relationship between God and man. Fundamentally Theology, like Philosophy, explains and justifies the relationship between the First Cause and all other causes. It is placed second on the list because Philosophy is a necessary prerequisite to the fruitful study of God and of man's relation to Him.

There is an infinite beauty of thought as well as incalcuable inspiration of the will in the truths of Dogmatic Theology. As part of the core curriculum Theology demands an intense application of the highest rationalized powers. In the liberal arts college Theology courses should equal seminary courses in difficulty of content and in demand on the student's intellectual powers.

148

3. *Language.* Language is the tool of thought and vehicle of thought expression. In addition to a thorough knowledge of the mother-tongue a liberally educated man should know not only language, but languages. The attempt to translate shades and differences of thoughts into another language sharpens the intellectual process and helps the thinker to a more accurate reproduction of his idea in thought-symbols.

*Summary of core curriculum.* From Philosophy and Theology the student learns to think easily, precisely. Precise thought loses its value unless the thought-expression in language be equally exact.

## B. THE SPHERAL CURRICULUM

This refers to the study of the six subjects not included in the core. They give the student a broad yet comprehensive acquaintanceship with a wide field of knowledge. History, Mathematics, Natural Science, Social Science, Literature and the Fine Arts have their own disciplinary effect and particular influence in drawing out, strengthening, and maturing mental powers. The effects we seek, in combination with the core, develop in an individual qualities of mind and heart associated only with the wise and self-controlled person.

1. *History.* History is vicarious experience. Through history a student becomes acquainted with all men. History provides a second type of rational explanation as it traces through the ages of the past a sequence of cause and effect in loves and hates, religious beliefs, greed for wealth, and lust for political power. The study of history will diminish that insularity which is the external work of inexperience. All facets of life have their past, present and future. History, like Philosophy, therefore has universal incidence.

2. *Mathematics.* A system of abstract reasoning, it might be included in the core. Mathematics is an indispensable tool for the pursuit, at a higher level, of all scientific study, natural and social. As the most abstract of sciences it disciplines the mind vigorously in precision, logical sequence, and coherence in thought processes.

3. *Natural Science.* Over and beyond keeping up with modern discoveries in this field and its significance to modern life, the important reason for including science is the specific training by inductive reasoning that such subjects afford the intellect. The methodology of laboratory science will be an example of objectivity and precision in approaching problems which a liberal arts student cannot afford to lose.

4. *Social Science.* The liberally educated person has a great opportunity for service to a community (not paid service) in sharing the privileges and responsibilities of community life and solving contemporary problems of political science, economics, sociology, education and psychology. The study of social science is necessary for this.

5. *Literature.* Literature concerns itself with the noblest thoughts and highest aspirations. It makes available the finest and most deeply inspirational thinking of every yesterday. Not only does it appeal to the intellect but it strengthens the will which can easily weaken under the constant attack of things selfish and ignoble. For its humane values literature stands high.

6. *Fine Arts.* This discipline is too often slighted in colleges of liberal education. Fine Arts studies the expression of the beautiful in sound, color and form. We cannot omit courses which teach the principles, if not the practice, of beauty — beauty that contributes beyond expression, powerfully and permanently to the education of the whole man. Fine Arts can also be taught by indirection; the most effective way to teach beauty is to surround the individual with it.

*Summary of the spheral curriculum.* This area secures proper breadth in the six fields of cultural inheritance, not by assimilating every detail but by becoming acquainted with the highlights of the arts and sciences and understanding the principles on which each discipline is based. Attention must be paid to the integration of each branch of learning with the total of human knowledge. The student can proceed to a detailed study in any general area of knowledge or can continue his education along these lines under his own guidance.

C. PERIPHERAL CURRICULUM — *The field of concentration.*

Here the problem of depth is cared for. Only by depth of investigation will students realize the impossibilities of one field. Students develop an understanding and respect for intellectual ability and acquire an appreciation of thoroughness, of perseverance under difficulties, and of self-reliance which independent work, even under the direction of a counselor, is bound to produce. The full effect of a liberal curriculum cannot be secured unless one field is grasped thoroughly in principle and application. By peripheral, we do not mean subject matter different from any of the nine fields but the manner in which one small segment of the wide area of knowledge is handled. This is the undergraduate major.

D.  RESUME OF THE RELATIONSHIPS AMONG CORE, SPHERE, AND
         PERIPHERY.

The core is a group of basic subjects sufficiently handled to provide depth as well as breadth. The spheral curriculum is comprehensive enough to provide for breadth. The periphery is one of the fields chosen at the student's option and on advice of his counselor; in this area the student's work is intensive.

## INSTRUCTIONAL PROGRAM

Upon entry into College the student is presented with a definition of Philosophy and the diagrammatic and schematic picture of all knowledge which explains why the Core curriculum revolves around Philosophy and Theology. Because Cosmology and Psychology deal with the more tangible, they and the Natural Sciences should be taught the first year. What would be comparable to two years of Language is offered during the first year followed by a qualifying examination. During the second year the remainder of Philosophy and Theology are given with Humanities and Social Sciences. Excluding the Natural Sciences and Language courses the first two years are integrated. A comprehensive examination is required at the end of the second year.

During the last two years the student may concentrate in some areas of Liberal Arts or Professional training. An option is available for those who want one semester abroad during the Junior year, but it must fit the program. A Comprehensive examination occurs at the end of the last year. Four academic years of two semesters each would be demanded of all. The work would be strenuous enough that a regular summer session would be inadvisable. The summer would be used for reading programs, strengthening any weaknesses noticed during the year, or gaining empirical knowledge through work.

Since Grades and Credits would be issued only upon demand of a transcript from a college (e.g. transfer), all faculty members would be advisors and would keep the student aware of his progress so he could pass the comprehensive examinations. Papers and problems would be the order of the day with infrequent testing left to the discretion of the faculty.

The Faculty would be adept in using the Library in their fields of concentration and would have bibliographic assistants. The Librarians should have subject competence and may teach each year. Adequate mature Library clerical help would also supervise student help.

151

The Method of Instruction follows this pattern: One class period is used for a formal lecture by the best of teachers, preferably over kinescope to allow repeated use and exchange with other institutions. The second meeting would be in as large a discussion group as could operate (circa 15). These groups would be handled by the remainder of the faculty to allow full play for other viewpoints and orientation to the course purpose. These two meetings are the only formal classes during each week. The rest of the time would be spent in directed independent study. Each faculty member would lead four or five discussion groups and direct their study each semester.

Code:

1. Philosophy
2. Theology
3. Language
4. History
5. Mathematics
6. Natural Science
7. Social Science
8. Literature
9. Fine Arts
10. Field of Concentration

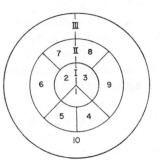

# Breadth Versus Depth

*SISTER HELEN (SHEEHAN)*

ONE OF THE PROBLEMS in liberal arts education is that of breadth versus depth. Conceivably, a student could spend four years in a smorgasbord-type curriculum with one introductory course in every area of human knowledge. Such a program would sacrifice depth and produce a dilettante knowing less and less about more and more. Choices must be made for a modicum of concentration.

The usual argument is that after graduation the educated man will continue to learn and investigate the subjects omitted during his formal schooling. National studies have verified our suspicions that this just isn't so. Motivation, opportunity, and direction are low or lacking for continued self-education by college graduates.

Good reading lists are available, such as the American Library Association's "Reading for an Age of Change." But how capture the dispersed degree-getters after commencement? How capitalize on the almost universal regret that college years left so many subjects out of the student's program? Why not try the same idea — directed reading — *before* graduation? And why not utilize the best of newer educational and technological devices?

This is a proposal to make use of:

1. Computer or electronic data processing for identifying intellectual lacunae.
2. The teacher-bibliographer or librarian-teacher for providing direction.
3. Independent study during senior year for filling the educational gaps.

1. *Identifying Lacunae.* — Some form of punched card equipment is universally used for registrars' records. During the last term of the junior year these records could easily produce a list of areas unexplored during high school or college. Then this could be matched against a master list, an outline of "What every educated man should know." This master list would itself be on punched cards, tapes or discs for computer use.

2. *Providing the Directed Program.* — A team of teacher-bibliographers, librarian-faculty, would have compiled short, highly-selective reading lists — only four to six books — on each area of the master list. When the student's needs were identified corresponding sets of book lists would be printed out to provide a personalized reading list at college level.

3. *Filling the Gaps by Independent Study.* — Each student would devote up to one-fourth of his time during one term of the senior year to independent reading in the previously underdeveloped areas of his studies. Students would be given the opportunity to indicate sections apparently untouched by schooling but covered by informal education.

Of the twenty to thirty major fields offered by the average small college the typical student might find six to ten unfamiliar to him. Certainly no one claims that four books give adequate knowledge of a major field or that they could be equated with a college course but surely it is better for a physicist to have read four books each on art, psychology, modern drama, and problems of government, than none at all. For the art major, there might be need for reading in physical science, sociology, contemporary philosophy, and communications arts. The possibilities are endless.

If it were considered necessary, supervision and testing could be provided by the team of teacher-bibliographers. Probably a test similar to the Graduate Record Examination would disclose the results of this program of "Independent Reading for Breadth."

# Students as a Specialized Audience

*PATRICIA B. KNAPP*

IN HIS ARTICLE "The Uses and Users of Recorded Information," Philip Ennis draws a series of distinctions between "general" and "special" audiences:

> First, let us consider the distinction between general and specialized audiences. As noted above, each has generated a typical kind of question which, in turn, has shaped its research traditions. For general audiences the studies have been designed mainly to arm librarians, educators, and publishers in the perennial struggle to create and maintain an adult audience of readers. A key element in that struggle was the instilling and sustaining of motivation to read. Thus, a good deal of inquiry was devoted to discovering the techniques to get people to read and to evaluating the efficacy of those techniques.
>
> For specialized audiences on the other hand motivation to read has been taken for granted. It is assumed that a specialized audience, in seeking information, is carrying out some well-motivated performance of an occupational role, for example, scientist, physician. Being informed and keeping up with the literature are part of that role.
>
> There is another way to describe the difference between a general and a special audience. It is in the relations—quantitative and qualitative—between their readers and writers. Quantitatively, the difference may be described in terms of the ratio of writers to readers. One can define the degree of specialization of an audience partly by its absolute size and partly by the extent to which the number of writers approaches the number of readers.
>
> Qualitatively, the difference between a general and a special audience is the kind and amount of feed-back from reader to writer. In the special audience there is more of the tendency for a member to be, at alternate times, reader *and* writer, with the channel of recorded knowledge being part of mutual communication. In the general audience the reader simply tends to say yea or nay (accept or reject) to various items transmitted. In brief this is the difference between two-way communication and one-way communication.[1]

---

[1] *Library Quarterly*, XXXIV (October, 1964), p. 307.

This analysis provides a useful framework for reflection on student use of recorded information. Let us leave aside the question of the student as a general reader; the chemist, too, is a member of the "general" audience except in the field of chemistry.

Motivation for the student can be more or less taken for granted. On this criterion, then, we might say that he falls into the category of the specialized audience. On the other hand if we infer that the motives of the specialist can be taken for granted because they are internalized, the classification is not so easy. The motivation for most student reading is so patently external.

On the quantitative criterion the student is clearly in the general audience. Textbooks are his principal recorded sources of information, and though there are too many textbooks, the number of textbook writers is still very small in comparison to the hordes of students. The evidence shows, moreover, that even when the student goes beyond the textbook in preparing term papers and reports, he relies at least through his first year or two in college almost exclusively on relatively popular books and on mass circulation magazines.

On the third criterion the student once again falls into the category of the general audience since he is not both writer *and* reader of the books and articles in his field. But in this criterion there is also suggested a style of use, a stance toward sources of information which comes into play more and more as the student moves toward subject specialization. As he proceeds through college, moving from the freshman "library" paper through the term paper, the senior essay, the master's thesis to the doctoral dissertation the student is increasingly expected to engage in a critical dialogue with sources of information, though to be sure his "feedback" is almost always an unpublished communication to his professor.

Note, however, that this development occurs *within* the student's own special discipline. Assuming that the critical-interplay style is desirable in the use of all materials do we assume there will be a spill-over into other fields? When we insist that every student should have a "major" to ensure that he explore one field "in depth," are we admitting that most education does not provide much opportunity for critical interplay with resources *below* the level of the advanced courses offered to majors? Or are we bowing to what many faculty members would regard as a self-evident truth, *viz.,* a critical interplay with resources is impossible until it is based on a solid foundation of knowledge — vocabulary, concepts, methodology, information.

156

However these questions are answered the undergraduate student must be placed closer to the "general audience" than to the "specialized audience" on the Ennis continuum. But would we not agree that it is the mission of education, at least of higher education, to develop in the student the *style* of the specialized user of recorded information? We would like the student's motivation for such use to be internalized. We would like him to belong to an audience which does not merely passively accept or reject but to one which *responds* in one fashion or another. Even if he never writes we would like him to read in a spirit of critical dialogue using many and diverse sources of information and ideas.

We would like this development to take place moreover in all students not just in those recruited into graduate work and ultimately into the ranks of the specialist audience itself. And if we have faith in the spill-over theory we would like it applied to all fields of study, not just the major.

What can we make of all this for the Library-College? It suggests teaching which de-emphasizes "coverage" (How often do we hear that miserable wail "There's so much to cover!") and emphasizes instead a style of thinking *including* the use of resources. Faculty in the Library-College should examine their own use of resources to determine how, how much, and how quickly they could induct their students into a similar style of work. There would be at least two dangers to guard against here. One, symbolized in its worst form by the freshman "research" paper is the confusion between the form of scholarly paraphernalia and the substance of the scholar's method of inquiry. The other is the tendency to teach not only what we were taught but as we were taught — thus arises the fetish of "coverage." The librarian can help with this problem for it is the librarian's business to be an expert in the use of resources *without* the specialist's basic foundation of knowledge.

# The Underprivileged Student

*BRUCE LEE*

AT JAMESTOWN my tail-end minority report was spoken in jest. Now my approach to the workshop is serious for its application to one of the United States' major problems: the crisis in education.

Almost every current publication indicates a troubled awareness of public education. According to the NEW YORK TIMES, January 5, 1966, the 1966 national expenditure for education will be nearly $25.8 billion. This is a tremendous sum, and it will require the dedication of many citizens to make sure funds are forthcoming to run our educational institutions satisfactorily.

The American system of public education seeks to develop each child's potential in traditionally successive steps from elementary through secondary schools. It is hoped that such exposure will optimally prepare each child for life, job, and perhaps further education.

This is the hope of education, but in reality the best optimum education for each child often does not happen. In spite of the large amounts being spent it is becoming increasingly difficult for many American children to secure adequate educational preparation for the trades, college, or for facing life. Students are going through elementary and secondary education and emerging stunted and crippled intellectually. And, many rebel at the education to which they are exposed and drop out. All are available for the society-market which has no place nor need for them or their limited potential.

This non-education is a tremendous loss and is creating a class of people who contribute nothing to contemporary society through their lack of awareness of opportunities or ability to take advantage of them. The WASHINGTON POST of January 16, 1966 quotes Kenneth Clark as saying the predominantly Negro schools of the North are so bad that they are turning out thousands of graduates who cannot read, write, or do simple arithmetic.

There is national concern over this developing class. Some feel the situation to be the fault of educators, yet there is growing evidence that

158

educators are the recipients of forces acting upon them; they are but the receivers of human refuse from the disorganization of society still working in a traditional framework.

The middle class is a bulwark in the power structure of the urban community and is often static and deeply concerned with perpetuating itself. One method has been to develop middle class communities increasingly located in peripheral areas away from the inner city.

Suburban residents have fled leaving social upheaval in the inner city. They hope to find in the suburbs peer relationships economically, socially, racially, and religiously. The flight is often uncoordinated. But what has this done to the deserted inner city? Large social groups left there are unable to escalate in the middle class manner. Invariably they are from the lower income groups and like their peers in economics, race, lack of opportunity and motivation, are poorly educated, even though public education budgets and expenditures are large in their regions. The proven formulae for middle class education often fail when applied to lower economic classes. The result of a poor education is poverty and lack of opportunity and presentation to the labor market of those "educated" in ghetto schools.

Many students produced in the traditional educational process have good native intelligence which has become dulled instead of elevating their horizons and sharpening their thinking. One of the greatest resources of the country is its youth and much of it is currently being squandered. This waste must be stopped.

The current process for college entry means that a student must take prescribed courses, supposedly geared to equip him to handle college materials and experiences. In most schools college material is presented by the traditionally formal lecture-recitation system. Small, non-directed classes are rare. Also, in most classes the teacher-pupil ratio is large, often out of healthy proportion for effective learning.

The ghetto is a place of restraint and confinement having an adverse effect on learning. The urban ghetto which is the symbol of the present day American dream for the minority person is found in every city. It is an area set aside where minorities are forced to reside and recreate exclusively. Nothing is creative there; it exists for the exploration of its inhabitants through higher rents and payments for provisions or services. It is at the same time self-destroying and self-perpetuating. Exit is usually discouraged by the majority group by overt or convex means with the existence of the ghetto assuring the majority group of a feeling of sta-

159

bility and security in their suburban residences. Residence in the ghetto has as its prerequisite race, religion or culture. Since ghetto residents work for the majority in providing services, ghetto doors open at 8 a.m. and close at 5 p.m. The ghetto lacks opportunity, education and hope, and its residents are socially immobile with insular thinking, suspicion, and non-awareness of the world about them or aspiration to change.

The rural ghetto extends for hundreds of miles and its cage is immense but still it has certain similarities — economic peer relationships, lack of opportunity, conservative thinking, fear of the national government and inability to conceive the world beyond.

However, the situation is not going unnoticed. Many government and private agencies have initiated programs to counteract the corrosive effects of the educational experience. These include the Poverty Program, Office of Economic Opportunity, Citizens' Crusade Against Poverty, religious and private agencies, crash programs, Higher Horizons, Great Cities programs. They have called forth comments from such writers as Sexton, Mayer, Meyer, Deutsch, Schrieber, Brown and Grant, and yet, the scattered pitifully small recoveries are meager.

Jamestown College is in a unique geographic location for dealing with this crisis in American education. It is located far from urban areas and students who go there will be "sentenced" to learn, far from the possibilities of returning easily to city confusion. Jamestown's area is one of plains, flat, seemingly endless, and romantic.

Jordan's seven elements of a liberating education have a direct application to my ideas for the Library-College catering to students from urban and rural ghettos. Occasionally ghetto youth have been successful in higher education. Jamestown must identify potentially promising students by using standard and unique methods. Other traditional sources can also be tapped for identifying candidates such as local governments, social and religious organizations. In order for the recruitment team to function successfully it must develop finesse in dealing with ghetto types.

It is my hope for the Jamestown Library-College that one quarter of its first entrance class be of ghetto origin. Following preliminary interviews in ghettos the candidates would be contacted and invited, expenses paid, to Jamestown. Considering a possible entrance class of 120, 36 candidates might well be ghetto. Broken down into three groups of 12 each they would be subjected to a battery of tests to define areas of strength, weakness, interest potential, and relationship to the world outside the ghetto. The testing team should include a clinician or psychiatrist in constant attendance to resolve emotional problems and render assistance.

The College must make strenuous efforts to integrate the ghetto student into the freshman class. Education which was formerly looked down upon must be stressed as the means of escape from the ghetto. Full support should be provided for each student. It would not be wise for students to work in the first year. Their energies should be directed toward accomplishing this change from a non-directed goal-less ghetto to the college-oriented library-centered program which is a definite means to escape to life.

# Faculty Development

*DAN SILLERS*

THE COLLEGE striving for distinctiveness must acquire faculty members who are intellectually honest, adequately trained in their major disciplines, dedicated to the development of the whole person, capable of communicating ideas, and willing to relate with others beyond the level of superficiality. Very few universities are educating college instructors with such objectives in mind. A few graduate schools have designed programs for college teaching which entail practice teaching in college classrooms under supervision. However, this does not accomplish the aforementioned objectives which are stated by at least one-third of all colleges.

These goals, however, lead to a possible paradox. For instance, Mary Owen[1] states that many of the advantages of the small college, such as low student-faculty ratio, individual attention, and small classes can also become disadvantages if the faculty member is not motivated or prepared to work with students in a person-to-person relationship. Being human, college faculty members have idiosyncrasies, personal deficiencies, communication problems, desire for status quo rather than dynamic change, and at times show immaturity. They also have biases and often overemphasize their own disciplines to the detriment of a broad liberal education. Yet, the goals of a liberal education require faculty to help students eliminate these same human frailties. Thus a program is needed which assists faculty to become aware of their own weaknesses so they may help students know themselves.

Perhaps then it is relevant for the Library-College to set as a goal the development of opportunities for students to broaden and mature through interpersonal as well as academic relationships. Therefore this paper will suggest a model for faculty development consistent with Library-College objectives.

---

[1] Owen, Mary S., "The Small College-A Faculty Perspective," *Liberal Education,* (May, 1963,) pp. 258-267.

162

## BASIC ASSUMPTIONS

The proposed model is predicated on the following assumptions:

1. That individuals' attitudes, perceptions, and certain personality characteristics can be changed.
2. That these changes will most likely occur under the following circumstances:
   a. When new knowledge is acquired, discussed, and evaluated.
   b. When one becomes aware of his present attitudes and actions and their effect upon interpersonal relationships.
3. That the degree of attitude and personality change is enhanced through participation and total involvement.
4. That in learning to understand one's self the possibility of understanding others is improved.
5. That an understanding of the principles of learning, and behavior and means of measuring and evaluating them contribute to teaching effectiveness particularly when working with individuals and small groups.
6. That faculty teaching in small colleges gain personal satisfaction from interacting with individuals and small groups, thereby being so motivated to want to improve.
7. That attitudes, values, standards, and emotional campus climate can be quantified to a degree and thereby measured.

## THE PURPOSE

In order to implement these ideas effectively total involvement and participation is demanded of college leadership (faculty and administration) based on a common goal and philosophy.

We propose to achieve this participation through a multiple approach:

I. To establish a model for administrative and faculty professional leadership skill development consistent with Library-College objectives, that is, those objectives emphasizing the importance, growth and worth of the individual, and then teaching them in a climate enhancing man's dignity.
   A. An in-service program for faculty improvement of undergraduate instruction.
      1. Develop an awareness of how individuals learn.
      2. Develop concern and capability in working with individual students and groups.
      3. Improve classroom emotional climate to enhance opportunities for maximum learning.

163

     4. Improve small college teacher effectiveness through new knowledge.

     5. Improve teacher effectiveness by increasing his emotional maturity through personal counseling.

     6. Improve the faculty's understanding, use, and acquaintance with the library.

  B. An in-service program for administration to improve collegiate climate for learning creativity.

     1. To develop awareness of mental health principles and apply them to administration.

     2. To improve personal maturity through counseling.

     3. To obtain skill in establishing a climate of learning and creative experience for students and faculty.

II. To establish personal counseling for faculty and administration. The counseling staff must be well qualified and interviews strictly confidential with separate counselors for administration and faculty.

  A. To allow personnel an opportunity for emotional release and ventilation with minimum negative effect on the small intimate community.

  B. To allow personnel an opportunity for personal growth and maturity by having professional assistance. Many of our ideas should be tested by those less personally involved. Working out problems we gain in understanding the effect of personal problems on our day-to-day work and interpersonal relationships.

  C. The counseling interviews and periodic evaluations will record the emotional strains, personal feelings, and reactions of those involved as well as the changes that may take place. The recording of the process of this program and possible change may be the most important contribution to education, administration, and the social sciences.

  D. Counseling interviews may reveal important factors which could improve hiring practices.

     1. Personality characteristics important in selecting faculty and administrators for the Library-College.

     2. Personality characteristics that adapt to change.

III. Specific in-service training activities.

  A. Personal counseling for administration and faculty.

  B. Visiting lecturers discussing learning climate in and out of the classroom.

164

C. Visiting lecturers discussing specific disciplines in relation to the liberal arts.

D. Weekly discussions and projects concerning immediate problems of instruction and the points raised by visiting lecturers.
   1. Various areas of the library
   2. Motivating students
   3. Developing bibliography

E. A week-long seminar to analyze the experience of the academic year on a group basis.

F. A month-long seminar during the summer to work on several topics from the in-service program as well as develop next year's courses in view of past educational experience.
   1. Library Workshop
   2. Reading improvement

G. A week-long seminar preparing specifically for the new students and new academic year.

IV. The faculty and administration will design an in-service course on "emotions, learning, and the college student in the Library-College setting." This will entail such topics as:

   A. Understanding learning
      1. Theories of learning
      2. Psychological and sociological concepts of the learning process.
      3. Intellectual and non-intellectual factors in learning.

   B. Understanding college students.
      1. Emotional health and behavior of college students
      2. Problem behavior
      3. Meaning of behavior

   C. Using learning resources
      1. Using reference materials
      2. Reviewing new publications

   D. Motivating college students

   E. Creativity and the college student

   F. Working with groups

   G. Evaluating learning

   H. Mental health methods and philosophy of teaching

   I. Understanding one's self.

Such a program has far-reaching implications for faculty training at the graduate level as well as for faculty selection by the institution itself. As the Hawthorne studies demonstrated so clearly the act of paying attention to and obtaining participation from relevant people almost invariably brings about an improvement in performance.

# Library-College Faculty

## ENTHUSIASM

*JOHN COYNE*

IN THE JANUARY *Esquire,* the editors present their "Annual Dubious Achievement Awards, 1965." Under the heading "Fat Lot of Good It Will Do" there is the statement: "There are now more college students in California than in Western Europe."

As this statement ironically points out and as such episodes as the Berkeley riots dramatically emphasize, the problem of numbers in the sixties pose a challenge to the quality and texture of American education. Attempts to meet this challenge have been feeble and self-defeating. President Kerr's multiversity designed to swallow the overflow crop of students has been incapacitated by a massive attack of indigestion. And the new program of federal scholarships promises to turn this attack into a permanent condition.

Under such circumstances the program outlined by Jordan is desperately needed. At a time when universities are being crippled by size and apparent inability of both faculty and administrators the role of the liberal arts college becomes increasingly important. A plan such as Jordan's may save the liberal arts from complete extinction.

There should be little doubt that the proposed Library-College is workable and that it should be set up soon. Of course, its ultimate success depends on a number of factors. Someone has to provide money. Many academic presuppositions must be combatted. The most important factor, however, will be the types of people who staff it.

There are certain obvious personnel requirements. Staff members should be broadly learned and capable of intellectual excitement. The

167

staff must also be conversant with the latest developments in teaching technology.

But such requirements do not concern me a great deal at this point. There is one requirement, however, one staff quality to be discussed. This quality is enthusiasm which should permeate Library-College atmosphere. This enthusiasm should spring naturally from a deep-rooted concern for the future of American higher education and for the student too often victimized by educators' inadequacies. Staff members must feel deeply for their students, must be determined to counter the discontent engendered by pedants. There must be enthusiasm for a program to rescue education from slow strangulation.

Perhaps the most important personnel policy will be the rigorous screening out of time servers. Because they have turned their backs to the world they are incapable of concern; without concern there can be no enthusiasm, and without enthusiasm the Library-College will not work.

Often in today's multiversity the only product of academic programs is anarchism. The student rebels against authority which provides no sensible direction for his abilities. Many students resort to individualism in desperate attempts to preserve their integrity because no one can offer a better way to make their university experiences meaningful. The Library-College could show a way to channel and direct this energy. Its program combines the best features of the individualistic and the social. The student is taught to learn for himself through sympathetic personal and intellectual contacts with people who know his name and respond to his enthusiasms. In the Library-College the social will complement and refine the individualistic and the individualistic will benefit the community.

Those who feel concern for the college student need not simulate enthusiasm for the Library-College. Old methods are breaking down and a new approach is desperately needed. They will be enthusiastic for they will realize that they are helping to provide that approach.

# Personnel Factors

*ROBERT GAYLOR*

PERSONNEL IS FUNDAMENTAL to successful library operation. In a Library-College it is imperative that personnel be superior in every respect.

The faculty must work together as a team, not only in the administrative-teaching sense, but as a team generating ideas; the program will rest upon the ideas and abilities of the team. They must be willing to adapt and make quick decisions.

The most important aspect of personnel will be an energetic administrator. According to Knapp, one of the problems at Montieth was the administrator's inability to persuade all faculty to carry out plans. The administrator must be able to persuade his faculty to carry out the program fully. The Dean must support the Library-College concept and bring librarians and faculty members into a functional entity. He must be dynamic, full-time, and in residence.

## Proposal

A team of librarians and scholars should be recruited to form the core of the creative teaching faculty, men with ideas highly motivating students. The size of this team could vary greatly depending on funding. Ideally, there might be five participants in this capacity. Their major function would be to develop specific Library-College programs. This team should be nationally prominent and advise the Dean. They would set up programs and machinery but not be in residence, instead meeting quarterly on the campus.

On the campus an experimental team would be responsible for student general education and would offer a liberal education consistent with college purposes, emphasis and new programs. This experimental team should be convinced of college library importance.

The faculty would devote two-thirds time to teaching and one-third to assisting students. Faculty load must not force a separation between faculty and students.

169

In previous and unsuccessful attempts at establishing Library-Colleges lack of complete dedication from all participants was probably a cause. If an "all-out" attempt is made again, all factors must be ideal to insure success.

## Additional Considerations

1. Clerical/faculty ratio
   a. 3½-4 clericals to every faculty member
   b. Pay more than average salaries
2. Cost Analysis
   a. Raise salary rates 20-30%
   b. Student-staff ratio 15 to 1
3. In-Service Training Program
4. Rotating Personnel
   a. Rotate staff from outside
   b. Rotate 20% every year
5. Big Brother Program; i.e., College Adopted by Larger College

# Library and Classroom Faculty

*JOHN HARVEY*

PERSONNEL REQUIREMENTS for the Library-College are of vital importance. No area of college activity is more important than personnel. Certain colleges are known to be outstanding because they have excellent faculties and staffs, not primarily because they have superior student bodies, physical plants or alumni groups. A superior student body is attracted primarily by an excellent faculty.

My discussion will be divided between the two areas of (1) developing an excellent faculty, and (2) developing an excellent library staff. Our first concern with a faculty member is for his basic character, personality, integrity, initiative, ambition, conscientiousness, and interest in students. By this is meant the faculty member must be a very superior individual to start with. Then he must be successful in the usual ways in which we expect faculty members to be successful as well as having a strong concern for the importance of the library and the audio-visual center in higher education. If we have a strong individual who is destined to go far in whatever field of higher education he enters, we have the best possible start.

It is important that we have an individual who is already a successful instructor. The more common classroom instruction techniques will undoubtedly be used to some extent in every Library-College so it is necessary that this individual be a successful instructor, be well informed about good teaching techniques, and be eager to teach his students how to learn.

Also, such individuals should have research interests. At the Library-College research may not be primary, but on the other hand it helps to keep faculty members alert and interested in their subject fields. Therefore, each faculty member should have a research program. And if the entire Library-College is regarded as an experiment and therefore a research project with proper controls and data collection, the college atmosphere will be much more exciting.

171

Finally, this individual must have a strong interest in the use of books and audio-visuals and a considerable understanding of them. Of course, by in-service training courses and experience, we can improve his understanding after he reaches the campus, but he must already have a great interest in the Library-College idea or he will be out of step with the rest of the faculty. In the average college, some faculty members resist the library, others are disinterested in it, and a great many have no idea how to use it in their teaching. There is no room for these types of faculty members.

A distinction can be made between library staff and faculty because it seems likely not all the faculty will be doing cataloging and acquisitions work and that there will be some separation of duties based on experience and education. The Ph.D. in English will probably spend most of his time working directly with English students rather than cataloging English books in the library, and the library school graduate with acquisitions experience may be expected to deal more with the library's acquisitions program than with English teaching. Of course, all library and faculty members will have full faculty rank, title, vacations, faculty privileges and salary commensurate with their qualifications, however.

Now we come to the library staff members. They should be selected on the same bases as teaching faculty members as outstanding people, but also on the basis of their ability to work closely with students and faculty members on course material, rather than on their cataloging skills or interest in reading. Their technical competence is assumed but they must have outgoing personalities since they will be working closely with faculty and student body.

We must have as leaders of this library staff, as director and assistant director, individuals who can be respected by the rest of the faculty for forceful leadership qualities. The director must be regarded as a major campus educational and administrative official, ranking certainly as a major department head and probably as a dean. Other library administrative staff members must have sufficient personality, ability and leadership qualities to be respected as campus leaders. It is reasonable to assume that the library department heads will rank with academic department heads.

Where are so many paragons of excellence to be found for this faculty and staff? First, we must resign ourselves to the expense of such a staff. If recruiting is successful, these people will expect relatively good salaries, many of them above $12,000 per year. One of the devices used

172

recently by Parsons College, that of paying well for relatively large teaching loads, can help justify high salaries.

Undoubtedly some of the faculty members can be found on the faculties of other superior colleges. The Ivy League colleges plus Swarthmore, Carlton, Grinnell, Knox, Cornell, Lawrence, and others come to mind immediately. It is also possible to identify a few faculty members across the country who have written or spoken on library use in their teaching so are faculty possibilities. Graduate school placement officers will occasionally identify students particularly interested in library use. A faculty young in age and high in enthusiasm is to be recommended.

We should avoid "bookworms" who spend much time in the library and have therefore developed an interest in it. Sometimes such persons attend library schools where they become identified as "lemons," failures in dealing with people. This is not the kind of person we need.

Where will we find library staff members? They may be found in outstanding liberal arts colleges also. They will be identified by the respect of faculty members for them, their knowledge of subject bibliography, and their reputations with other librarians.

How can we develop these staff members within the library schools? These schools must recruit superior individuals, not merely scholastically but in personality, ambition and ability. Exposing them to the Library-College idea in course work is also important as well as encouraging them to be creative in their approach to librarianship.

Let us not forget that such a library will need staff members to work behind the scenes. It will be necessary to attract librarians who have mastered the basic skills of librarianship. Not all library staff members will be spending their time working closely with faculty members in their offices or in classrooms in developing course work. The usual college library activities will be carried on with certain ones intensified, but the unglamorous cataloging, indexing, classifying, acquisitions, book selection, book preparation, and shelving must be done also. With energy and courage we will find what we need.

# Inter-Library Support

*JAMES HOLLY*

My PURPOSE is to provoke discussion rather than provide a definitive statement. Precedents for the type of cooperative support being proposed are limited and not necessarily relevant. Librarians are cooperative when it is profitable but they also can be quite selfish and institutionally centered.

Well-known cooperative enterprises such as the Farmington Plan, the PL 480 Program, U.S. Book Exchange, regional bibliographic centers, the Hampshire Interlibrary Center and the Center for Research Libraries have limited applicability. Recent developments in Arkansas, Missouri, and Minnesota hold more promise.

Perhaps certain assumptions can open the discussion of cooperative support.

1. *The Library-College Will Have Limited Library Resources.* — No matter how excellent a library collection is available it will often be inadequate for the wide-ranging type of inquiry anticipated in the Library-College. This would be true even if Dartmouth or Oberlin spawned a Library-College. After establishing a sound basic collection the college must develop bibliographic resources permitting students and faculty to identify quickly and exactly materials relevant to a particular line of inquiry and provide quick access to such materials located elsewhere.

2. *Conventional Inter-Library Loan Facilities and Practices Are Inadequate.* — They are wasteful and time-consuming, primarily for graduate student and faculty use, and fail to recognize the importance of sustaining undergraduate curiosity and enthusiasm.

3. *Students and Faculty Prefer to Work with Recorded Knowledge in Conventional Forms.* — How the conventional form is produced is of no concern, whether it comes from a library shelf, pamphlet file, film, magnetic tape, or more sophisticated storage device is unimportant. But the recorded material must have no umbilical cord, it should be

174

capable of being stuffed in a briefcase, digested in bed, in a coffee shop, under a tree on a pleasant day, marked or even cut up.

4. *We Have the Technology and National Wealth to Develop the Ideal Experimental Concepts.* — Probably more interest and support for libraries generally and academic libraries especially is available now than ever before. This is reflected in federal legislation, foundation activities, and recent industrial alliances between electronics and publishing firms, e.g., General Electric and Time and Silver Burdett, or Xerox with University Microfilms and Wesleyan University Press. Cooperative support can involve banding together several educational institutions to develop local, state, or regional experimental information centers.

*Phase 1.* — As participating libraries build up basic collections and bibliographic resources the information center would contain a comprehensive microfilm collection of journals. Characteristics of its operation would include:

a. Rapid print-out facilities using equipment such as the Xerox 824 and 914.
b. Rapid local delivery by a center panel truck or mail out daily in response to telephone and mail requests.
c. Capability of utilizing data processing equipment.
d. Capability of performing centralized purchasing and processing.

*Phase 2.* — Here the center exploits fully modern electronic means with fast retrieval and transmission of requested materials, and ties into similar centers. In each library would be a small electronic facility through which, having established bibliographic identity, students and faculty could request a specific item by voice, dialing or punched code. The request would go first to the local center. Response with an adequate print out might be obtained with a delay of minutes. If the material was not in the local center the request would be relayed automatically to another local center, or to a regional, national or international center with print-out response in a matter of minutes or hours. Poorly identified items might cause delays as they do now. The information would be received in an immediately useful form. Probably the material would be turned over to the student without any attempt to process it into the local collection since it would be less expensive to request the same information again at a later date through the center.

# Educational Channels

*THEODORE SAMORE*

EXCEPT FOR THE teacher the book has long been the oldest of the "new" media. Indeed books whether in codex or scroll have been the major medium of the scholar and student since Plato's academy. Yet the book is still regarded as one of the newer media. On what grounds can it be considered a newer medium? Over 50 years ago Thorndike pointed out:

> Two few teachers know the purposes of the text-books they use. Too often a teacher uses a book section much as a savage might use a coat to cover his legs, or as a child uses a saw to cut a string, scissors to cut a board, or a padlock as a bracelet.[1]

On the whole the improvement of printed directions, statements of facts, exercise books and the like is as important as the improvement of the powers of teachers themselves to diagnose the condition of pupils and guide their activities by personal means. Great economies are possible by printed aids, and personal comment and question should be saved for its unique contribution. A human being should not be wasted in doing what forty sheets of paper or two photographs can do. Just because personal teaching is precious and can do what books and apparatus cannot it should be saved for its peculiar work. The best teacher uses books and appliances as well as his own insight, sympathy, and magnetism.

The fundamental concern underlying the use of all media, including journals, books, graphics, films, video tapes, records, magnetic tapes, etc., is the process of human learning.[2] All media, both old and new, are various means of recording knowledge in an orderly manner, storing it, and yet making it accessible for use. Media of all kinds are *carriers;* they carry various signs, signals, symbols, and other representations which reflect the reality or phenomena to which the communications refer.

---

[1] Thorndike, Edward L., *Education, New York:* Macmillan Co., 1912, p. 167.
[2] The last four are sometimes referred to as "projected media."

Crucial to the learning process is the principle that the structure of knowledge needs to be analyzed and then organized to provide the best possible conditions and means for enduring learning. Put another way, the principle holds that the . . .

> main function of a college professor becomes one, not of dispensing knowledge in the classroom, but of motivating, encouraging, and helping the student to make effective use of the abundant sources of knowledge now available. The professor's most challenging responsibility is that of helping the student learn how to learn. Becoming efficient in the process of learning on one's own is at the heart of the educational process.[3]

Instruction then, can be conceived as those "arrangements of materials, methods and activities which provide the conditions increasing the possibilities that learning of desired kinds will occur."[4]

"Send me a man who reads" is a joke in an age where education is almost a life or death matter. Nonetheless new media have moved in where books either have been misused or failed. Two directly related areas are involved in a study of new media. These are: (1) the rationale and development of the newer *materials* of instruction, and (2) trends and developments in the *hardware* or devices used with the newer media. There is an abundance of information about both, to be sure, but this information exists in many places and much of it is inaccurate. In any event this paper deals primarily with the *rationale* of using new media in college instruction.

Using new media is sometimes known as "automating the teaching profession." Yet, a Library-College will use new media only if they do work that the printed media cannot do as well. Probably teaching will begin with the lecture and what the lecture cannot do well either projected or printed media may do better. Basic to the whole program is the premise that whatever medium can contribute most to the learning process should be used in preference to any other medium. Furthermore a combination of media is likely to be more effective than any single medium. Of course lecturing and discussing are media as are journals and phonorecords.

The major thrust behind the new media arose from a variety of fac-

---

[3] "Using Groups in Independent Study" *Antioch College Reports,* (June 1963), No. 5, p. 1.
[4] Carpenter, K. R. "Strategies of Learning and Learning Resources" In the *Proceedings of the National Conference on the Implications of the New Media for the Teaching of Library Science.* Edited by Harold Goldstein. University of Illinois, Graduate School of Library Science, 1963, p. 10.

tors outside formal education. In any event the issues involved in using the new media for instruction present formidable problems especially for the Library-College since this sort of institution is traditionally oriented toward the printed media.

The basic problem may be expressed in three questions: (1) How are printed media more effective for learning than projected media? (2) How are projected media more effective for learning than printed media? and (3) How much can the media be mixed for maximum learning?

These three problems involve four common aspects: student, teacher, curriculum and administration. The three problems should be resolved in relation to all four — student, teacher, curriculum and administration. Let us briefly take up in turn the questions which each poses:

*The Student*

1. Can the new media help meet the social and educational problems generated by the rapid increase in enrollment?
2. Can the new media increase student involvement with their courses?
3. Do students learn more through one medium than another?
4. Do some new media restore the tutorial relationship in mass higher education?
5. What contributions to student motivation may grow from using the new media in college teaching?

*The Teacher*

1. Can the new media improve large-group instruction?
2. Can the new media yield higher quality instruction? Which is the best way—alone or in combination with large-group presentation, discussion groups, tutoring, independent study, and programmed learning?
3. Can the new media contribute to effective self-instruction and thus free the professor for more face-to-face contact with students?
4. How can professors be motivated to adopt more imaginative approaches to instruction and to learning outside the classroom as well as within it?
5. How can professors learn to communicate more effectively what they know, what they can do, and their attitudes toward their disciplines?
6. Is it possible that experimentation with new media may lead to improved effectiveness of the professor as well as extension of his influence?

178

*Curriculum*

1. Within the time available for education can the new media increase the total amount of knowledge that can be taught well and thoroughly learned?
2. Can the new media speed up the process of learning?
3. Will the new media have contributions to make both in bringing the materials of instruction into harmony with the requirements of our time and in keeping them continuously current?
4. What kinds of subject matter can best be learned through new media?
5. Does using the new media impair the repute of the subject matter itself? Why do most prestige colleges shun them?
6. Will the new media contribute significantly to the quality of research performed by students and faculty?

*Administration*

1. Will the new media "work" over a long period of time?
2. Will the new media increase efficiency of instruction enough to offset cost rise?
3. Can the new media be justified by greater educational results rather than dollar savings?
4. What effect will the new media have on the traditional library?

Workers in new media are convinced that projected media provide proven benefits:

1. Greater service to greater numbers.
2. A conservation of teacher time.
3. An enrichment of the learning process itself, a sort of esthetic dividend.
4. Facility of independent study.
5. Greater understanding of the dynamics of learning.
6. Efficiency and economy in time, effort, and money.

Yet it is very difficult to "prove" that one method of instruction is better than another or that one medium is more efficient than another, or to "prove" the sources of student success in college. For example each of the following statements has been "demonstrated" through research:

1. Students do better in small classes.
2. Students do better in large classes.
3. Students do better with inexperienced teachers.
4. Students do better with experienced teachers.

179

5. Students do better when they use their libraries extensively.
6. Students do better when they do not use their libraries.
7. Students do better in old classrooms.
8. Students do better in new classrooms.

Here then may be one of the chief opportunities of the Library-College, to demonstrate decisively what the new media can or cannot do as compared to the traditional media.

In order to do this Library-College goals should be defined and defended. The following statement by Harold Taylor seems fitting:

> The curriculum will contain those studies and will foster those experiences which are significant in the individual lives of the students and are at the same time relevant to the needs of the society in which the students will live ... If their college education has been successful they will be prepared to take the role in society for which their talents are best suited, and they will at the same time be liberally educated; that is to say, they will be interested in the arts, in ideas, in thinking critically and creatively about their society, in forming standards of taste and judgement about the culture which surrounds them.[5]

The Library-College should consider seriously whether the new media (or the traditional media for that matter) will contribute directly to these objectives. I believe they will.

## BIBLIOGRAPHY

1. Brown, James W. *Administering Educational Media.* New York, McGraw-Hill, 1965.

2. Center for Programmed Instruction. *Programs '63; A Guide to Programmed Instruction Materials Available to Educators by September 1963.* Ed. by Lincoln F. Hanson. Government Printing Office, 1964 (OE-34015-63).

3. Committee on Utilization of College Teaching Resources. *Better Utilization of College Teaching Resources.* New York: Fund for the Advancement of Education, 1959. 63pp.

4. Coulson, John E., ed. *Programmed Learning and Computer-Based Instruction.* New York, Wiley, 1962.

5. Erickson, Clifford G., and Chausow, Hymen M. *Chicago's TV College: Final Report of a Three Year Experiment.* Chicago: Chicago City Junior College, August 1960. 98 pp.

---

[5] Taylor, Harold, "The American Idea" *Current Issues in Higher Education 1960,* edited by Harry Smith. Washington: Association for Higher Education, 1960, p. 43.

6. Hauf, Harold D., and others. *New Spaces for Learning: Designing College Facilities to Utilize Instructional Aids and Media.* Troy, N. Y.: Rensselaer Polytechnic Institute, 1961. 122 pp.

7. Hubbard, Richard D. *A Study of the Reasons Given for the Limited Use of Certain Audio-Visual Materials at Syracuse University.* Doctor's thesis. Syracuse, N. Y.: Syracuse University, 1960. 229pp.

8. Lumsdaine, Arthur A. *Learning from Films.* New Haven, Yale University Press, 1958.

9. Lysaught, Jerome D. *A Guide to Programmed Instruction.* New York, 1963.

10. McClellan, James. *Automated Education: A Philosophical Approach.* New York: Center for Programmed Instruction, 1962. 28pp. (Mimeo.)

11. McLuhan, Marshall. *Understanding Media; the Extensions of Man.* New York, McGraw-Hill, 1964.

12. Mowrer, O. Hobart. *Learning Theory and the Symbolic Processes.* New York, John Wiley & Sons, 1960. 473 pp.

13. Skinner, B. F. "Teaching Machines." *Scientific American* Vol. XXV Nov. 1961, pp. 90-102.

14. Smith, M. Daniel. *New Instruction Media: Self-Instruction, Guided Instruction, and the Role of the Teacher.* Richmond, Ind.: Earlham College, 1962. 70 pp.

15. Thomas, R. Murray, and Swartout, Sherwin G., *Integrated Teaching Materials.* New York, Longmans, Green and Co., 1960. 545 pp.

16. Wittich, Walter Arno, and Schuller, Charles F., *Audio-Visual Materials: Their Nature and Use.* New York, Harper and Brothers 1962, 3d ed. 500 pp.

## A SELECTED LIST OF INSTITUTIONS ACTIVELY USING THE NEW MEDIA

| | |
|---|---|
| Case Institute of Technology | New York University |
| University of California, Los Angeles | Ohio State University |
| Chicago City Junior College | Oakland Community College |
| Florida Atlantic University | Pennsylvania State University |
| Grand Valley State College | Purdue University |
| Indiana University | San Francisco State College |
| State University of Iowa | State College of Washington |
| Johns Hopkins University | Stephens College |
| Miami University | University of Texas |
| University of Michigan | University of Washington |
| Michigan State University | University of Wisconsin |

181

# The Library-Centered College

*CHARLOTTE FLETCHER*

THE LIBRARY in a Library-College is both head and heart of the college: the library shapes the program for the whole college and also pumps life-giving books into the collegiate arteries and capillaries. The faculty will be a library faculty.

In the ancient church all men were saints; in our Library-College all men are students. Some are undergraduate students, some are librarian-teachers, some are teacher-librarians, but all are students.

The College will try to develop the individual intellectually through thoughtful reading of books in all forms and through other communication media like classroom discussion, occasional lectures, examinations, written reports and essays, recorders and computers.

The avenues open for fruitful study in the College are legion, although there are several inherent limitations. Since there are no laboratories and only a limited serials collection original research in the natural and social sciences cannot be carried on. There can be courses in the history of science, and seminars and papers based on analysis and interpretation of scientific hypotheses.

As a matter of fact any kind of research leading to copious library note-taking should be discouraged as well as lectures leading to copious classroom note-taking. All search and reading should occur in a free and thoughtful manner not hampered by over zealous foot-noting. Emphasis should always be on thoughtful reading.

Students who want laboratory and research experience can go to the state university for a term. It is possible, of course, that some substitute for the laboratory will be found satisfactory.

Except for these limitations placed on research the curriculum includes all the major disciplines pursued in any liberal arts college. After certain basic courses in mathematics, language and science are completed the student maps out his own program with a faculty adviser. The kind of independent enterprise which the student must cultivate can be nurtured in the library framework which provides flexibility with willing mentors always at hand.

182

There should be a simple faculty organization to implement the curriculum. Two Committees will meet regularly throughout the year. First there must be an Instruction Committee to name the basic courses and the general areas for individual reading and to decide when a course of reading has reached a good stopping-place. Second there must be a Library Committee to plan collection growth and recommend books for program reading.

The two Committees together will schedule students for specific library hours just as laboratory periods are now scheduled in colleges. The two Committees must give special attention to the schedules of students employed to operate the library and the librarian-teachers who supervise the library operation. They must make sure a student works no more than ten hours and the librarian-teacher no more than twenty hours a week in the library operation.

Moreover the responsibility assumed by an employed student should not exceed ten hours. The librarian-teacher, however, must bear responsibility beyond his scheduled time, but his maturity should see him through. His total immersion in the library as worker and reader will make him a better librarian. The benefits of this kind of scheduling of library personnel which allows time and energy for reading will outweigh both the difficulties and expense incurred.

The Library Committee should be composed of three professional librarians and two instructors. Chairmanship should last for two years and revolve among the professional librarians. The Chairman will also be the Head Librarian and final responsibility for library functioning will be his.

The library should be organized so it is never necessary for more than one faculty librarian to be on desk duty. All routine jobs will be performed by student assistants; during certain times they will man the library alone. Even so, the number of faculty members assigned to the library must be larger than the usual college library staff, for it will be open fifteen to eighteen hours a day and the College will operate all year. Faculty vacations will correspond to one of the four terms of the college year. And sabbaticals will come around regularly ten years after permanent faculty appointment.

The Library Committee will have an office in the library. The only offices grouped around the working lobby will be designated for definite functions: cataloging and classification, acquisition, and circulation.

The St. John's College motto encircles a seal which shows seven books grouped around a balance. The translated motto reads: I make free men from children with books and balances. At St. John's the books represent the seven liberal arts and the balance represents the laboratory sciences. In the context of the Library-College program the books could mean books and the balance could mean justice.

What we plan here has gone on surreptitiously in libraries for a long time. The September 26th, 1965 issue of *BOOK WEEK* surveyed American fiction with comments from contemporary authors. One was submitted by John Barth, author of SOT-WEED FACTOR who wrote: As an illiterate undergraduate I worked off part of my tuition filing books in the Classics Library at Johns Hopkins which included the stack of the Oriental Seminary. One was permitted to get lost for hours in that splendrous labyrinth and intoxicate, engorge oneself with story. Especially I became enamored of the great tale-cycles and collections. If anything ever makes a writer out of me it will be the digestion of that enormous surreptitious feast of narrative.

So, in scheduling students hours some slack must be built in.

# The Library As Coordinator

*FRANKLIN FAUST*

THE DEVELOPMENT of a library centered college will require a greatly extended concept of the nature of a library. It will be necessary to expand library resources and consider new means of utilizing them. The library will become the center of a completely unified administrator-librarian-instructor staff which must formulate a workable set of principles and goals to guide development of the institution's program and direct selection of library resources.

This new library should be considered the center of all educational stimulation. Normally college educational stimulants are separated by department and variety of educational activity. With little coordination the student receives the spoken and written word, facts, ideas, experience through experiment or exercise, sounds live or recorded, visual exhibitions, art, film, drama or dance, social contacts, physical activities, and so forth. The new library would bring these stimulants together and coordinate them. It would no longer be the storage house of knowledge but the nerve center of educational stimulation.

Determining the range and character of the stimulants brought together in the new library would be of primary importance. Purposeful selection will be a necessity and a great opportunity. The staff should formulate clear institutional purposes and principles in order to select library material and develop methods of library use stimulating students to achieve the institution's goals. Since all means of education will be coordinated in the library, the college will realize its educational aims much more fully.

The library-centered college idea does not determine the institution's nature or purpose. Conceivably it could be a professional institute, a discipline-oriented college, a research center, or a liberal arts college, each requiring a different kind of library to stimulate students and a different structuring of the educational process.

No doubt some points will hold true for any library-centered college. First is the need to formulate a clear purpose, for this must precede

185

even the commitment to a library-centered college. All other points are dependent on the first since the educational stimulants making up the library must be directly related to this purpose, not simply be an indiscriminate collection of available resources. The administrator-librarian-faculty will also require close coordination in carrying out a program to fulfill college aims. Students too must understand the institution's purpose and be screened to assure their capacity for sustained effort toward this goal. Finally, a close staff-student relationship must be established to utilize the library's stimulants most effectively.

Isn't the library going to be entirely different, beyond even your conception, just as the institution will be beyond our present conception? Will the library take as much initiative in changing itself as it is asking of the rest of the college? In my own conception of the library as center of all stimulation, it is not limited to recorded material or stored material in a physical sense at all.

My field of painting is being preempted, in fact overshadowed. What traditionally has been done with painting can now be done so much better by film or thru advancement in technology by drama. Probably the college would deal with films as well as books.

We're planning a Library-College before knowing what it is to do. Are we merely accepting the purpose and principles of the liberal arts college that we're opposing, which has failed, or are we going to develop a new set of principles and values?

And finally comes the selection of material which takes us back to our conception of the library. The library which becomes a collector and accumulates all possible materials would be valid only in a college requiring research in every possible area, but this is not what liberal education requires. One of the dangers for the library-centered college is that of attempting too much. The library might possibly become smaller rather than larger in a library-centered college. Rather than expanding the library it would become more selective and be a more important tool in forwarding the institution's ends.

# Campus Design

*BRUCE MANWARING*

THE LIBRARY-COLLEGE should extricate the student from the impersonal lecture room and give him more direct confrontation with ideas through extensive library use, practical experience in the laboratory and studio, and personal experience in small group and individual discussions with professors.

With this in mind the following ideas on campus design and architecture are presented, not as separate entities in terms of a physical plant in which the process of education and creation merely exist, but as an overall plan homogeneous with these processes.

When selecting a college, one of the first things a prospective student looks for is the physical nature of the campus. Intangibles such as course offerings, staff quality and concepts of education can be discussed in interviews and read in catalogues and can be fully realized only when the student has integrated himself in the process of becoming educated. The student can use only a fraction of all available resources. The physical structure, however, should have a very positive effect upon him in a wisely and imaginatively planned campus. Of primary consideration, then, in inaugurating a college is to integrate the total design of campus facilities with the curriculum structure, faculty, and philosophy of education.

A student's surroundings should not interfere with his freedom or concentration. At best physical surroundings should stimulate serious study and be compatible with student objectives. Buildings, laboratories and classrooms should be sufficiently flexible to accommodate several different uses. A college campus should provide a functional environment that is also pleasant, comfortable, and stimulating. Institutional buildings can be cold edifices reflecting the impersonality common to public and educational buildings, but they should also serve as subtle reminders of the tradition of academic learning.

Space is of primary importance and should be used to its fullest extent; architecture and grounds should contain a feeling of openness and freedom consistent with the spaciousness of the surrounding plains. Fu-

187

ture college expansion should be considered both in students and buildings thereby allowing for architectural growth as the need arises.

The library should become the central and dominant campus feature. Perhaps the campus could be organized around the "spoke" theory with the library as campus hub, the largest building with easy access. The campus would be divided into four sections: (a) administration, residence, cafeterias; (b) science and laboratories; (c) social science; (d) fine arts, studios, theater, exhibition hall. Each division would radiate from the library with administrative offices and classrooms closest to the center and laboratory-studios on the perimeter.

The buildings would not be rigidly set in a definite row-upon-row pattern but would be juxtaposed against each other to allow maximum movement throughout the campus. Open courtyards should be placed between separate buildings or completely enclosed with larger buildings such as those of Scripps College.

Rather than confine each division to one large building there could be several small buildings clustered together thereby eliminating the feeling of one large vague and impersonal structure. We might take the fine arts division as an example. The main building closest to the library would contain offices, lecture and classrooms; extending from this building around one large central court-yard would be the various studios, the theater and exhibition centers. Each building would be accessible from the main office building. A network of connecting tunnels for winter use could be arranged to culminate in the library.

All structures need not conform to a rigid architectural pattern. Each should be designed according to its specific function since the architectural form would be suitable for all purposes. Each building should be designed for maximum flexibility and expansion. Such non-functional areas as courtyards and lounges should be designed for enjoyment and warmth. Courtyards between buildings would be links tying the campus together into a homogeneous unit. A great deal of imagination can be used in landscaping, pools, fountains, and sculpture which can be appreciated the year around.

Each divisional office and classroom building should contain a small professional library branch for immediate reference use. Offices should be large enough to accommodate small informal discussion groups or should have "round table" rooms adjacent. Separate audio-visual facilities should exist within each main building. Classrooms should be designed with flexible, sound-proof, moveable walls.

Each main divisional building could repeat the "spoke" lay-out of the whole campus. Audio-visual facilities could be contained at the center, and spreading out from it would be class-lecture rooms with tiered seating, lecture platforms, and screens. Surrounding the class-lecture rooms would be a circular corridor with extensive wall space for displays and exhibits. On the outer perimeter would be offices, informal discussion rooms, and the divisional library. Natural and interior lighting, sound-proofing, and acoustics should contribute to the personal yet open feeling of the entire campus.

Encircling the campus would be a road making the campus itself entirely pedestrian. Where public use is involved parking lots should be adjacent to necessarily accessible buildings such as the theater, gymnasium, dormitories, and administration buildings.

As the center of the student's academic life and educational experience the library should receive primary consideration in the functional design. Such a library would present a tremendous opportunity for imaginative architectural design. As the most widely used building the library would dominate the campus and would present both a reminder that education is the primary purpose of the student's college years and that a liberal education is a total experience, a co-operative interchange among all disciplines.

A large structure of glass, steel, and concrete is envisioned here. Perhaps a round plan could be used which would enclose a central courtyard or be raised above the ground with the bottom level containing bookstore, cafeteria, smoking rooms, and courtyards. Its interior structure should remain flexible with few stationary walls. The outer walls could be composed primarily of glass with steel and concrete buttressing to allow as much openness and natural light as possible.

The stacks should be easily accessible and built on several levels around an open central hall housing check-out desks, card catalogues, and reference material. At the bottom level would be library administrative offices, rare book collections, periodicals, microfilm facilities, and cataloguing department. Interspersed between every other stack should be small study alcoves or groups of tables and chairs allowing the student to study material near at hand. A feeling of privacy should prevail throughout. If the student is expected to spend more time on independent study the surroundings should be conducive to privacy and moderate comfort without turning the library into a lounge. Lighting should come from indirect sources with individual reading lamps and as much natural light as possible.

Contained within the library would be audio-visual rooms sound-

189

proof and separate from the main reading room. A main auditorium for general lectures and convocations would be designed for theater and public use as well. Sound and stage studios for taping lectures and programs could be contained within the central building core where provisions for natural light would not be necessary. Sufficient space should be allowed for exhibitions of educational material and for showings of group or individual art works in a small museum, permanent or interchangeable. Departmental offices should be contained on one floor adjacent to divisional campus sections. Perhaps faculty studies and small seminar rooms could also be contained in the area.

The entire library structure should be logical and well integrated presenting maximum accessibility to all building areas with the stacks and reading rooms at the center. The architecture should be simple, uncomplicated, and flexible, yet as warm and personal as possible.

# PART THREE

# The Jamestown
# Library-College

# Introduction to the Workshop

*DAN SILLERS*

WITH A GREAT DEAL of pleasure I welcome you to this workshop, to the campus, and to North Dakota. Jamestown College is one of the state's two oldest institutions of higher education. Its reputation among North Dakota educators is of the highest quality. It is now the only four-year, coeducational, accredited, private liberal arts college in the state.

Briefly, this is how the workshop came into being. For the past two years the faculty Curriculum Committee has been studying ways of improving the educational process as well as improving themselves to contribute to that process. After having worked with a number of consultants plus doing their own research, when they read Jordan's Library-College paper many felt this idea had some of the features they were seeking. At the same time the Board of Trustees had asked for a thorough college survey and evaluation. A national committee chaired by J. L. Zwingle carried out this study, indicated the quality of the institution and its basic need for a new library to accompany renovation of its curricular offerings. It seemed only natural that further studies be pursued to show how to design and make more efficient use of such a facility. Thus with the help of many of you and particularly with the push of Bob Jordan and Winslow Hatch we decided to have this workshop.

Earlier a proposal had been developed to test some of the ideas Jordan presented in his Syracuse Workshop paper. However, most potential funders of such a program felt it should contain greater detail so this was an additional reason for the Workshop.

It is not the purpose of this Workshop to develop a program for Jamestown College. This would be too selfish and restricting. Its purpose is to develop in moderate detail an ideal design for a Library-College applicable to an independent four-year liberal arts college.

We hope, then, to develop this design and present it to funding sources to allow further research and evaluation and eventually make the idea become a reality.

A basic assumption is the idea that the library is the central resource

193

from which knowledge can be obtained. This is not meant to imply that knowledge is not gained from the interaction of individuals and evaluation of self. As we go more deeply into these ideas many of our previous concepts of the teacher's role and of educational practice may be changed. First, we should "brainstorm" many ideas to be considered in improving the educational process while keeping in mind the library as the major central resource. Then we must evaluate these ideas and put them into a concrete concept with moderate detail and finally develop a proposal.

We hope this vast geographical environment will encourage open-mindedness, creativity, and removal from everyday organizational restrictions. May our horizons in ideas and aspirations be enlarged! And, at this particular time of year we may give birth to a new concept which will affect the education of mankind so His dignity shall be continually enhanced.

A major question is "How can you staff such a program?" The answer lies in the idea that we are preparing students to believe learning to be a continuing endeavor; therefore, the same assumption can be made for faculty. We will take faculty members with the intellectual and personal skills adaptable to such a program and develop an in-service training program to give them emotional security and the technological know-how to gain personal satisfaction from this kind of educational interaction.

There is no reason why an educational institution should not use in-service training as industry does. Thus, after a period of years the principles of such an educational in-service program would be invaluable for the perpetuation of the goals of a continually changing institution. But one can dream even beyond this for universities have never trained liberal arts instructors in any great degree, particularly for the smaller colleges where interpersonal interactions are of great importance. In fact, the present trend toward specialization carries one farther and farther from this concept. However, the possibility can be seen of bringing in persons who have done all their course work toward a doctoral degree, have them spend a two-year internship in such an institution, and then encourage them to spread this concept beyond the mother institution. Probably we would then find major universities developing similar educational programs.

We must also allow for the human factor in the transitional period and thereby will be less likely to revert to old practices when high ideals are not reached in a single bound.

194

# Library-College Charter

THE PURPOSE of the Library-College is to increase the effectiveness of student learning, particularly through (though not limited to) the use of library-centered, independent study with a bibliographically expert faculty. This charter assumes that the "Library-College concept" can and should be adapted to colleges with varying objectives and philosophies. The curriculum of a particular Library College must emerge from its objectives and philosophy.

I. Library-centered, independent study with a bibliographically expert faculty requires:

   A. Library materials: As conceived in this statement, library materials represent varying viewpoints and typically include the following organized for independent use:

      1. Reference sources representing knowledge in all pertinent fields.

      2. The Good Books (basic editions of the great monuments of human thought — the time-tested classics).

      3. Representation of the better current literature in all pertinent fields, including hard covers, paper-backs, serials, etc.

      4. Graphics (maps, globes, charts, pictures, dioramas, realia, etc.).

      5. Projections (transparencies, slides, film strips, microfilms).

      6. Transmissions (disc, tape, radio, TV).

      7. Resources (human, social, natural).

      8. Mechanical, automated, electronic, computer, programmed and other "new educational media."

   B. Independent study: With faculty assistance it will typically include:

      1. Definition of goal or problem.

      2. Selection of methods of study or investigation.

3.  Conduct of study or investigation.

4.  Report of findings.

5.  Evaluation of findings.

C.  Bibliographically expert faculty: The faculty will be expert in knowing:

1.  Library materials as defined in A above in their respective fields.

2.  How to use library materials as defined in A above as vehicles of learning in their respective fields.

D.  Students at Library-College: Students will be expected to achieve competence:

1.  In reading, writing, speaking, and listening.

2.  In critically using resources of learning (including library materials defined in A above) in independent study and investigation.

3.  In intelligently relating these resources to the educational objectives and philosophy of the particular college in which they are enrolled.

II.  Library-centered, independent study, with a bibliographically expert faculty will typically—though not invariably—require:

A.  Abundance of appropriate materials as defined in IA above.

B.  Merging of present library and classroom teaching functions in the same individual — the new breed faculty member.

C.  Library facilities which appropriately permeate the campus.

D.  Varied syllabi, bibliographies, and reading guides.

E.  Abundance of activity related to varying views on controversial ideas and issues.

F.  Cooperative exploration, discovery, and synthesis by faculty and students rather than perpetuating a "master-disciple" relationship.

III.  Since life is broader than library-centered independent study students will have planned experience in other and varied aspects of living. To this end library resources will be used as much as possible to enrich such activities as the following to

196

be selected on the basis of the objectives and philosophy of a given college:

A.  Worship and meditation.

B.  Participation in the fine arts.

C.  Conducting scientific and other experiments.

D.  Participation in discussions, forums, and lectures.

E.  Participation in citizenship and community service.

F.  Participation in the practical arts.

G.  Participation in recreation and social activities.

H.  Engaging in field work.

---

Charter Committee: *Johnson,* Shores, Armstrong, Jordan.

# Curriculum Report

## General

Curriculum was discussed in relation to the goal of liberal education while leaving to other types of colleges the problems of developing curricula for their goals. Liberal arts does not necessarily mean specific courses, areas, or coverage, but does imply breadth.

The ultimate goal of a liberal arts education is usually stated as the intellectual development of the student, but there is SOMETHING MORE suggested by such terms as religious, moral, service, commitment, involvement, whole man, etc. This goal we affirm with the insistence that each college determine its SOMETHING MORE.

In the Library-College the curriculum should not be fragmented but inter-disciplinary. To attain this end we propose the following procedure:

The faculty and students should scrutinize the curriculum. Beginning with the present curriculum but looking at educational advances elsewhere, they should identify knowledge, values, techniques, ideas which are crucial to themselves. From these crucial elements those aspects should be chosen that fulfill the purposes of the individual college.

These elements should then be woven together, the whole to indicate a progression of experiences, ideas, understandings which will serve as guidelines for independent study to be conducted under the guidance of the bibliography expert faculty. Inquiry should not be helter-skelter, nor narrowly directed — this way one term, another way the next term. We can conceive of the curriculum being organized in at least three ways.

1. A foundation core permeating the four years such as Philosophy and Theology; Philosophy, Theology and Language; History, Art, Religion, Science.

2. A pluralistic approach which might include some elements organized by discipline, some by large subject areas, some by culture, etc.

3.  A completely interwoven curriculum in which no one element is specifically identified.

Whatever the organizing framework students should develop an awareness of the interrelationship of all knowledge as they strive to attain their individual evolutional goals in keeping with institutional objectives.

### PREAMBLE

As its basic purpose the Library-College curriculum has the development of the individual student. Such a curriculum would imply a learning program individually tailored for each student. It would be implemented through participation of one or more faculty members jointly with each student in the process of inquiry in directions to be determined by the student's interests and goals rather than the faculty member's specialized discipline.

### THE GOALS AND INTERESTS OF THE STUDENT

A.  If the student enters college with ill-defined goals and diffuse interests, the program will stress exploratory experiences deriving from these interests. The assumption is not that such exploration would necessarily result in the formulation of explicit and specific goals but that a continuing mode of living and learning in a creative and exploratory way is justifiable as a goal in itself. Indeed, it is a desirable underlying goal also for students who enter college with well-defined interests and specific vocational goals.

B.  If the student entering college has broad interests with possible emphases, for example, in the arts or in areas of human relationships, his program will be planned to capitalize on these interests but, at the same time, to develop breadth and understanding of significant interrelationships.

C.  If the student enters college with specific goals in mind, his program will be highly directed toward the achievement of his specific aims. For example, the student who wants to enter graduate work in physics will be guided in the development of a program which will ensure his preparation to meet graduate school requirements; the student who wants to be a teacher will have a program which will prepare him to meet certification requirements.

The method of the curriculum will be non-classroom and will employ instead individual use of all sorts of learning resources with the guidance of bibliographically expert faculty members. It follows that the learning resources should be abundant, that they should be organized for maximum accessibility, and that they should include not only books, audio-visual materials, and the newer media, but also people (faculty, staff, guests, townspeople, other students), field experiences in the community and the area, etc. The nature of the individual program will determine what kinds of learning resources would be used at what levels of study. For example, where the objective is mastery of specific terminology, facts and information, it is likely that highly programmed materials and media will be most appropriate. Beyond this level in the stage of independent *inquiry* the student's learning experiences could be varied, involving laboratory experiments, field work, reading, listening, viewing, discussing, and, indeed, sheer reflection.

## THE QUESTION OF EVALUATION, GRADES, CREDIT, ETC.

1. *Basis.* Evaluation is characteristically based upon measures of the student's achievement of predetermined goals, upon his growth and development in terms of his capacity, or upon the time spent. Any of these three bases can be used, depending upon the student's individual program. For the student preparing to enter a specialized profession achievement must be a crucial factor. On the other hand for the student who wishes to explore the liberal arts time spent in such exploration may be a perfectly appropriate measure.

2. *Method.* At least two faculty advisors will work together, involving as many others as need be to arrive at an evaluation. This evaluation will make clear the basis on which the evaluation has been made in terms which are reasonably easily translatable into grades for the benefit of the record, as needed for transfer, for admission to graduate school, for job applications, etc.

3. *Frequency.* Evaluation will occur as often as needed depending upon the unit of learning (or time) or upon the needs of the individual student.

---

Curriculum Committee: *Knapp,* Bell, Faust, Lang, Mason, Shook, Sillers.

# THE LIBRARY ORGANIZATION OF
# RESOURCES AS THE CURRICULUM;
# MINORITY REPORT                                        Patricia Knapp

LET ME MAKE CLEAR that this is not a minority report in the usual sense of disagreement with majority views since I am thoroughly in accord with the Curriculum Committee Report which sets forth guidelines for what can be a truly excellent educational program.

My problem is semantic. The report proposes a program not for a "Library-College," but an "Independent Study College." The Committee defined the library as including all resources for learning — field trips, lectures, indeed the physical environment of the campus. In my view a word used in such diffuse fashion loses its precision and thereby its conceptual effectiveness.

There are two elements in my definition. The library — not just any library but *the* library — encompasses *recorded* resources of society and *organizes* them for use.

It would be quite possible for a student to spend four years in independent study without going beyond the resources of a good paperback bookstore. In the process he could get a fine liberal arts education. Similarly a student can get a fine scientific education through a judicious combination of lectures, textbooks, and laboratory work. Either of these possibilities would be open in the Curriculum Committee program.

In contrast the curriculum of a Library-College would capitalize on the unique contribution inherent in the nature of the library as an *organization* of resources. That organization is not simply the classification and catalog of the holdings but the total network of systems through which ideas are recorded, transmitted, indexed, abstracted, classified, and so on. Any given library can be the source through which the individual gains entry to the system. The bibliographical and reference tools through which the vast body of records is organized and the ways in which these tools are themselves organized moreover reflect, always imperfectly and tardily but with considerable accuracy and completeness, the conceptual and social structures which shape scholarship and inquiry. These structures are not static. As presuppositions change, new concepts are born, and new evidence found, new vocabularies and tools are developed, new classification schemes devised, old evidence re-evaluated and new summaries written.

All of this might be beside the point of undergraduate education except the most impressive work now being done in curriculum construction (see the work of Jerome Bruner and that of the curriculum study commissions in mathematics, physics, and the biological sciences) emphasizes the conceptual structure of the discipline as the foundation upon which curriculum planning must rest.[1]

"If students discover how one body of knowledge succeeds another, if they are aware of the substantive structures that underlie our current knowledge, if they are given a little freedom to speculate on the possible changes in structures which the future may bring, they will not only be prepared to meet future revisions with intelligence but will better understand the knowledge they are currently being taught." Joseph J. Schwab, "Structure of the Disciplines: Meanings and Significances," in G. W. Ford and Lawrence Pugno, *The Structure of Knowledge and the Curriculum* (Chicago: Rand, McNally, 1964), p. 30.

This, then, is my case: Educators maintain the curriculum should be based on the structure of the discipline. The organization of the library reflects that structure. Where better than in the Library-College can we try out the notion that there might be some merit in relating the two?

---

[1] The curriculum of a subject should be determined by the most fundamental underlying principles that give structure to that subject." Jerome Bruner, *The Process of Education* (Cambridge: Harvard University Press, 1960), p. 31.

# Personnel Report

I. Administration and Faculty should consist of:

  A. A Board of Trustees — should we try to infiltrate the Board with leading idea men?

  B. An Educational Advisory Group of such people as presidents of experimental colleges, "hardware" manufacturer representatives, and prominent proponents of the Library-College. This group should meet once or twice a year to discuss the progress and philosophy of the College, help the College refocus ideas, and help the President find outstanding personnel.

  C. The President and Director of the Library who should be the same person. He should have a good subject field background, a good library background, and be a forceful administrator. He should attend a superior library school.

  D. A second administrative person who should be a public relations director, alumni association secretary, and fund raiser.

  E. A dean-registrar who strongly supports the idea of the Library-College and presides over an academic and student affairs steering committee.

  F. A business manager, a progressively oriented accountant.

  G. No separate subject departments, divisions, or department heads. However, working committees will probably be needed.

  H. Faculty members with the following characteristics:

    1. First of all they must be skilled at teaching undergraduates how to think. In order to do this, however, they must teach them how to learn.

    2. Broad interests and knowledge.

    3. Unusual awareness of good library and audio-visual resources and successful experience in using them in teaching. This is the most unique faculty characteristic in the Library-College.

203

4. Desire to continue their own education.

5. Desire to work in other subject fields.

6. Participation in and deep concern for society as a whole.

7. Ability to accept people as they are and to be adaptable.

8. Independent thinkers.

9. Unusually good empathy and ability to work with young people.

10. Belief in the Library-College program.

11. Doctorates for some but by no means all.

12. Versatile in several fields — a variety of backgrounds (majors) in one person being desirable.

13. A small faculty-student ratio, one to twelve should not be exceeded.

II. Other personnel characteristics of the Library-College should be the following:

A. Faculty and staff will be hired by selecting from applications received in response to announcements of college establishment and also through correspondence and interviews with well qualified individuals at good colleges.

B. The intimate contact and interaction of the students and faculty should be an important stimulus to learn at the Library-College.

C. The librarian and subject-matter instructor will share responsibility for all aspects of course development and teaching. They should be encouraged to participate in all areas of activity. Team teaching will be desirable.

D. Both library staff and faculty should have full status, rank, title, and equal privileges according to background and ability and should form one unified instructional staff.

E. While library staff members will be directly involved in teaching, the routine work of indexing and the supervision of student assistants, for instance, in the audio-visual center and library must receive sufficient staff attention.

F. Staff cost will be high because of the need for a larger than average and superior professional and clerical staff.

G. A faculty and staff orientation program should make each person an expert in book and media resources and their use.

H. Student assistants should play an important role as teaching and library assistants.

J. There should be a basic flat salary rate for all faculty with higher rate for president, fund raiser and dean. Salary differentials should be based on years of service at Jamestown, education, and experience elsewhere.

K. The basic faculty salary should be $7500 for twelve months with $750 increment per year of service to a limit of $20,000.

L. Clerical pay rates should equal the federal minimum rate, $1.50 per hour.

M. Based on faculty and student evaluations there should be a rigorous weeding out of less satisfactory faculty members in their first 2-3 years of service.

N. Distinguished visiting faculty members should be brought in occasionally at high salaries for special teaching assignments.

O. This document is well supplemented by the memorandum, "Faculty Development in a Library-College" by Dan Sillers.

Personnel Committee: *Harvey,* Armstrong, Coyne, Fletcher, Gaylor, Halvorson, Lee, Sillers.

# Library Supporting Media Report

I. Auxiliary Devices: These are recognized but do not change the system. Aids used: typewriters, tape recorders, Xerox, microfilms, etc.

II. Teaching Machines: Interplay between machine and user in a general way. User control.

   A. Qualities
1. Capture of audio and visual material for later retrieval.
2. Infinite patience.
3. Independently used.
4. Flexible in content.
5. Instant feed-back for the student.

   B. Limitations
1. The designer must anticipate response.
2. Tedious due to small segments of subject matter.
3. Interpretive aspects of education are beyond machine scope.
4. Implies large number of students (users).
5. Most useful at freshman level; usefulness becomes less as more contemplative studies are sought.

   C. Catalogue of kinds of devices

| Device | Cost |
|---|---|
| 1. Tape recorder | |
| 2. Single concept film | |
| 3. Slide projector | $ 50 |
| 4. Video-sonic (sconoscope-synchronized tape and slide presentations) | 300 |
| 5. Overhead projectors | 100-500 |
| 6. Edex | 6,000 |
| 7. Socratic machine — Computer plus | |
| 8. Computer | 20,000 |

9. Telephone technique
10. Program instruction book
D. Physical facilities characteristics
1. In living areas — giving a 24 hour a day learning laboratory.
2. Centralized facility — such as library.
3. Indisciplined areas on campus.

These are not mutually exclusive. Modifier for all would be:
1. Facilities that do exist.
2. Relationship with teacher.
E. Management of facility
1. Central technical processing (devices and materials).
2. A need for special maintenance, service and storage.
3. Selection
   a. Recommendations
      (1) From the entire community.
      (2) Decision made by the person who has overall responsibility for instruction.
   b. Circulation, inventory and control
      (1) Decentralization controlled by central area.
      (2) Function of material and physical facilities.
4. System evaluation
   a. Continuous evaluation of the entire system.
   b. The evaluation group should be independent of the operating group.
   c. There are professions (e.g., industrial engineer) especially trained for this type of work.
5. Management structure
   a. Teaching machine facility should be responsible to one person.
   b. Teaching facilities group should have clearly drawn lines of authority and responsibility in college.

III. Non-student Control, One-way Instructional Devices
A. Closed circuit TV is basically a logistic problem. Since the small college is usually centrally located with adequate large classrooms there is no advantage in TV facilities.

B. Types
1. Television
2. Radio
3. Motion Pictures

C. Advantages
1. Dispersement of facilities.
2. Increase in flexibility of class schedule.
3. Conservation of instructor time.

D. Disadvantages
1. Production cost.
2. Equipment use and availability.
3. Technical aspects.

IV. Computer
A. Scope within the college
1. Administrative
a. Business office
b. Student personnel
c. Library mechanization
(1) Central processing
(2) Circulation
d. Community use
2. Instructional tool
a. Teaching machine
b. Evaluation support
c. Information retrieval
3. Subject for separate instruction

B. Advantages
1. Does repetitive clerical routines fast and accurately.
2. The college has an instructional responsibility for a universal tool.
3. Extends the institution's bibliographic capabilities.
4. Economic way of retrieving material repeatedly.
5. Wide variety of combinations of units and storage.
6. Multiple-simultaneous remote access to stored information.

C. Disadvantages
   1. High conversion cost for present records.
   2. Trained personnel required.
   3. Need for internal and external standardization (queries, spelling, facilities, etc.).
   4. Demands strict accuracy.

D. Catalogue of different kinds
   1. Punch-card machines
   2. Sorter
   3. Printing device
   4. Collator
   5. Automatic data computer
      a. Tape devices
      b. Random access devices
      c. Remote facilities

E. Physical facilities
   Data processing is found in central places due to equipment characteristics.

F. Management of data processing facilities
   1. Special maintenance, service, and storage.
   2. Airconditioning is a factor in central station.
   3. Personnel: Operators, system designers, etc.; not maintenance.
   4. Training:
      a. Administration, faculty must have minimum competence in operation and design of program.
      b. College should provide training for every student.
   5. Selection does not apply.
   6. System evaluation:
      a. Continuous
      b. Permanent evaluation person.
   7. Management structure:
      a. A single man should be responsible for installation and operation.
      b. Clear lines of authority should be drawn.

V. Analogue Devices

Analogue devices have been conceived primarily for lab measuring and assimilating, therefore we have not considered them in this report.

VI. Recommendations

A. Introduction

The essence of the Library-College is active student involvement, use of library-centered independent study and a bibliographically expert faculty. Therefore, the learning media should reflect these concepts whenever relevant. Each format or medium has a peculiar pertinence to the individual learning situation. The unique strengths and weaknesses of each of the classes of educational media, from textbook through television including programmed manuals and computerized devices, should be an integral part of faculty equipment. In accordance with these principles and the intent of the charter the committee recommends the following:

1. Personnel: The College could acquire personnel to do systems analysis in individual disciplines; however, in accordance with the charter and our evaluation of the institution's needs, we recommend hiring a systems analyst for studies of the whole college system. This step should be taken as soon as a basic college philosophy has been stated.

a. Salary: Annual — $10,000 plus

Consulting: — $100 per day

Part-time: — Comparable with visiting professor appointments.

2. Scope of facilities: A centralized community facility should be considered. However, administrative regulation should give priority to instructional and institutional use.

a. Do not consider these devices only in terms of specific uses but rather in terms of over-lapping services (multi-purpose operations).

210

b. Faculty members in charge of operation could serve in other areas (Teaching classes, instructing training courses, etc.).

3. Management of Organization: The administration of supporting media should come under the Academic Dean and not under business or service offices. This recommendation is based on committee experience, rather than the concepts of the Library-College.

4. Cost: The cost of these devices in comparison to their usefulness and efficiency within the academic institution is such that they should be given early consideration and evaluation.

5. Systems simulation techniques should be considered as a tool in the design of the proposed college and its subsystems.

6. These recommendations for use of supporting media are not contingent upon a change of institution philosophy.

Supporting Media Committee: *Minder*, Brown, Holly, Samore, Tirrell, Westley.

# *Architecture Report*

The present collection of 30,000 volumes shows strength in some areas but is obviously inadequate for the program envisaged for the future. To bring up this number to the needs of a Library-College the committee proposes aiming at 150,000 volumes with a ten year program:

Annual additions 1966 through 1969 of 10,000
    volumes each year          40,000 volumes

Annual additions 1970 through 1976 of 12,000
    volumes each year          84,000

              Present collection    30,000

                          154,000

           Necessary discarding    4,000

                          150,000

To process these books for the shelves additional personnel will be necessary, as a minimum one professional and one full-time clerk. This presumes faculty book selection and their cooperation in supplying buying information.

For book selection the list prepared for the California university system's new campuses should be available within the year. The University of Michigan undergraduate library list can be purchased on cards, microfilm or in book form, but is already somewhat out of date as is the Harvard Lamont list. Until the California list appears depend on individual faculty members' and librarians' selections of key books in their fields chosen from personal knowledge and available bibliographies.

The committee recommends the use of Title II funds, hopefully available in early 1966, for filling basic collection gaps. College appropriations might be used for current publications. The minimum of 10,000 volumes will cost $45,000. Average cost of college books runs around $6, but advantage can be taken of the excellent basic collection titles in paper-back. They should be bound or reinforced at $1 apiece.

Title II provisions include a 1-to-1 matching grant of up to $5,000. The matching amount can come from any source except federal funds but must be over and above the college's usual (average of 3 years) appropriation. This $10,000 plus the college's previous appropriation of $10,000 leaves $25,000 to be raised from other sources. Title II contains provision for supplemental grants up to $10 a student; it would appear that Jamestown could qualify for an outright grant requiring no matching. Also under Title II are provisions for special purpose grants, on a 1 to 3 basis. Title VI provides funds for instructional materials — for non-books.

During the years of space shortage until the new building is available much material could be purchased on microfilm. Price is about the same on the average. Readers are now available at $100. Valuable back files of periodicals are examples here.

The periodical collection should be checked against the curriculum to make sure all subjects are adequately represented. The amounts given above do not include current periodical subscriptions, but both proposed additions and book costs include bound back issue periodicals and microfilm.

## *LIBRARY ARCHITECTURAL ORGANIZATION*

I.  General Principles.

A.  Library facilities must be functional. Interior functions must take priority over exterior, i.e. planning from the inside to the outside.

B.  Flexibility and adaptability should be high considerations for it will be impossible for an experimental project to plan in detail far ahead and tragic for new ideas to be hampered by structures.

C.  Where certain areas require specialization, for instance, special wiring for electrical equipment, effort should be made to permit new integrations with other functions. Keep non-reassignable areas to a minimum.

D.  The architectural format should reflect a spirit of freedom and reason compatible with existing structures yet without preconceptions of matching previous styles to the detriment of various functions.

E.  Attention should be given to future expansion, preferably laterally rather than vertically. The number of plans should not exceed five; possibly three is ideal.

213

II. Major Concepts of the Library-College Library.

A. The library will not be primarily a building but will be the materials of all sorts called the collection of resources to be used by students.

B. Because of the reference function, because the basic book stack will include much little used material, and because all knowledge is so filled with interrelations, central facilities must exist for housing most of the collection. Many other functions would be provided in this central facility — the main catalogs, listening rooms, ordering, cataloging, processing, and other library and teaching staff offices.

C. Dispersal will be accomplished through a flexible and unlimited loan system so special collections can be established on a term basis at any point. Provisions for small collections should be available at any point where there is need — in dormitory areas (for browsing), in professors' conference rooms, and in departments (though this does not mean the development of large permanent departmental libraries). Books in considerable demand should be held in multiple copies. Since students will be engaged primarily in individual study projects there will be little need for reserve rooms.

D. This program of creating a book environment throughout the campus will call for adequate staff to control various collections. A daily delivery service with quick surveys and frequent inventories will be needed to keep the dispersed collections active and in order.

E. Full advantage should be taken of modern technological developments such as copying devices, tape recordings of special programs, lectures, unexpendable recordings, and microfilms. Projecting and playing equipment should be available whenever needed, and the entire Library-College should be adequately connected by intercom, telephone and other systems. Consideration should be given to teletype communication with a comprehensive bibliographic resource center to expedite interlibrary loans. Centralized storage should be provided for such teaching aids as motion pictures, realia and dioramas.

## PROPOSED SPACE REQUIREMENTS AND COSTS
## FOR JAMESTOWN COLLEGE LIBRARY

This library is planned to accommodate the proposed expansion of the student body to 800.

| | | |
|---|---|---|
| 150,000 | volumes at 15 volumes per square foot | 10,000 sq. ft. |
| 800 | student studies at 25 sq. ft. | 20,000 |

| | | |
|---|---|---:|
| 70 | faculty office-conference rooms at 100 sq. ft. | 7,000 |
| 4 | seminar rooms, approx. 15 x 20 ft. | |
| | (4 x 300 sq. ft.) | 1,200 |
| 2 | group listening-viewing rooms, 25 x 20 | |
| | (2 x 500 sq. ft.) | 1,000 |
| | Preparation, cataloging, binding, and other work areas for staff of 8, at 250 sq. ft. per person | 2,000 |
| 4 | Carpeted lounge areas, possibly with fireplace at 500 sq. ft. | 2,000 |
| | Storage for A-V equipment & materials | 800 |

|  |  |
|---|---:|
| | 44,000 |
| 40% of above area for non-assignable space and for card catalog service stations | 17,600 |

| | |
|---|---:|
| | 61,600 sq. ft. |

| | |
|---|---:|
| At $25 per sq. ft. including airconditioning | $1,540,000 |
| 10% of above amount for furniture and equipment | 150,000 |

| | |
|---|---:|
| | $1,690,000 |

Costs of equipment for 500 students. Additional equipment and newer models can be purchased as enrollment increases; it would be unwise to purchase extensively now for later use.

| | | |
|---|---|---:|
| Tape recorders (1 for 10 students) | 50 at $200 | $10,000 |
| Single concept film projectors (1 for 20) | | |
| | 25 at $100 | 2,500 |
| Slide projectors (1 for 10) | 50 at $ 50 | 2,500 |
| Videosonics (1 for 50) | 10 at $300 | 3,000 |
| Overhead projectors (1 for 50) | 10 at $100 | 1,000 |

| | |
|---|---:|
| | $19,000 |

Some of these equipment pieces are to be in the library, others in instructional areas such as laboratories and studios, and others in living areas.

For use with portable equipment, student studies—conventional carrels or other type—should be wired for outlets. Carrels of this type made for

Oakland Community College sell at $75 each from McNeff Industries, Dallas, Texas. Their cost is included in the figure given for furniture and equipment.

---

Architecture Committee: *Warner,* Hample, Helen, Jordan, Manwaring, and Tirrell.

## LIBRARY SPACE REQUIREMENTS
## AND COST; MINORITY REPORT                              John Tirrell

| | | |
|---|---|---|
| 1. | Housing 75,000 volumes at 15 volumes per square foot | 5,000 sq. ft. |
| 2. | Seating 25% of the student body of 800 at 25 sq. ft. per student | 5,000 |
| 3. | Seating 30 of the faculty at 70 sq. ft. per person | 2,000 |
| 4. | 4 seminar rooms (4 x 300 sq. ft.) | 1,200 |
| 5. | 2 group listening rooms (2 x 500 sq. ft.) | 1,000 |
| 6. | Preparation rooms on proposal | 2,000 |
| 7. | 4 lounge areas (4 x 500 sq. ft.) | 2,000 |
| 8. | Allowance for audio visual equipment and materials | 800 |
| | | 19,900 |
| 9. | 40% of the net space for gross area | 7,600 |
| | | 26,600 sq. ft. |
| 10. | At $25 per square foot | $665,000 |
| 11. | 10% for library furniture and equipment | 66,500 |
| 12. | New media (100 carrels) as proposed | 27,000 |
| 13. | Computer | 20,000 |
| | | $778,500 |
| 14. | Contingency | 50,500 |
| | | $829,000 |

With rise in construction costs and other unforseen events a one million dollar goal is in order.

## COMBINING THE LIBRARY AND
## THE DORMITORY; MINORITY
## REPORT                                                  Robert Jordan

WITH INCREASING emphasis on individual study there is a tendency to provide library carrels for an increasing proportion of students. The ultimate conclusion of this trend is the provision of a carrel for every student as advocated by Louis Shores and exemplified at Oklahoma

216

Christian College. Admittedly it is expensive to provide two sets of study facilities, one in the dormitory and one in the library.

If we can make two assumptions about the college this excessive cost may be substantially reduced without sacrificing the principle that every student should have a library study area.

First, let us assume the optimum college size is 400 students or less, the maximum size for first name acquaintance among all faculty and students.

Second, we must decide in advance that a particular college will *never* grow beyond this size. If the educational community must grow, a sister campus can be added as bees add another cell of honey.

Large group facilities and other expensive services can be shared in common by a group of cluster colleges.

Given these conditions we can design an essentially circular combined campus library in one completely integrated complex *incapable* of expansion. Paradoxically, such rigid inflexibility provides certain special advantages perhaps never before realized on American college campuses.

It becomes possible for the first time to bring student living areas in an outer circle into close physical proximity to the library-faculty office-seminar areas which occupy inner circles.

Private individual student offices including individual telephones can occupy a concentric circle a few feet outward from the library-faculty office-seminar area and a few feet inward from student living areas. Thus, one set of individual student offices can replace the traditional dormitory desk and library carrel. Schematically this plan would look like this:

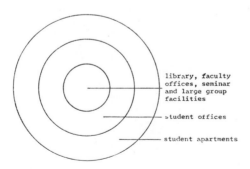

library, faculty offices, seminar and large group facilities

student offices

student apartments

Looking at the same schematic diagram edgewise in a three story complex the library is basically on one floor, faculty offices and seminar rooms on the floor below, large group facilities on the floor above, and student offices and living quarters on all three floors (if necessary), on the extreme outer perimeter.

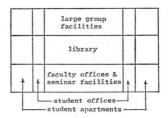

By providing an individual office for each student, the need for individual sleeping rooms becomes less pressing, and considerable savings can be achieved by returning to the practice of placing two or more students in one room or efficiency apartment.

Such a structure need not be one monolithic windowless unit. Terraces, light wells, courtyards, etc., can be incorporated in one complex unit that is compact, yet combines indoors and outdoors where appropriate and aesthetically desirable.

# Summary

*B. LAMAR JOHNSON*

IT IS OBVIOUSLY impossible to summarize this Workshop. Any valid summary must emerge from the experiences each of us as individuals has had during the past three days. All of us hope President Sillers, the faculty, Trustees, and students of Jamestown College will translate into action the idea of the Library-College. This will be the summary that counts.

With this background some of the reflections of one participant will be presented under four headings: (1) A few regrets, (2) Some achievements, (3) Limitations and cautions, (4) Suggestions for action.

Although this has been the first workshop on the Library-College it will not be the last. Accordingly, as a basis for planning future workshops we should note features of this one which might be changed if we were doing it over again.

## A.   A FEW REGRETS

1.  We have had few professors and administrators (outside of Jamestown College) and a high proportion of librarians, including myself, here. We have been holding conversations among those already converted. Because of our backgrounds and commitments we have been able to advance our thinking farther this way than with a more diversified group. Nevertheless, if the Library-College is to develop, leadership must emerge from administrators like Presidents Sillers and Tirrell and from professors committed to "library teaching." If pressure for the Library-College comes only from librarians they will be accused of representing vested interests. The support of presidents and professors must be elicited so they will take the initiative in launching proposals for Library-Colleges.

2.  Some of us have been so discursive that there was no time for formal statements from several workshop members.

3.  There has been relatively little *active* participation by Jamestown professors. Those who have been here have merely listened. If

219

the idea is to be translated into action, active faculty involvement is essential. Also, excluding the President, none of the faculty members in attendance has a doctorate. Does this suggest that the professor with a Ph.D. is less receptive than other professors to new ideas?

4. Finally, it is regrettable that Workshop members have not been better informed regarding the present Jamestown curriculum. We have been interested in applying the Library-College idea to Jamestown, and yet, we have been working in a vacuum. If they had been better informed, Workshop members might have been more helpful to Jamestown.

## B. SOME ACHIEVEMENTS

The achievements have far more significance than the regrets.

1. Holding this Workshop was a major achievement, particularly bringing national leaders on this concept together during a holiday period.

2. A second achievement has emerged from the advances in our understanding of the Library-College concept. When we assembled many felt we shared a common understanding of this idea. However, our recent sessions have led to increased understanding of it.

3. This increased agreement is epitomized in the Charter. Any college which wishes to be guided by the Charter, however, should develop a specific curriculum, staff, plant, and facilities on the basis of its particular purposes and philosophy.

4. Colleges may be committed to varying and conflicting educational philosophies and still be Library-Colleges. A Library-College may hold a rationalist, neo-humanist, or instrumentalist approach to its curriculum. Jordan expressed this view when he asserted, "A library-oriented college could come in as many shapes and varieties as a classroom-oriented college." A Library-College may be open door or may cater to the intellectually elite. President Tirrell has suggested that an open door community college of several thousand students can be a Library-College, also.

5. The specific recommendations for action in the committee reports on curriculum, personnel, plant facilities, supporting media, and others represent an achievement valuable for Jamestown.

6.  Workshop members have been introduced to systems analysis sufficiently to make us aware of a systems approach to operational problems. And we have noted such varying approaches to information-gathering as personal contacts, laboratory work, and literature.
7.  The imaginative suggestion addressed to the Jamestown faculty of a highly individualized program tailored to the needs and interests of each student represents a break with tradition which may epitomize the truly experimental Library-College program.
8.  The Workshop achieved agreement that library materials may include graphics, projections, transmissions, electronic, computer, and programmed media, and opened the door to revolutionary developments.

## C. LIMITATIONS AND CAUTIONS

Most members of this Workshop are committed to the Library-College idea. Some of us are Library-College evangelists. Accordingly, at times our enthusiasms may have gone beyond realistic expectation. Upon occasion we have gotten the impression that the Library-College idea might permeate the public school system, but at other times it has seemed that the idea would be so costly as to be restricted to a few institutions.

1.  Plans for any Library-College must be based upon financially realistic costs. Taxpayers and donors demand a rigorous examination of expenditures and expect high efficiency in higher education. All proposals for staff, plant and holdings must be subject to rigorous analysis, not only initial but also operating costs.
2.  If we expect the Library-College to have a major impact upon American higher education, we must recognize the reality of the large college and the commuting college. Sixty-five percent of college students are attending large institutions, and the percentage is increasing there and in commuting colleges also. In seeking funds for a Library-College it might be helpful to keep in mind implications for large colleges and for commuting colleges.

## D. SUGGESTIONS FOR ACTION

This was conceived as an "action workshop." We have been partially successful in developing a Library-College design. Where do we go from here?

Here are some suggestions for action: (1) Nationwide, and (2) for Jamestown. Each of us should spread, study, and instrument the Library-College idea. A variety of Library-Colleges should develop in several states. Some may establish study groups, others work through committees, and through established organizations. The Library-College idea should have an important place in conference programs. In addition, we can publish papers and books. In such action we should involve administrators and professors in discussions and study. The success of the idea will depend only in part — and perhaps small part — on librarians.

If a Jamestown Library-College is developed, it must be consistent with college purposes and philosophy and be developed from faculty study and recommendation.

1. A three to five day Jamestown College Faculty Workshop on the Library-College should be held during the Spring, 1966, with the following program:

   a. Consideration of "A Charter for the Library-College."

   b. Consideration of committee reports from the December, 1965, Workshop.

   c. Consultation with

      1) Professors who now do library-centered teaching:
         Jay Rush Sullens (or one of her associates) at Stephens College in literature.
         Samuel Postlethwaite of Purdue University in the biological sciences.

      2) Experts in the Library-College idea.

      3) Presidents of experimental colleges.

   d. A specific proposal for a Jamestown Library-College.

2. Re-examine and revise the proposal for a Jamestown Library-College, Summer, 1966.

   a. Faculty.

   b. Consultants including systems analysts.

   c. Educational Advisory Committee as recommended by Personnel Committee.

3. Present proposal to possible funding sources, 1966-67.

4. Hold two-month workshop for entire faculty on teaching in the Library-College, Summer, 1967.

5. Initiate Library-College program, 1967-68.

222

## E. CONCLUSION

In discussing general education Edgar Dale identifies that "over the ground" approach in which students are expected to "cover the tests." Dale, on the contrary, advocates the "uncover the ground approach" which has been characteristic of this Workshop. We have opened opportunities for exciting achievement in varied Library-Colleges. Why not a Library-College movement which emerges from the Jamestown College Workshop of December, 1965, with the first such college established here at Jamestown!

# Appendixes

# APPENDIX A

# The Library-College Workshop of Jamestown College

## *TIME*

The workshop has been scheduled for Saturday, December 18 through Tuesday, December 21, 1965. Participants will arrive Friday evening and depart Tuesday morning.

## *PURPOSE*

The primary function of the Workshop will be developing an ideal design, in moderate detail, for a Library-College. Such a design is needed on an ideal basis not related to any particular campus. This design, however, will be limited to the independent four-year liberal arts college. Only broad efforts will be made to restrict the design to Jamestown College. This will reduce blocks to creativity. Later, an ideal program could be related to the Jamestown situation.

A second objective will be the development of the second and third steps which might make the Library-College a reality.

## *TOPICS FOR DISCUSSION*

A number of participants have been invited to write and bring brief papers on a specific phase of the Library-College of special interest to them. Papers should be between two and ten pages in length. Several main categories have been selected as topics for the papers and as beginning points for discussion. These include: architecture and campus design; curriculum and instructional program; personnel; student and faculty counselling; co-curricular and community activities of college staff and students; new media; programmed learning and computers; and finance.

227

## JAMESTOWN COLLEGE

Basically a four-year, coeducational, private liberal arts college, Jamestown has a relatively young faculty and administration both of whom are constantly striving to improve the College program. Teaching and improving the learning situation are the prime functions of professors.

A predominance of the Jamestown student body comes from the Mid-West although an increasing number are coming from eastern and western states. The average student in the present freshman class ranked in the upper one-third of his high school class and scored a composite of 24 on the A.C.T., 518 mathematics and 530 verbal on the S.A.T. The largest number of graduates in recent classes has entered graduate school immediately after graduation. The second largest number enters the teaching profession. Both college and specific departments maintain formal and informal placement bureaus to aid students.

The Thaw Memorial Library was erected in 1912. Rapidly growing inadequate, the structure and a nearby annex hold the college library collection. After study by an outside committee and extensive self-evaluation the immediate College capital goal is the design and construction of a new library within the next two or three years. It is hoped that this workshop will provide ideas useful in this venture.

## JAMESTOWN, NORTH DAKOTA

The home of Jamestown College is a small (population 17,000) mid-western city serving a large rural grain-farming area. Jamestown is 100 miles west of the twin cities of Moorhead, Minnesota, and Fargo, North Dakota, the state's largest city, and 100 miles east of Bismarck, the state capitol.

Jamestown is served by daily schedules of Northwest Orient Airlines, the Northern Pacific Railroad, and several bus lines. It is also on U.S. Interstate 94 and three state and United States highway routes.

# Outline of Topics:

## THE DESIGN OF A LIBRARY-COLLEGE

*ROBERT JORDAN*

Resumé
    Campus design
    Recorded knowledge
    Inquiry (curriculum)
    Personnel
    Control

Campus Design
    Acquisitions
    Aesthetics
    Architecture
    Arrangement (inter-relations)
      Relationships
      Space Utilization
    Cost
    Design and building programs
    Facilities (buildings)
      Eating
      Meditation
      Mobile
      Etc.
    Interiors
      Air control
      Equipment and furnishings
        Carrels
        Operable walls
        Etc.
      Lighting
    Location, sites
    Maintenance

Recorded Knowledge
    Media
      AV (new media)
      Computers
      Laboratories and technical aids
      Mechanical learning aids

229

Printed materials
   Books
   Paperbacks
   Periodicals
   Etc.
Programmed learning
Etc.
Organization
   Acquisition
   Representation
      Bibliographies
      Catalogs and indexes
      Reading guides
      Syllabi
      Etc.
   Storage and Obsolescence
   Searching
   Dissemination
      Loans
      Sale
      Etc.

The Process of Inquiry (curriculum)
   Content (topics)
      Academic subjects
         Abstract sciences
         Arts
         Language
         Natural science
         Social science
      Chronological
      Conceptual
      Interdisciplinary studies
         Area studies, cultural areas
      Problem orientation
         Community service
            Political
            Social
            Etc.
         Topical problems or questions
         Etc.
      Vocational fields
   Methods
      Conferences
         Inter-college
         Community
         National
      Course system

Discussion
Independent study, projects
  By the individual
    Essays and reports
    Reading
  By the group
Individualized instruction
  Correspondence
  Programmed learning
  Tutorial programs
Laboratory method
  On-campus labs, demonstrations and clinics
  Field trips
  Work-study
  Family living
    Foreign country
    Minorities
    Etc.
Lecture, recitation and quiz
Research
  Institutes
  Educational
  Faculty
  Undergraduate
Grouping
  Size
  Grade level
    Graded (Freshman, Sophomore, etc.), homogeneous
    Ungraded, heterogenous
    Remedial
    Honors (tracks, ability groups)
  Alumni
  Continuing education (adult education)
Alternatives and Requirements
  Options (electives)
  Common experiences
    Core or common requirements
    Campus-wide experiences
    Common syllabi
  Courses of study
  Specialized experiences
Resources
  Recorded knowledge (see above)
  People (see above)
  Community (see above)
  Real time communication systems
    Audio

                    Computer
                    TV
            Location
                On campus
                Off campus
                    Local community
                    Regional or national
                    International
        Personnel (people)
            Staff
                Assistance
                    Aides
                    Consultants
                    Instructional methodology
                    Psychological counseling
                    Released time
                    Secretarial
                    Students
                Compensation
                    Benefits
                    Salaries
                Evaluation
                    Efficiency
                    Promotion, tenure
                    Etc.
                Functions
                    Administration
                    Communication services
                    Counseling
                        Bibliographic
                        Community
                        Educational
                        Group
                        Personal
                        Social
                        Vocational
                    Library services
                    Teaching-tutoring
                    Research
            Load (responsibilities)
            Organization (deployment)
                    Projects
                    Subject departments and divisions
                    Teams
            Rank
                    Non-professional

232

Marriage
Sex
Activities
Functions
Organizations
Government
Community
Student
Health
Mental
Physical
Inter-group relations
School-community
Academic freedom
Off-campus experiences
School-parents
Parent week-ends
Student-faculty
Extracurricular involvement
Student equality
Student-faculty ratio
Morale
Community
Group
Individual
Orientation
Control
Administration
Deans
President
Trustees, boards
Change and innovation
External relations
Accreditation
Alumni
Articulation
Secondary-higher
Transfers
Undergraduate-graduate
Post-college
Community, regional, national, and international
Cooperation
Sponsorship
Finance (budget)
Endowment
Fund raising

234

```
        Plant improvements
        Operating expense
        Research and projects
        Student financial aid
        Tuition
    Founding (implementation)
        Development programs
        Priorities
        Schedule
    Interpretation (PR)
    Organization
        Calendar
            School year
            Semesters, etc.
        Satellite colleges
        Schedule
            School day
            School week
    Planning (development)
        Aims (purpose)
            Aesthetic competence
            Concerned citizenship
            Creative ability
            Custodial maintenance
            Democratic method
            Critical judgment
            Enthusiasm
            Ethical values
            Facts—principles
            Flexibility
            Individual responsibility and initiative
            Inquiry, Competence in methods of
            Intellectual development
            Love for fellow man
            Reading competence
            Sensory-motor skills
            Vocational training
            World orientation
        Campus environment (press)
        Innovation and change
        Philosophy of education
            Learning theories
            Theories of knowledge
        Surveys
            Evaluation
            Self-studies
    Research and measurement (validation)
```

# APPENDIX B

# *Library-College Newsletters*

NUMBERS 1-4, MAY-DECEMBER, 1965

All portions of these issues are included except the bibliographies in numbers 1 and 4 (now consolidated with an earlier bibliography in Section C of the Appendix) and an editorial by Patricia Knapp (now in Part II).

## Newsletter on Library-College Integration (and Related Experimentation in Undergraduate Higher Education)

Rotating editors: Robert T. Jordan
Patricia Knapp
Daniel Patrick Bergen
Louis Shores
H. Lee and Mildred Sutton
George Bailey
Theodore Samore
John Harvey
Gilmore Warner

### INTRODUCTION

Typically the areas between major disciplines are vague and grey. Individuals at the center of each discipline find their direction clear and their career cues neatly laid out. The more non-conformist, those inclined to restlessness, and wide-ranging in their curiosity, gravitate to the inter-disciplinary boundaries.

This newsletter is conceived as a venture into such a grey area. We believe the area between librarianship and higher education to be rich in untapped potentiality.

### PROCEDURE IN DISTRIBUTION OF NEWSLETTER

Each of the rotating editors will take turns (monthly?) in responsibility for an issue. Each editor will be free to develop his own emphases and objectives. The Newsletter will function as a medium for the exchange of information, ideas, or hortatory appeals on topics of common interest to some or all of us. Please send announcements, comments, reports, new techniques involving the library in the educational process, surveys, questions, proposals or calls for assistance in developing an activity to the next editor.

The Newsletter is being sent to 33 people (plus the seven "editors"). This is a reasonable limit for any one editor to distribute. In order to make it possible for additional individuals to receive the Newsletter, we are asking each of the 33 to route the Newsletter to three to five additional people, using a routing slip. Each of the 33 are invited to add two additional names. More than this may be added if desired, but five would seem a reasonable maximum for most routings. In this way, the Newsletter should reach an eventual total of 200 people.

Please send the names and addresses of any individuals added to the routing lists to Pat Knapp — she will print the entire list of 200 recipients in the next issue.

We are anticipating that a few of the 33 might not want to participate in this "Scheme." In this event, please return the list of three addresses to Robert Jordan.

If you *do* wish to participate, merely forward three stamped self-addressed, *long* envelopes to Patricia Knapp. (This paragraph is directed to the 33 only.)

At his own option, the current editor will at times use large manila envelopes, and will forward the unused smaller sized envelopes to the next editor.

## EDITORIAL — AN INTERPRETATION OF THE EDUCATIONAL OBJECTIVES OF THE NEWSLETTER

The educational objective: the most effective possible education, in the generalist tradition, with emphasis towards modern world problems. The world is integrated, there is no longer any place to hide, we are now truly neighbors and brothers to all mankind. We can no longer afford the luxury of warped and over-specialized men developed only in one narrow area. Paradoxically, as the complexity of the world demands more and more specialists, the world becomes less and less viable, unless all men are at once specialists and generalists. Not only must we have a sophisticated appreciation of all cultures, but we must

237

also be capable of making personal sacrifices to insure that all people in the world have increasing opportunity for material necessities and individual development.

Since the world is truly integrated, that macrocosm of the world, the college campus, must also be integrated. We are appalled at the development of "massversities," with hundreds of entirely insulated, parochial little empires. We cannot break up our huge universities into small independent colleges, but we can develop an integration of subject matter, academic program research activities (optional) and informational resources, in units on a human scale of size. In summary, we hold that there must be a physical and procedural integration of the campus and the academic program, if we are to expect the development of the integrated student, with a sense of responsibility to all areas of life.

In terms of sheer educational effectiveness, we maintain there is a potent dynamic in bringing the students into constant and intimate association with the unexplored intellectual riches and variety of the library. The library is itself a symbol of the integration of the world, with all subjects developed in one arrangement, with one common staff, and with representation of all viewpoints.

Just as we expect students to become at one and the same time both specialists and generalists, we expect that the faculty at our Library-College of the future will be both librarians and faculty members. Just as we find it impossible to split away the specialist from the generalist in such men as Albert Schweitzer, Albert Einstein and Martin Luther King, so will we find it impossible to split the professional staff of the Library-College into "librarians" and "faculty members".

## CLEARING HOUSE ON COURSE-RELATED LIBRARY ASSIGNMENTS AND OTHER TECHNIQUES INVOLVING THE LIBRARY IN THE EDUCATIONAL PROCESS

The Newsletter will function as a bulletin board for information about student assignments, procedures, curricula, and techniques that in any way involve the library directly in educating students, *beyond* the traditional general "orientation" of new students.

## INITIATION OF A LIBRARY-COLLEGE

Many of us are interested in finding a way to initiate a full-fledged Library-College, where the classroom cannot physically or philosoph-

238

ically be distinguished from the library. Such a college was projected by Harper at the U. of Chicago 60 years ago, was again revived by Louis Shores more than 30 years ago, and has been partially carried out at Stephens under B. Lamar Johnson, and more recently at Monteith. The College Talkshop, held at Kenyon College in 1962 considered several conceptions for the design of a Library-College. Plans for a strongly library-oriented college were unveiled at a conference sponsored a year ago at Florida State University. But nowhere, as yet, is there a prospect for a *complete* integration of library and classroom, so that, in effect, all educational activity would be directed from the library, or conversely, all faculty would be dually qualified as librarians and faculty.

Will anyone take the initiative in setting up another meeting, to more specifically discuss the program for the Library-College? Once the program is developed in moderate detail, it should be possible to negotiate with the increasing number of universities that are deliberately searching for promising orientations for yet-to-be-established undergraduate colleges within the university.

## SURVEYS, COMMENTS, CRITICISM, SUGGESTIONS, PROPOSALS, QUESTIONS, CALLS TO ACTION

This Newsletter will serve as a general medium for exchange of ideas.

### REGISTER OF EXPERIMENTAL COLLEGES

Much of the current experimentation in higher education has strong implications of involvement with the library, and converseley, the most receptive environment for development of the Library-College and related concepts will be found at the experimental colleges. So there is a natural affinity between experimental colleges and the Library-College. But there is no national "register" of experimental colleges. Hence, this Newsletter will attempt to carry listings of experimental colleges that come to our attention.

## PROPOSED & PROSPECTIVE EXPERIMENTAL COLLEGES

### Antioch

Not quite a "college within the college", Antioch will inaugurate this fall a radical new program for freshmen. Classrooms and grades will be eliminated. The library will spread into the dormitory where

239

students will be in close association with preceptors throughout the first year. Academic offerings will consist of seminars, large group lectures, independent and programed learning.

### University of California, Berkeley

Plans are far advanced for an experimental undergraduate campus at Berkeley. Also, a "Free University of California" has developed as an out-growth of the great upswelling of student and faculty protest this past year; classes have been held on an informal basis according to student interest.

### University of California, San Diego

Will open this fall to undergraduate students. As at Santa Cruz, plans are to eventually accommodate 27,500 students, but here the autonomous satellite colleges will average twice as large in size as at Santa Cruz, and will not be so exclusively undergraduate oriented.

### University of California, Santa Cruz

Will open this fall; will ultimately consist of 20 to 40 autonomous satellite colleges. The first of these will be patterned on the Swarthmore model, straight liberal arts. The second will be oriented towards political science, the third toward science, and the fourth toward urban problems and regional planning. Each college will have its own library of 10 to 15 thousand non-course related books and records with a heavy emphasis on paperbacks.

### Florida State University

Plans are underway for an autonomous undergraduate college with an emphasis on world problems and the unity of knowledge. The staff will include "faculty-librarians". Books and other media will pervade the campus. Students will be limited to 300 or 400, and will be a cross section of FSU students, as at Monteith. The curriculum will emphasize the humanities, will cover areas rather than courses, will include a foreign stay, and will not include grades. The library will include 50 to 100 thousand books, will be open 24 hours a day and students will be allowed to keep materials as long as desired. All staff will share in administration of the college. There will be a room for meditation and introspection. The key element will be a co-extensive welding of all facilities and personnel into one unity.

240

## Illinois

The establishment of a new experimental college was recommended in a master plan for higher education published in 1964 to be concerned with utilization of the new media and reaching effectively the students from culturally deprived homes.

## University of Michigan

Robert Hynes, Vice President has plans for an autonomous college combining dorms, classrooms, and library.

## Novatech (Nova University of Advanced Technology, Fort Lauderdale, Florida)

Proposed new university, land already acquired (?), building plans being developed, aim is to compare with MIT, CIT, initial emphasis on graduate level, an ungraded undergraduate level, with free movement of students into various areas according to ability and achievement. Use of AV to free professors from routine work. James Killian on advisory board.

## Palo Verdes State College, California

Not yet in operation. Will include satellite colleges.

## Parsons College, Fairfield, Iowa

Parsons is sponsoring the opening of two new colleges this fall, one at Scotts Bluff, Neb., one at Denison, Iowa, and two more in 1966. Lee Sutton is helping to find librarians for these colleges, salary up to $14,000, as well as additional staff for his own library. He writes there is a fighting chance that any one of these five colleges, including Parsons, might be developed as a library-centered college.

## Purdue University

Ad hoc talks, similar to those held at the "College Talkshop," are being held by librarians, humanists and scientists.

## San Bernadino State College, California

A new college, to be in operation in 1968. Will include satellite colleges.

241

### United Presbyterian Church in the USA

In recent years, this church has sponsored one fairly experimental college, Florida Presbyterian. Plans are underway for two additional colleges, Eisenhower College in New York State, and one in Oahu, Hawaii.

### World College, Brookville, Long Island

Will open 9-65 with 30 students and 4 teachers, Quaker sponsored, plans eventually to operate through seven study centers in representative parts of the world, with faculty and students representing many of the world's religions and cultures. Plans include Soviet Union and China. Seeking students concerned about the more menacing problems of the time. Annual tuition of $2,625 will include transportation costs as well as board and room.

## EXISTING EXPERIMENTAL COLLEGES

Here is the beginning of a list of currently prominent existing experimental colleges: Goddard, Monteith, Antioch, Reed, University of the Pacific, Stephens, Parsons, Shimer, St. John's (Annapolis and Santa Fe), Trinity at Washington, D.C., Marlboro, Mount San Antonio, Florida Presbyterian, Bard, Kalamazoo, Upland, Stetson, Michigan State, University of Michigan, University of California, Grand Valley, Oakland, New College, Delaware, Berea, and Cornell (Iowa). Not included are the two dozen or so universally acknowledged elite (and usually experimental, as well) colleges in the East. Which colleges would you add to this list?

It has been suggested that Talladega, Jarvis Christian, Virginia Union and Wilberforce are among the more experimental Negro colleges.

## EDITORIAL COMMENT —
## THE LESSON OF CALIFORNIA

There is a natural relationship between the concepts of the Library-College, the college-within-the-university, and human scale in education. While we might take some satisfaction in saying "we told you so" to Berkeley, at the same time we might also feel guilty that as librarians we have made such meager contributions towards developing a more viable, meaningful and humanly digestible scale in our colleges and universities.

For 115 years California has often led the nation in adopting new ideas and institutions (see Carey McWilliams' "California"). At the same time that one trend toward gigantism and impersonality has reached its disturbing climax, dialectically, within the same university, plans have been under development for many years for new campuses on a more human scale, and plans are far advanced for an autonomous experimental college at the chief multiversity itself.

Unfortunately, the lesson unfolding at Berkeley will undoubtedly take several years to penetrate to all of our "massversities." At this moment universities are planning undergraduate libraries to serve up to 6,000 seated students at one time — mass education with a vengeance.

## NEW IDEAS — THE "JORDAN PLASTIC BOOK BOX"

The current Newsletter editor has attempted to visualize physical and procedural conditions in the library that might contribute to the success of the Library-College concept. It is not without significance that we enthrone the circulation control area, with its picayune detail and clerical staff, in the most prominent locations in the library. Our deeds belie our ideals. It is visibly obvious to every student that the major concern of the library is minute and detailed accounting to ensure that no one keeps a book beyond a rigidly prescribed period of time. What is the answer? How can clerical routines be reduced in visibility? How can the circulation desk be removed from the library? How can clerks be removed from visibility to users? How can we arrange our libraries so the first staff seen by the student is the librarian, or librarian-counselor, or librarian-faculty member?

In the 1920's, the typical university library building was built with a large reading room on the second floor, reached by formal paired stairways. As one entered the building, on the first floor, the first sight that greeted one were two doors, leading to the men's and women's toilets, between the pair of stairs. Today, we have progressed to the circulation desk occupying the position of key prominence. We must progress one logical step further so the librarian himself and his direct personal relations with the student will be located in the architectural focus of the building.

The current editor thinks he has discovered a concept that might make possible a fundamental redesign of library buildings and the procedures therein. This is the "Jordan plastic book box," an individual box for each book in the library. Although an extremely basic and simple concept with far-reaching implications for user self-service, such a

243

box makes possible retrieving, circulation, and shelving. The circulation desk can be eliminated, and with it the large proportion of staff time that it represents. Alternately, it would be possible to install low cost fully automated shelving and retrieval. Would you like to know more? Read the forthcoming convention issue of the *Catholic Library World,* or write Robert Jordan for a preprint. Your criticism is invited. Volunteer libraries are needed for a demonstration of this concept.

## NEWS ITEMS, MEETINGS, ANNOUNCEMENTS

ALA sponsored a conference at Airlie in Virginia, (March 29-30) on "Education and the Nation's Libraries." Among the half dozen major recommendations was one urging that librarians participate actively in the planning and development of educational programs.

There will be an invitational brainstorming session at Aspen this summer on designing new experimental colleges. Robert Blackburn at Shimer College is involved in setting up this conference.

The American Documentation Institute is sponsoring an invitational conference on the documentation-education "interface" at Airlie House, in early September. For information, write Fred Goodman, E. R. I. C., Office of Education, Wash. 25, D.C.

A number of the editors or recipients of this Newsletter will be speakers at the "National Conference on the Junior College Library," to be held at UCLA July 12-14, 1965. About 200 are expected to attend, one-third junior college presidents, one-third faculty, and one-third librarians. Lamar Johnson is organizer.

A conference on "The Library and the College Climate of Learning" will be held at Syracuse June 20-23, 1965. Two of the Newsletter editors are among the six speakers.

REPORTS AVAILABLE (no charge)

A few copies of the College Talkshop proceedings are still available in Microcard format. Also, copies of a talk on the Library-College given at Syracuse in Nov. 1964 are available. Write to Robert Jordan.

Knapp, Patricia. Independent Study and the Academic Library. Special Report Series. E.R.I.C. (Educational Research Information Center) OE.

The long range plans and academic plans are available from UC-Santa Cruz and UC-San Diego.

Smith, Seymour A., Prologue to the Future. Stephens College 1964.

## No. 2, July, 1965, Issue Editor: Robert Jordan

### EXCERPTS FROM RECENT LETTERS

To: Patricia Knapp                                                    February 2, 1965

From: Robert Jordan

But since your proposal for a clearing house was not exactly received with wide open arms, perhaps you will be in a frame of mind now to revive the idea of an ad hoc group and an ad hoc newsletter. I think the reasoning would run something like this. If educationally oriented librarians are to get anywhere with their ideas, carry out the vision of Shores and the implications of Monteith's project (instead of being buried in the files at OE), we *must* in some way get together, exchange notes, associate ourselves. This is a first principle. We just can't expect that our ideas can be translated into reality if we remain in isolation; we must organize, in a word. On the other hand, I don't think very much organization is needed. Just a little effort, a moderate amount of groundwork, a moderate amount of concerted and consistent organization by two or three individuals working together can achieve important results. There are many indications that the time is right for a full fledged trial, for the first time in history, of a college organized from scratch with an all-out library-oriented philosophy.

Now, I agree with you, and always have, in your repugnance of further splintering ALA. I don't think we should operate outside ALA. True, ALA, as presently constituted, does not positively encourage, as I think it should, the formation of ephemeral ad hoc groups revolving around specific issues. At the same time, there is nothing to prevent us from starting an ad hoc group—eventually, we might get recognized as a "committee." George Bailey has been intensely interested in the idea of a library-oriented college, would very much want to be included in any new group on this subject, and would see that we were sufficiently related to ALA. He attended Louis Shores conference in Florida last spring.

245

In order for your idea of a clearing house to be properly nourished and cherished it must be handled by those who are already "converted" so to speak. You can't expect that technicians who believe librarians should stay in their place would be receptive to what they consider a rather esoteric and entirely peripheral concern.

I see that the primary motivating, organizing and inspiring concern for a group of educationally oriented librarians would be the design and founding of a Library-College. As a spin off there would be a variety of benefits. One of these would be a clearing house. A second would be a newsletter. This could be a fairly painless operation, I believe, each of us could take turns in getting it out, accumulating material and enclosures in between the irregular issues.

But the initial motivating force should be the organization of a national semi-invitational meeting, preferably pre- or post-ALA Detroit. The purpose more specifically than at the first College Talkshop, would be to develop the design of a Library-College and get the machinery in motion for its actual development as a new autonomous college, preferably in Michigan, associated with Wayne, University of Michigan, or Michigan State.

Now, this national meeting doesn't have to be complicated or expensive to organize. The first College Talkshop was developed quite painlessly and effortlessly at minimal cost by deliberately *not* seeking subsidy or foundation support. We should have no trouble in finding a dozen or two dedicated and worthy souls who would subscribe to a statement of general principles for a Library-College, who would want to contribute positively to its development, and who would, moreover, be willing to come at their own expense, especially if many of them would already be in the vicinity for ALA.

As further confirmation of my conviction on working within ALA, despite its deficiencies, I am enclosing a paper that has not been seen by anyone outside my office with the exception of Castagna. He has urged that it be published, but I am not confident that this would be the most constructive and convincing method for achieving some of the suggested reforms.

\*　　\*　　\*

To: Robert Jordan                    Received March 26, 1965

From: Patricia Knapp

I agree that an initial motivating force for the formation of a circle of converts might be interest in the design of a Library-College. But I have reservations:

I'm less than enthusiastic about your proposed procedure of starting with the design of a Library-College and then moving toward its actual development as a new autonomous college. Maybe this reaction is completely subjective, too. Maybe I've lost my missionary zeal, though I'd hate to admit it. But here's at least a rationalization: I have a feeling that the people who do the best job on curriculum design, educational philosophy and the like are the worst at founding, money-raising, etc. At Monteith, for instance, what got the money from Ford was one good but naive and impractical (the inversion of class size, small classes for freshmen and large for seniors) and another good but hardly novel idea (that good professional education should be based on good general education.) The experimental flavor, the "style" of Monteith was largely supplied by those recruited by the founders; but I'm pretty sure that these latter would be quite ineffective as initiators, founders and money-raisers. I know I would be, and that is why, perhaps, I feel that designing such a college would be fun, but "academic in the wrong sense of the word.

All of this sounds awfully dreary, I'm afraid. Perhaps if I get away from administration and back to teaching next year my enthusiasm for new undertakings will revive.

*     *     *

To: Verner Clapp                                   March 11, 1965

From: Patricia Knapp

My thinking about what next on the Monteith library program has gone through several stages. At first, I assumed that the next step would be to resubmit without much change the proposal, rejected last year by the Cooperative Research Branch, to implement and test the effectiveness of the four-year sequence of library coordinated assignments. But two sorts of difficulties appeared. First, we've had some turnover on the Monteith faculty and the new people, like most faculty members, think of library competence as either something that can be acquired in a couple of weeks in Freshman English (or better still in high school) or as command of the bibliography of a specialized subject field which is useful only for graduate work. In time I could have convinced them or, at worst, carried a vote against them, since most of those who had experienced the pilot project had been converted. But another difficulty arose from the fact that the "model" sequence was developed two years ago and that some of the assignments in it would not be scheduled for testing for another four or five years. The Monteith curriculum is not and I hope never will be settled down, so the assignments we dreamed up would require revision. Since they were designed to illustrate principles concerning the *process* of using library resources, rather than any specific content or tools, they could theoretically at least be devised to coordinate with whatever approach and materials were being used at a particular time. But the faculty was fearful about what seemed to them like a commitment too far in the future, and I was discouraged by the prospect of the work involved in adjusting to changes again and again.

To avoid this impossible choice, I have decided to turn my attention away from people, both students and faculty, and toward bibliographical organization. I am satisfied (though I have not scientifically "proved") that the early assignments in the Monteith "model" program are feasible, i.e., workable with fairly large numbers of students and educationally effective, i.e., that students can derive valid generalizations about the organization of library resources from such experiences with aspects of that organization.

247

I intend now to work on the assignments which were planned to occur later in the sequence and which were suggested by the faculty but were never really tried out. I want to find out whether or not the bibliographic machinery will actually bear out my notions about general principles concerning the organization of scholarly and scientific literature, principles which might be teachable as part of general education and which might be derived from quite individualized library experiences—if these principles were to be identified as "general" rather than specific to specialized subject fields or disciplines.

\* \* \*

To: Robert Jordan March 31, 1965

From: Louis Shores

More than ever as we move into universal higher education, Library Learning must replace classroom contact as a measure of higher education. I said this at Stetson to about 250 librarians and higher educationalists assembled at a banquet. The reception my "far out in left field" thesis got was heart-warming especially since I took the extreme position that the classroom contact, the separated specialized courses, and teacher-centered higher education, now predominant, are all on their way out. I also paid my respects to automation and programmed learning and my belief that these are part of the generic book and must be kept in proper balance. More than ever I believe you and I and the others must work on librarians as much as on college presidents to destroy this ancillary complex which librarians more than educationalists suffer from. I touched upon this several times in recent articles: The College of Library Arts, 1984, which appeared in the *Journal of Education for Librarianship;* "The Quiet Force" which appeared in the *Hawaiian Library Association Journal.* Perhaps if you and I can keep hammering away at this and librarians will read the metamorphosis may come about.

\* \* \*

To: Robert Jordan December 3, 1964

From: Dan Bergen

About an experimental college it might be possible to develop an institution that would comprehend the last two years of high school and the lower division years of college. This is an old idea of course (cherished by both Hutchins and Harper of Chicago), but one which may be ripe for implementation given current pressure from graduate schools and strong academic high schools. Chronologically, such an experimental college would occupy the position of the *gymnasium* in Germany or the *lyceé* in France. It would, however, be much more concerned with integrated general education than either of those institutions.

I agree with you that Pat Knapp would be the ideal leader of such an institution. In addition to her library work at Monteith she has served as Secretary of the College and is well acquainted with the program of general education there. That program, by the way, looks a little like Shimer's—no academic ranks and division of the social sciences, humanities, and the natural and biological sciences.

I am very interested in founding an experimental college. I believe it should be tributary to a cultural center, but not subject to the pressure which might prevail in a larger setting like Monteith or U. of C. (Santa Cruz). I am not certain, however, whether I now have the experience for such an undertaking. Probably both of us should spend some time teaching in an experimental college. Why don't you write Pat Knapp of our interest in establishing an experimental institution?

## ADDENDA

In a letter dated April 30, we learn that Pat Knapp will be leaving Monteith, and will teach full time at Wayne's Department of Library Science in the fall.

She also writes that the final report on the Monteith Library Project might be published in the Library Science Series by the Free Press. She has thought for some time that a review of the Project by a group of librarians might be desirable. She wonders whether the prospect of publication should have any bearing on such a reviewing conference. "Would it be better before or after publication, for instance? Could, in fact, deliberations of such a review be included as part of a published report?" Pat will gratefully receive your comments.

She has further news to report, as follows:

> "I enclose a copy of a letter I just received from Dean [D. Gordon] Rohman of the new [Justin Morrill] College being established at Michigan State University. Since he seems to see the library as the central focus for the development of an independent study program, we might have an opportunity here to pursue our crusade.
>
> "Did you know that Ralph Shaw has received a grant from the Carnegie Foundation to develop a program at the University of Hawaii having to do with determining 'whether (and, hopefully, how) the college experience can be made to develop habits of mind that lead to continued intellectual interests and growth throughout life for a substantial segment of the student body'? I have been invited to serve on an advisory committee which will be meeting in Honolulu early in June, so I shall have more to report later. (The quotation above is from an early statement of the project proposed. One copy of the whole draft is enclosed)."

Dan Bergen reports the following:

> "Beginning in the fall of 1965, Sam Baskin will be on half-time leave from Antioch to serve as President of the newly formed

Union for Research and Experimentation in Higher Education. The initial membership of this association includes Antioch, Bard, Chicago Teachers College North, Goddard, Hofstra, Monteith, Nassan, Sarah Lawrence, Shimer and Stephens. Sam writes that 'the stress within the group will be on experimentation and exploration of new program ideas and new ways of teaching and learning as well as on research and evaluation of the effects of change.' "

Winslow Hatch, Director of the Clearinghouse of Studies on Higher Education at the U. S. Office of Education is proposing to issue a *New Dimensions* series on the subject of educational initiative in the library. He conceives that this might take the form of an anthology, bringing together the scattered and heretofore uncollected writings on this subject. Your nominations would be appreciated.

Hatch is also hoping to issue another *New Dimensions* pamphlet on quality in higher education, something of a more concise up-dating of Sanford's *The American College.*

Finally, Hatch would like all of us to feed copies of articles, reports and experimentation on the general topic of the library as it affects the educational process to his *Current Awareness Alerts.* He considers this topic of prime importance now, and suggests that the climate is right for major "break-throughs." The kind of material published in *Current Awareness Alerts* in the next few months can help establish trends and will have a major influence on how the new Federal money will be spent. *Current Awareness Alerts* is replacing the *Reporter,* and will be distributed at frequent intervals to a mailing list of 8400. OE will abstract, if we don't, but the process will be expedited if we furnish an abstract along with the document. Preprints or advance typewritten copies are preferred. We are the only group that has been asked to forward material on this topic.

Does anyone have a suggestion for a permanent "home" for this Newsletter? Our rotating publication and the routing slips might be all right for an interim period until the novelty wears off; but in the long run, we should probably have a more stable and conventional institutional base, although we might want to continue with the rotating editors.

In the first issue of the Newsletter, the question was asked "Does anyone think that we are at the point at which a meeting of any kind

250

would be advisable" (during the week of the ALA conference)? Since that was written, an opportunity has developed which has the potential of developing into the Library-College concept. Dan Sillers, President of Jamestown College, Jamestown, North Dakota has for some years been thinking along lines similar to ours but not perhaps as clearly formulated as the ideas of Patricia Knapp or Louis Shores, for example. After exposure to some writing on the concept of the Library-College evidently he shouted, "Eureka — this is exactly what we need to revitalize our college!" At any rate, he seems to be full of genuine and informed eagerness to work out "something." As yet nothing has crystallized but it appears that we might have the opportunity we have been looking for.

Sillers has a talent for fund-raising and community relations and is confident about the financial picture. Jamestown College has a good endowment for a college of only 500 students but practically no staff time has been devoted to fund-raising in the past few years. Sufficient money will be secured to support the above mentioned initial "team" over and above the regular faculty and teaching requirements.

In addition, Sillers is proposing to raise at least one million dollars specifically for constructing a new library. If we can develop a realistic and workable program for a Library-College, it is not inconceivable that we can participate in the design of a major new structure that would carry out this philosophy in its physical arrangement.

Conceivably, at Detroit, we might recommend the following: First, that a workshop be held at Jamestown to develop a tentative plan. Second, appointment of a national Advisory and Visiting Committee of 3 to 5 people who would develop plans in more specific detail, and during the next 2 or 3 years would advise the "experimental team in residence" at Jamestown. Third, appointment by Sillers of the initial first year "experimental team in residence" to carry out the plans.

As far as we know, this is the first time this kind of approach has been taken to experimental higher education.

For the first time in anyone's memory at Jamestown the students are alert and interested in educational innovation and might be expected to carry a major role in developing and implanting a program.

Sillers, a psychologist by training, specializing in mental hygiene is a congenial and perceptive person and seems to have the talent to hold together such a dynamic situation. He is realistic about such a venture and is quite prepared for a flop as well as a success. If the former he has no doubt that the attempt would still be a plus for the College in stirring up controversy and challenging old ideas.

The team would function as a "Department of New Ideas" in all matters affecting the college, and might be responsible for developing such major innovations (for implementation in 1966 or 1967) as a four year program beginning at age 17 replacing two years of high school and four years of college, or a work-study program including development of local employment opportunities (the population of North Dakota is declining), or an alumni and adult correspondence program integrated with: the library — home delivery of books — traveling book centers — programmed learning — state-wide TV and special week-end or week-long campus residential sessions.

Also, can you bring to Detroit one or two pages of ideas in reaction to this admittedly hasty and sketchy outline as to how we might best proceed in implementing a Library-College?

Also, if there is any possibility that you might be persuaded to join the team at Jamestown next year, please determine the likelihood that you might obtain a leave of absence for that period of time.

Finally, could you ask the above questions of others of your acquaintance, particularly young librarians (or faculty members who "act" like librarians) who would be qualified and eager to participate as junior members of such an "experimental team in residence"?

Sillers promises the salary can be at least equal to anyone's existing salary plus the provision of furnished living quarters in Jamestown, either for an individual or a family. However, he would like to complement more experienced team members (commanding higher salaries) with younger members (at lower salaries).

*Robert Jordan*

## No. 3, August 10, 1965, Issue Editor: Louis Shores

1. *"The true University* is a collection of books." Quoted freely (even by college presidents who don't understand the significance). I reread Carlyle's words in context (Heroes and Hero worship: Lecture V. "The Hero as Intellectual" (Delivered Tuesday May, 19, 1840.).
   "If we think of it, all that a university or final highest school can do for us, is still but what the first school began doing—teach us to *Read*. We learn to *Read* in various languages in various *sciences* ... It depends on what we read, after all manner of professors have done their best for us. The true university of these days is a collection of books."

Further, Carlyle observed, "Literature . . . is an 'apocalypse of nature,' a revealing of the 'open secret' . . . a 'continuous revelation' of the god-like in the terrestrial and common."

"Once invent printing, you metamorphosed all universities or superseded them. The teacher needed not now to gather men personally round him that he might speak to them what he knew; print it in a book."

## TEN EXPERIMENTING COLLEGES AND ANOTHER

reported at a colloquium at Wakulla Springs, Florida in the spring of 1964. Key in all of the experiments are accents on (1) independent study; (2) unity of knowledge through interdisciplinary approaches; (3) library learning.

1. *Antioch:* (Esther A. Oldt, Research Associate, Antioch Education Abroad)

   "Now under consideration . . . an experimental program for the freshman year which . . . will incorporate independent study techniques into the entire program from the first year on.

2. *Stephens:* (Ralph C. Leyden, Director of Educational Development)

   "The largest and physically the most dominating building of the learning center is the resources library . . . equipped with learning carrels . . . recorded materials . . . individual television sets for programmed materials . . . listening rooms . . . wall space for the display of pictures which are later checked out for student use in dormitory rooms . . . open stacks . . . secluded reading and study areas . . . browsing areas, conference rooms and an informal reading area around an open fireplace . . . . The Stephens College Learning Center Project is especially significant because of its departure from previous educational patterns . . . This attempt to saturate one (area) with all the tools available and appropriate for instruction . . ."

3. *The University of California, Santa Cruz:* (Chancellor Dean E. McHenry) "The library will be the intellectual heart of Santa Cruz campus. From the beginning it will be molded by four formative influences:

   (1) Centrally located undergraduate collection . . .
   (2) The residential colleges will have substantial libraries . . .
   (3) The emphasis on humanities and social sciences will require extraordinary support for the library . . .
   (4) . . . through inter-library loans and travel-by-reader the vast resources of the Berkeley and other University Libraries . . ."

4. *New College:* ("Q minus five months")    (John W. Gustad, Provost and Dean)

   "Several basic assumptions . . .

   (1) Each student is responsible in the last analysis for his own education . . .
   (6) Liberal education requires an appreciation of the unity of knowledge

253

...the student who has learned to read history with insight and perception...can be left very largely alone to accumulate the essential body of facts.

5. *Parsons College:* (Lee Sutton, Librarian)

"I was convinced that library techniques were the ideal method to educate. Within the library a student could be informed while being forced to find and select valid information, draw inferences, and weigh conclusions. In a library students could be taught to think.

To this end . . . all upper division courses and selected courses in the core were to have term papers or equivalent library projects...

Nevertheless, I had made a primary mistake... Having convinced Deans and faculty senate, I assumed the rest of the faculty agreed. I should have known from the writings of Patricia Knapp and Harvie Branscomb that the speculative or exploratory method of learning and teaching which is involved with library-oriented study is alien to most faculty members since their own training on the undergraduate level was not conducted in this way . . . Because of this failure 'the library way...did not work out. It is a good way toward improved education and in time...it can become the Parsons College way."

6. *The University of the Pacific* (Samuel L. Meyer, Academic Vice President)

"...the first of the 'cluster colleges' should be a liberal arts college but it should differ."

(3) ...curriculum was to indicate the unity rather than the departmentalization of knowledge.

(4) ...place emphasis on inter-disciplinary concepts with the resulting cross-fertilization and stimulation of ideas.

(6) ...emphasis was to be on *learning* rather than on *teaching*...

"The instructional methodology features seminars, tutorials, independent and directed study.

7. *Florida Presbyterian College* (John M. Bevan, Dean; the students call him "The Burning Bush")

"Too frequently the teacher stands in a place similar to the mule driver who has had animals equipped with blinders as he holds tight to the reins and cracks the whip...

"One of the primary aims...is to develop a program in which independent study might become an academic way of life. In the evaluation of such a college atmosphere the following conditions were initiated and the following procedures pursued:

(1) Admittance...of better than average students...(initially)

(2) Selection of faculty...decidedly interested in experimentation in independent study.

254

(3) Elimination of . . . required class attendance . . . grade point system . . .

(4) Establishment of small housing units . . .

(5) A reading proficiency requirement . . .

(6) Open-stack library program . . .

(7) Open door classroom policy . . . sit in on any lecture . . . take a a comprehensive examination.

(8) Initiation of the Winter term (inter-semester) . . . period of independent study.

(It is the Issue Editor's opinion that Florida Presbyterian is further along on the way to a true Library-College in both concept and execution than any other institution.)

8. *University of Michigan Dearborn Campus:* (W. E. Stirton, Vice President and Director)
"Industry's need for quality manpower and a $10,000,000 gift provide an opportunity to prove that professional and occupational competency can be reconciled with a culture curriculum." The Library's contribution can be as creative as the campus opportunity. Dearborn will be watched hungrily because of the Dr. Stirton's acumen.

9. *Michigan State University:* (Paul L. Dressel, Director of the Office of Institutional Research)
"Residence Hall-based instruction as it is being designed for the first three new halls—Case, Wilson, and Wonders, provides for a library with the "Learning Resources" trappings out of which may yet develop at least one library-centered learning program.

10. *Wayne State University, Monteith College:* (Woodburn O. Ross, Dean)
"A grant by the Office of Education made possible . . . a program which sought out means of uniting library staff members with each instructional staff, deriving much of the intellectual development of students from the library thus . . . making the library . . . the center of the learning process which it should and frequently may not be." (Patricia Knapp has amplified this in a study of the Monteith Project which will be published).

## AND ANOTHER

11. *Florida State University:* An *ad hoc* committee began meeting informally in 1963 once a week in the home of each of seven faculty members and academic leaders to review the state of higher education in the U. S. and particularly on this campus. As Hugh W. Stickler put it, the Committee came to two conclusions:

(a) "all is not well in undergraduate education in larger American universities."

255

(b) "A carefully planned and creditably operated experimental college holds considerable promise . . . of providing better undergraduate education in our institution . . ."

Inevitably, after the President's official appointment of this *ad hoc* group as the University's Committee on the Experimental College, different accents emerged. The two librarian members urged a Library-College, but as has been recorded before, it is difficut for a generation of classroom—habituated faculty to expel the "blinders" of "class contact" as the measure of education.

The report (R. R. Oglesby, Dean of Students) is an eloquent and balanced reflection of the committee consensus. "The library will be a focal point of learning . . . and what is proposed is certainly beyond library execution in most U. S. colleges. But to the Library-College advocate it does not go far enough."

To the newly appointed Senate Committee on the Experimental College, of which the original *ad hoc* committee leader is also chairman, the Issue Editor was invited to make the opening presentation. Two points are excerpted here:

### *Library-Centered Independent Study*

I propose for your consideration the adoption of the current library-centered independent study trend as the learning mode for the FSU experimental college. There would be departure in the fact that independent study would be extended to all students, not only the superior. There would be innovation in the fact that we would reverse the present relationship between class contact and library reading. Perhaps a half dozen times during a term, the student would attend a university-wide lecture in U.S. History, pertinent to his individual study. Each faculty member would prepare each term one or two of the university-wide lectures in his specialty, and these lectures would be of such scope and quality as to warrant publication.

Library-reading as a learning mode has, in my opinion, a number of advantages over the present classroom-contact pattern of education. Library reading is student centered; classroom-contact tends to be teacher-active, student-passive learning. Library-reading can cater to individual differences more effectively than can group-average lesson plans. Library-reading fortifies that "half of knowledge," which the quotation over the entrance to our former library building still celebrates, "Knowing where to find it." And as for the "other half" no small

256

part of it comes from the inter-disciplinary approach inevitable to a collection of books that represents all of man's knowledge. This is still another argument against dispersing our university collection to departmental libraries.

### Curriculum

I propose for your consideration that we go beyond this now "old hat" (Science, Social Science, Humanities) partial inter-discipline to an inter-area opportunity for the students. Our commitment to specialism, no doubt, must continue despite philosophical warnings that such commitment may drive us from frustration to destruction. I presume, for a long time yet to come, students will have to live an academic day in which from nine to ten in the morning God is a physicist; from eleven to twelve an economist; from two to three a grammarian. He will have to experience a universe which is constructed of certain subjects, more "substantive," more liberal, more respectable than others. Our experimental college cannot revolt all at once against the predatory rights of subjects. But our experimental college can make an inter-disciplinary contribution beyond the beginnings now found in this university.

I propose a foundation and a capstone for our subject specialities that is widely inter-disciplinary. The foundation will be inter-area relating the sciences, humanities and social sciences, as *Phy Sci* now relates physics, chemistry, geology, etc. It will be an encyclopedic course, comprehending generally the three-zero class of the Dewey Decimal Classification for books. Much as it may affront our specialism sensibilities, I would propose the generalism title for this inter-disciplinary reading as simply "Knowledge." It would attempt to summarize the deeds and thoughts of most significance to mankind.

## No. 4, December 8, 1965, Issue Editor: Patricia Knapp

### FLASH!

"Library-College" Workshop to be Held at Jamestown College,
Jamestown, N. D.
December 18-21, 1965

A number of the adherents of the Library-College idea (including several of our editors) will gather for the purpose of developing an ideal design for such a college. President Dan Sillers of Jamestown, host for the occasion, hopes the ideal plan will have considerable applicability to the Jamestown program.

## QUOTES WORTH THINKING ABOUT

In re: the library as an environment:

> "The environment is not a natural thing; it is a set of inter-related precepts, a product of culture. It yields food to the aborigine but none to the white traveller because the former perceives food where the latter sees only inedible insects." Edmund R. Leach, Culture and Social Cohesion; an Anthropologist's View," *Daedalus,* Winter, 1965.

In re: books and knowledge:

> "There is a widely spread misconception about the nature of books which contain knowledge. It is thought that such books are something the contents of which have to be crammed into our heads. I think the opposite is closer to the truth. Books are there to keep the knowledge in while we use our heads for something better . . . . . .
>
> I do not want to be misunderstood—I do not depreciate knowledge, and I have worked long and hard to know something of all fields of science related to biology. Without this I could do no research. But I have retained only what I need for an understanding, an intuitive grasp, and in order to know in which book to find what. This was fun, and we must have fun, or else our work is no good." Albert Szent-Györgi, "Teaching and the Expanding Knowledge," *Science,* Vol. 146.

In re: faculty-student relationship:

> "Another kind of value that media have is their ability to restructure or influence human relationships. One of the significant values of programmed materials is that the student can be freed from certain kinds of unreasonable or at least personal and idiosyncratic demands of the teacher. He need not be under the teacher's every whim, nor influenced by teachers' actions which reinforce his behavior toward adults rather than to rules of symbol usage. For instance, some studies of the Edison responsive environment, engineered by O. K. Moore, indicate that emotionally disturbed children can learn to read and write with the machine which they had not been able to do with teachers because of relational problems." Dwayne E. Huebner, "The Use of Printed and Audio-Visual Materials for Instructional Purposes: Elementary School," Conference, School of Library Service, Columbia University, November 22-23, 1965.

In re: the information-gathering patterns of students:

".. . For thousands of U. S. students pones, trots, crib books, outlines, digests, guides and crammers—in short, all the purported short cuts to good grades—have become an indispensable part of college life ......

"Part of the explanation for this explosion, of course, is the rapid growth of the college population. More important, the easy availability of the paperback book has encouraged professors to assign far more reading than ever before, and many students say they just don't have time to plow through the reading lists. Then, too, some students feel that teachers of mass "survey" courses prefer mastery of facts to original thinking. 'Intellectual curiosity and honesty are not really encouraged,' says Stanford philosophy major Kenneth Washington, 'because they're not rewarded as much as the ability to spew forth facts.' Students also tend to adopt a cynical attitude toward the whole highly competitive college world where marks are all-important. 'The object is to pass, isn't it?' *Newsweek,* November 22, 1965, p. 101.

## NEWS

Hampshire College, Hadley, Massachusetts.

The "New College," planned in 1957-58 by a group of faculty members from Amherst, Smith, Mount Holyoke, and the University of Massachusetts is to become a reality as a result of a $6 million pledge from an Amherst alumnus. As Hechinger notes in the *New York Times,* "It would be naive to suggest that the Hampshire venture is as revolutionary today as it would have been in 1958. Much of the 'New College Plan' has been adopted here and there across the country." Nevertheless, the stress on independent study and the centrality of the library's role will make this program well worth watching.

Nova University of Advanced Technology, Fort Lauderdale, Florida.

Concentrating on the physical sciences, with a total enrollment of 1500, only 500 of which would be at the junior and senior level. All faculty would be on the Graduate School faculty. The program would be located on the same campus as existing ungraded elementary, secondary, and junior colleges, all publicly supported, but Nova would be privately supported. Warren Winstead is the President, and the first students are expected in 1967.

City University of New York, Staten Island.

An upper division college, patterned after Florida Atlantic, will open in 1967.

Goddard.

Developing two new campuses to be erected alongside the existing campus. Each new campus will enroll 250 students.

Nasson.

Developing two new campuses to be erected alongside the existing campus. Each new campus will enroll 500 students.

Miami-Dade Junior College.

The library has been split squarely down the middle. Readers' services have been assigned to the Deans of Instruction on the various campuses. Technical services have been assigned to the Department of Learning Resources.

Chicago.

The College at the University of Chicago is being, once again, reorganized. Of particular interest is the new, fifth "Collegiate Division." (The other four are: Physical Sciences, Biology, Social Sciences, Humanities) Dean Wayne C. Booth describes it as follows: "Freed from the demand to provide traditional 'majors,' those who plan for this 'new college, as yet unnamed,' are expected to experiment with four-year programs that no one has ever thought of before, or that do not fit easily into other university departments and divisions." One will set up a major in "Civilization Studies" and will try to discover "The intellectual requirements for the study of civilizations, and . . . construct a new view of liberal arts on the basis of those requirements. Another possibility is a curriculum based on a re-examination of the traditional arts of grammar, rhetoric, logic, and dialectic."

"Free Universities."

A number of these have sprung up around the country, including Berkeley, Selma, and New York City. In the latter, a group of teachers rented a loft and held seven classes, sans grades etc.

Athens College, Gravel Pit, Athens, Ohio.

John Chandler, Chairman of the Board, is one of three faculty members at Ohio University who are involved along with a group of students in operating this ad hoc, extra-curricular "college." Founded in 1964-65, this group held a full-time session (?) during the summer of 1965.

260

# FROM THE JORDAN MAILBAG

From: Lee Sutton                                          June 29, 1965

I might as well use the occasion of this note to outline what I think the essential problems are with establishing a Library-College. I will not deal at all with the matter of library training since I feel that Patricia Knapp has worked out a good number of the problems in advance.

It seems to me that the basic problem is in the hands of those people who prepare course outlines. Very largely this is going to be faculty. I would suggest that librarians who are part of the initial team also have some teaching experience on the college level if possible—not the teaching of library science courses.

One key to the well developed library course is teaching organized around several key concepts. Not all courses are adaptable to this type of teaching, but a high percentage of them are. By concept teaching, I mean teaching where the necessary factual information is grouped around a set of ideas, insights or historical developments. These ideas automatically pose problems which can be dealt with in a variety of kinds of library projects.

Within my own teaching experience and from what I have observed, I can cite the following examples. In the teaching of Paradise Lost in a Milton course, the work can be approached in various ways. What is the role of Satan in this poem? How is Milton's theology reflected within the poem? Is the organization of the poem truly Epic, or did its early dramatic form determine the character of the poem? Any of these or other approaches can result in one or more papers or oral presentations, in the process of which the student must approach the poem as a whole. Since much has been published on such topics, the student must approach all the standard entrances to the library for literary subjects. The papers are thus part of learning the subject matter of the course—in this case Paradise Lost.

In history something similar is perfectly possible. In the teaching of medieval history, the problem of investiture, rightly considered, involves the relationship of all segments of medieval society. In American history, papers which concern states' rights, as opposed to federal power, would force the student to review a great deal of political and social history.

This type of teaching is something which must be planned in relationship to library holdings. I do not think I need to multiply examples, but it is upon this type of teaching that *meaningful* library work is built. It would take special course preparation, often *new* preparation, on the part of the instructor. It means that the instructor must trust the student with a good deal of responsibility for learning. With such courses, the library staff must be familiar with the demands the instructor is making and have some kind of idea of the courses themselves. It also means that the professor must have sufficient assistance (or small enough student loads) that he can make careful assessment of the resulting papers.

I should say, at this point, that one of the keys to library-related courses is the nature of some kinds of non-library related courses. It is

261

possible in philosophy, say, where four or five paperbacks are assigned, that the instructor insist that the student evaluate, in a very real sense, for himself. Beyond the library-related courses, it is important that speculation, originality and insight be appropriately rewarded. It is perfectly possible, even in philosophy or sociology, for an instructor to insist upon simple *recitation* of definitions or the capsulation of particular sets of ideas without criticism.

It would appear to me that perhaps the first requisite for a library-related college is an intellectual atmosphere that encourages thought even when that thought may not be entirely mature or reliable.

None of this should be construed as playing down the learning of specific library techniques or bibliographic "ways". At best these are learned within the context of a specific course for a specific purpose. Courses which do teach library techniques must be even more carefully planned, as Pat Knapp has demonstrated. Pat Knapp has also pointed out the necessity for some direct teaching, but I think one must always be wary of busy-work. But again, the chief thing to be wary of is the term paper on a narrow subject which is not related firmly to the over-all subject at hand.

One other but obvious thing must be said. Faculty must be involved in making the program from the very beginning. I do not mean heads of departments nor deans even if they teach. I mean faculty down to the lowest instructor. This is the most difficult thing to achieve. I know Pat Knapp had difficulties even when hiring for Monteith. Shores, using administrators for his committee to create a Library-College had faculty hackles up as soon as they heard details of the project.

From: John Harvey                                               October 25, 1965

I certainly enjoyed meeting you and learning more about the Library-College idea. It is heartening to know that there are others in the world who think the way I do. I had almost come to the conclusion that I was the only one who was worrying about what happened to the Stephens College idea. I am so heartened by the material which you sent and our discussions that I am willing to provide some material for the Newsletter.

Meanwhile, you asked about a list of colleges in which audio-visual service is directly under library supervision. While my memory is by no means perfect and my card files incomplete on many details, the following is a list of such libraries, most of which I have visited:

> John Hopkins University
> Bowie State Teachers College in Maryland
> Pennsylvania Military College
> Lock Haven State College in Pennsylvania
> Drexel Institute of Technology
> Moore Institute of Art in Philadelphia
> Trenton State College

Newark State College
Purdue University
Washington State University in Pullman
Ball State University in Muncie

There are probably a good many others and even some which I have been in where this relation exists.

You asked also about college libraries making a serious attempt to carry out a Stephens College type plan. I know of none. However, it can be reasonably assumed that many colleges which have a very high per student library expenditure are attempting to move strongly in this direction. In general, the Ivy League colleges and those of somewhat lesser eminence seem to have very good libraries with Princeton perhaps coming closer than any other I know to the Library-College ideal. However, in many cases their high expenditures are merely designed to build up book collections, not personalized service.

In our conference I did not mention some of my ideas about college library service which supplement those of Lamar Johnson. The college library should emulate the industrial technical information center which provides very personalized service. Selective dissemination of information, the extensive use of computer printed bibliographies and catalogs, personalized document retrieval, translation service, indexing and abstracting service, and the other facets of the modern technical information center should be transferred to the college campus. The upperclassmen and particularly the graduate student and faculty member deserve this type of service. It seems to me that this idea does not compete with the Library-College idea but expands and supplements it. Or perhaps it even carries it to its logical extreme. These ideas are expensive to carry out but if used to supplement the Stephens College Library idea would lead to outstanding library service.

If there is any interest in holding a further meeting concerning this idea, a new talkshop, I would be glad to be its host on the Drexel Campus. Undoubtedly the Jamestown meeting will be the center of such activities this fall, but if you would like to hold such a meeting during the coming spring or summer on the Library-College idea, I hope we can have it at Drexel. Undoubtedly, I would ask you to be director of this conference.

One of the distinctions which should exist in your mind in planning personnel for the Jamestown Conference is this. Will this be a brain-storming and imaginative session designed to produce many ideas, or will it be a session at which the practicalities of developing a Library-College will be hammered out in hard-headed detail? The two different kinds of sessions require different kinds of personnel. The imaginative brainstormer is seldom good at working out the practical details of operating a college.

# APPENDIX C

# *Typical Characteristics of a Library-College*

(from the ideas of Shores, Johnson, Knapp,
Jordan, Sillers, and Minder)

*Robert Jordan*

A. Learning Mode

1. Library rather than classroom-centered

2. Exploration of the bibliographic "way" rather than courses; the principal text is the library's unique organization of resources in a complex, inter-related network of bibliography, classification, indexes and catalogs

3. Student intellectual initiative and critical exploration rather than teacher-review and presentation of factual information in lecture-text-recitation

4. Greater emphasis on the process of learning, thinking and expression of thought than on the memorization of multitudiness minutiae

5. Joint student-faculty search and synthesis

6. Student, student-faculty and faculty team activity

7. Student-led "each one teach one" activity

8. The generic book in all its formats (from original sources through television) is the principal medium of communicating information

9. Faculty-constructed syllabi, bibliographies, guides and reading plans, supplemented by individual conferences, group seminars and planned occasional inspirational large group lectures

10. Off-campus community service and field work
11. Greater emphasis on ideas and problems than on geographic areas and periods of time
12. Regular speaking, writing, performing

B. Advanced students (faculty)
1. All educational community members are considered students, some more advanced than others
2. No groupings of the advanced students based on superior professional training
3. Essentially a cross between library-oriented teachers and teaching-oriented librarians
4. Includes both generalists and subject specialists with broad inter-specialty interest, and perspective
5. The advanced students are primarily counsellors, committed to encouraging and motivating, rather than informing and directing
6. No organizational separation between the library and the faculty
7. Students and faculty exchange roles at various times and places, in varying proportions, at varying levels of difficulty
8. The faculty set an example in continually learning, changing and adapting to new situations through competent use of the library and through personal interactions

C. Facilities
1. The academic facility is a library that acquires, organizes, interprets and disseminates all formats of the generic book
2. Individual offices in this facility for all students and faculty
3. At least one seminar room for every four faculty offices and 40 student offices

D. Educational channels (the generic book)
1. Laboratory materials and experiments integrated with other instructional resources
2. A minimum of 300,000 titles in the collection or 25,000 titles and access to a major research library
3. An abundance of materials related to varying views on controversial ideas and issues

265

# APPENDIX D

# Library-College Bibliography

selected, annotated, arranged chronologically

Shores, Louis. "The library arts college, a possibility in 1954?", *School and Society*. XLI (January 26, 1935), pp. 110-14.

Johnson, B. Lamar. *Vitalizing a College Library*. Chicago: ALA, 1939, 122 pp.

Hirsch, Felix E. "Use of the book collection in the teaching program of a progressive college," *College and Research Libraries* II (December, 1940), pp. 48-54.

Suggestions based on programs at Bard, Sarah Lawrence and Bennington. Report on extraordinary interest in reading, encouraged by lack of preconceived curriculum and by the close personal relationships between faculty, librarians and students.

Branscomb, Harvie. *Teaching with Books*. Chicago: American Library Association, 1940.

Textbook teaching is too uniform and is a surrogate for direct exposure to great literature. The library should not originate the educational program (this is the function of the faculty). Scholarly qualities are more important in the librarian than technical proficiency. Suggests auxiliary collections of core books and duplicates next to or in instructor's offices and classrooms (smaller and less complete than full-fledged departmental libraries). Suggests that all humanities or social science classes might be in the library. Pursues the thesis that the use of books is not an incidental aspect of instruction but is central and primary. There should often be a physical association of the three elements in

266

education, the student, the faculty adviser, and the book collection (including moving some instructors into the library as virtual assistants to the librarian). The instructor becomes an aid in acquiring and understanding knowledge rather than its source and final end. ". . . in place of specific assignments and set lectures, the student is directed to the literature of the subject . . . constant attendance at lectures is exhausting and except in the more favorable cases, destructive of zest and eagerness."

Orne, Jerrold. "An experiment in integrated library service," *College and Research Libraries* XVI (October 1955), pp. 353-59.

Describes the use of specially trained librarians as bibliographic assistants at Maxwell Air Force Base. These librarians spend most of their time in the classrooms or with faculty and students in the role of bibliographic experts in various subject fields.

Conference of Eastern College Librarians. *Library-instructional Integration on the College Level.* Chicago: ACRL, 1955.

Includes an excellent brief statement by Harold Taylor.

Knapp, Patricia B. "Suggested program of college instruction in the use of the library," *Library Quarterly* XXVI (July 1956), pp. 224-31.

The faculty should present library instruction as an integral part of content courses. Students should understand the kinds of information available in various subject fields, the nature of the bibliographic apparatus (the way books are listed and the function of literature searching). Library skill, including practice in the use of the library, *is* one of the liberal arts. There should be continuity through the four years, integration through repetition of unifying principles, and increasing breadth and depth in logical sequence. Includes a nine step program for persuading the faculty tactfully to adopt this program.

Givens, Johnnie. "The small and medium-sized college library," *Southeastern Librarian* VII (Spring 1957), pp. 12-15.

Suggests the development of teacher-librarians, to work with each class weekly, bi-weekly or monthly in exploitation of library resources.

Kuhlman, A. F. "Can we teach with books?" *Southeastern Librarian* VII (Spring 1957), pp. 5-9.

Reviews the history of interest in this topic from Justin Winsor in a Circular published by the Office of Education on "College Libraries as

Aids to Instruction" to all of the Carnegie sponsored activities in the 1920's and 1930's.

Scherer, Henry Howard. *Faculty-Librarian Relationships in Selected Liberal Arts Colleges.* Doctoral Dissertation. Los Angeles: University of Southern California, School of Education, 1960, 176 pp.

Available on microfilm from University Microfilms. P. Knapp's doctoral study suggested an investigation of the relationship between the instructor and the library. This work attempts to fill this need. A survey was made of hundreds of faculty and librarians relating to more than a hundred techniques and practices. Scherer's work summarizes the degree of satisfaction and the incidence of each practice. Almost all of the practices are conventional. There is no orientation towards a realistic integration of the faculty and library.

Scherer is now Librarian of the Lutheran Theological Seminary at Philadelphia.

Harvey, John F. "Library school instruction in academic librarianship," *Library Journal* LXXXVI (January 15, 1961), pp. 190-93.

A review of the history of instruction in academic librarianship and realistic evaluation of its place in the librarian's educational program, its strengths and weaknesses from the Library-College viewpoint.

Harvey, John F. "State of the college library art," *Library Journal* LXXXVI (February 1, 1961), pp. 513-15.

A realistic appraisal of the extent to which present American college libraries approach the Lamar Johnson-Harvie Branscomb ideal and why they are so poor.

Knapp, Patricia B. "The Monteith Library Project, an experiment in Library-College Relationship," *College and Research Libraries* XXII (July 1961), pp. 256-63.

Monteith College within Wayne State University emphasizes small discussion type classes in broad inter-disciplinary subjects with major library projects. The library furnished bibliographical assistance to the faculty and is conceived as organizing and controlling a complex network of communication systems.

Trump, J. Lloyd. *Focus on Change — Guide to Better Schools.* Chicago: Rand McNally, 1961.

Neither the classroom, the study hall, nor the library are adequate for independent study, which should take 40% of student time (plus

268

40% for large group lectures, films, etc., and 20% for small group discussions).

Proposes decentralized study centers in each major subject area or division, with carrells, AV and electronic facilities, an assortment of commonly used materials, including books, all under the supervision of a semi-professional, trained in the subject field and in materials management, and part of the library staff. All teachers will work in teams, and all librarians will be part-time members of teaching teams. The central library will contain only the lesser used materials. "It will be difficult to identify the library in the conventional sense because its services will permeate the totality of education."

Govan, James F. "This is, indeed, the heart of the matter," *College and Research Libraries* XXIII (November 1962), pp. 467-72.

Advocates greatly increased independent study to alleviate the crisis in enrollment, and to increase the quality of college instruction. Especially in the junior and senior year, two-thirds of the lecture hours should be cut out, to be replaced by wide reading within a broad bibliography. This should serve to open student's minds, help develop independent judgment, which has been stifled by the apron strings of dependence on instructor, textbook, or reserve list of specific readings. The instructor's role would be enhanced, not diminished in being freed from the role of presenting encyclopedia-like lectures; instead of being taskmaster, he can devote this time to acting as guide and critic, and prepare for performance at maximum capacity for his class periods.

More books will be needed, spread out around the campus, including paperbacks and dormitory libraries. No more erroneous analogy was ever drawn than the comparison of the library to the laboratory, as an adjunct or a support to instruction. "The library is no specially equipped area where principles and theories learned in a classroom are demonstrated. It is rather the repository of those principles and theories, the source to which the lecturer must go before he teaches. This is no adjunct, no support. This is, indeed, the heart of the matter."

Then Librarian at Trinity University, San Antonio, now at Swarthmore.

Moulds, Henry. "Why have teachers?" *Education Digest* XXVIII (February 1963), pp. 32-33 (originally in *North Central Association Quarterly*, Fall 1962).

Because of the shortage of excellent teachers, the availability of excellent books, and because of the impossibility of any real teaching to large groups, it would be best to eliminate all classroom teaching for general requirement courses and substitute syllabi, texts, assignments, study questions, examinations and consultation hours.

Singer, Len. "Florida Atlantic University," *Audio-Visual Instruction* VIII (April 1963), pp. 236-42.

The systems approach is used to design equipment, facilities and program to achieve maximum education experience. The library will be closely integrated into the instructional program as an integral part of a complex of "learning resources" activities, which include TV and radio, learning laboratories, graphics and engineering. The entire program is oriented to achieve maximum results, with minimum of traditional campus rah-rah and minimum faculty direction and supervision.

Bergen, Daniel Patrick. "Librarians and the bi-polarization of the academic enterprise," *College and Research Libraries* XXIV (November 1963), pp. 467-80.

Librarians, by nature of their training, are more ordered, conservative and conformist and more concerned with preservation than the faculty, and usually belong to a mutually exclusive sub-culture not that of the faculty. One example is the librarians' insistence on centralization. Suggests that librarians with the needed dual competencies in librarianship and subject areas, and with the service orientation of the special library should be trained in new schools devoted exclusively to the training of academic librarians. Only in this way can faculty-library integration be achieved.

Oxhandler, Eugene K. "Bringing the 'Dons' up to Date," *Audio-Visual Instruction* VIII (October 1963), pp. 566-59.

The Oxbridge Don system, based on individual counseling, highly individual and flexible program and independent study in a large library should be adopted in place of the traditional American system of mass or herd instruction to fully develop individual creative and intellectual capacities. The use of the computer to store all possible information about the student, the school, and teachers, the contents of the library and specific teaching machine programs, can make the Don system economically feasible in today's schools. This entire system will be coordinated by the AV specialist (audio-visual coordination or communicator). Such a system is the logical culmination of a trend that began

270

with Dewey and Parker, continued with the job-centered curriculum of the City and Country School, the large classes and team teaching of the Little Red School House, the contract plan (programmed learning) of the Dalton School and the Winnetka Plan, the core curriculum, and the giant step of the Trump plan.

Ellsworth, Ralph E. *The School Library; Facilities for Independent Study in the Secondary School.* New York: Educational Facilities Laboratories, 1963, 143 pp.

An expanded concept of the school library based on direct access by the student to a large quantity of materials of all types, not just books, which requires an "interfusion of materials and work space," not just a large study hall. The student and the teacher use the library in a wide variety of ways for independent study and research in association with all activities of the school. Seating, mostly in the form of semi-private carrells, is provided for 30 to 50% of the students, and the total quantity of materials jumps to the level heretofore considered adequate for a junior or senior college.

Dale, Edgar. "The teacher and technology," *Education Digest* XXIV (January 1964), pp. 24-27.

The teacher must become an organizer and manager of learning experiences, working with individuals and small groups, with more time for discussion and creative interaction, rather than presenting subject matter, giving and correcting tests, and assigning lessons. Students drawing upon a wealth of materials should become responsible for their own learning, through self-instructing techniques and programs, custom made for each student.

Bergholz, H. "Daniel Georg Morhof, overlooked recursor of library science," *Libri* XIV (1964), pp. 44-50.

Morhof was a German contemporary of John Locke and professor at Rostock. His "Polyhistor" represents "one of the latest single-handed attempts to encompass the essence of all human knowledge." Bacon had suggested an all-embracing inventory of human knowledge. . . . "It was left to Morhof two generations later to take up the challenge and produce an opus which is close to the Baconian inspiration. . . . Morhof not only discusses library science, he makes it the very foundation stone of his entire edifice and devotes a disproportionately lengthy first part of the first tome to this subject. . . . He justifies this procedure in the following manner: information and knowledge are most efficiently acquired through books and learned periodicals; therefore, the mentor must begin by furnishing advice as to which books and journals are the best in the various fields and why since the well-read scholar needs to know so many books, libraries have become an indispensable tool for him and an acquaintance with their organization and working methods is for that reason fundamental."

Eurich, Alvin C. "The commitment to experiment and innovate in college teaching," *Educational Record* XLV (Winter 1964), pp. 49-55.

College faculty are more loathe to adopt new methods in teaching than almost any other group in society, because of tradition, laziness, comfort, economy (in order to save time and money for teaching and research), existing building and equipment layouts, and lack of motivation. Change in higher education is resisted because of various false assumptions: that effective college teaching must be carried on in small classes, that there is a direct correlation between what the professor says in the classroom and what the students learn, that the student learns only when in the room with the teacher, and that there is an inverse correlation between technology in teaching and individual freedom. The goal of all education should be to learn without the teacher. A revolution might develop if only ½ of 1% of institutional budgets were devoted to educational research.

Gore, Daniel. "Anachronistic wizard: the college reference librarian," *Library Journal* LXXXIX (April 15, 1964), pp. 1688-92.

Proposes instruction in library and bibliographic techniques by a "new breed of teacher-librarian."

Shores, Louis. "Just suppose . . .," *School Libraries* XIV (October 1964), pp. 23-25.

Proposes an elementary school with only libraries and librarians.

Stickler, W. Hugh, ed. *Experimental College*. Tallahassee: Florida State University, 1964, 185 pp.

Reports on programs at nine existing and two proposed experimental colleges including the proposed library-centered college at FSU.

Gardner, John W. "Education as a way of life," *Science* XCLVIII (May 7, 1965), pp. 759-61.

"Traditional arrangements for education must be supplemented by

272

a system designed for lifelong learning" through credit by examination, television, correspondence study, self-teaching devices, libraries, and group study in various parts of the state, with the only requirements certification of the instructor, provision of the syllabus, and examination for credit. Employers will increasingly recognize the need for continuing education.

Tidwell, Roy. "The Oregon Plan," *Library Journal* XC (September 15, 1965), pp. 3686-89.

"Flexible scheduling, time for study in school, excellent physical facilities, adequate staffing, and strong collections all help shift the responsibility for learning from the teacher to the student. . . . Follows many of J. Lloyd Trump's recommendations but with important modifications" (such as a strong central library, in addition to departmental libraries) "on his free time student must decide where he can best use his unscheduled time (as much as 40%) — in one of the seven subject libraries, the main library, student unions, or various subject labs." This program is in effect at Marshall High School in Portland with 35,000 volumes in its collection.

Krohn, Mildred L. "Study in self-reliance — the Shaker Heights learning experiment," *Library Journal* XC (October 15, 1965), pp. 4520-22.

A Fund for the Advancement of Education Project in an elementary school. ". . . children can learn without the teacher being present if they are given access to many materials, motivation and skill to look for the answers themselves — and then left on their own."

Skinner, B. F. "Why teachers fail," *Saturday Review* XLVIII (October 16, 1965), pp. 80-81, 198-202.

There is no true technology of teaching. "College teaching has not been taught at all . . . It may indeed be true that the teacher cannot teach but can only help the student learn . . . The belief that personal experience in the classroom is the primary source of pedagogical wisdom" is an error. "It is actually very difficult for teachers to profit from experience. They almost never learn about their long-term successes or failures. . . . Teaching may be defined as an arrangement of contingencies of reinforcement under which behavior changes. Relevant contingencies can be most successfully analyzed in studying the behavior of one student at a time under carefully controlled conditions."

Dober, Richard P. *The New Campus in Britain: Ideas of Consequence for the United States*. New York: Educational Facilities Laboratories, 1965, 71 pp.

The philosophy of the "continuous teaching environment" has dominated the planning of the eight new universities. This is an attempt to develop "a physical form that preserves communication and contact between all parts of the institution while allowing external accretion and internal change. . . . Too often the rigid distinctions between instructional, communal, and residential buildings reduce the opportunity for casual and undirected attachment to a fixed point in space. A sense of belonging is lost, and easy communication between members of the institution may be blurred. . . . To avoid a split between teaching and social activities, housing is brought in close to the academic area, and facilities for leisure time pursuits are integrated with academic buildings." In some instances this has meant many facilities and services, including the library, have been combined into one complex. "The plan for York is based on an expanding series of "colleges" . . . whose size is the minimum number affording facial recognition after a year's regular contact" (400). Each college is largely autonomous.

Ellsworth, Ralph E. *The School Library*. New York: Center for Applied Research in Education, Inc., 1965, 116 pp.

Part of a subscription series, "The Library of Education," which cannot be sold separately. Includes an introduction by Louis Shores. Ellsworth's work heralds the amalgamation of school and library.

Hatch, Winslow R., ed. *Approach to Independent Study*. New Dimensions in Higher Education, No. 13. Washington: U. S. Office of Education, 1965, 73 pp.

An excellent "state-of-the-art" indicating a promising future for independent study and library-centered learning. See especially articles by Gruber, Knapp, Ballard and Leuba.

Overhage, Carl F. J. *Intrex*. Cambridge, Mass.: M.I.T. Press, 1965, 276 pp.

See pages 111-115, 243-253.

It is hoped that the library of the future will play a much more active role in the educational process as "the most powerful teaching instrument ever conveived." Reading for a degree is alien to most cam-

274

puses. Evaluation of the student's success would be based on what he selected and read, not on the structure of the corresponding course. . . . Exploring techniques designed to de-emphasize the traditional divisions among classroom, laboratory, library, dormitory, and lounge.

Perkins, Ralph. *The Prospective Teacher's Knowledge of Library Fundamentals.* New York: Scarecrow, 1965, 202 pp.

Responses by 4170 college seniors to tests designed to measure familiarity with libraries. Librarians seem to be the sole interpreters of the library. "Current methods are at an impasse." If the library is a necessity to education, all students should have training in its use, by teachers, in meaningful ways, and not as uncorrelated busy-work. "The greatest potential source of education for today's youth, the library, is being wasted."

Smith, Robert E. *A Review of Published and Unpublished Material Concerning College and University Learning Resource Centers.* Champaign, Illinois: Richardson, Severns, Scheeler & Associates, 821 South Neil Street, 1965, 96 pp.

Includes an annotated bibliography arranged by format and issuing agency (!). The unpublished material includes a concept for an "automated library" by Bruce H. McCormick. The best material in this mixed bag is a tentative proposal by F. J. Koenig, Assistant Dean at the College of Liberal Arts at the University of Illinois for a combined library, faculty office building and undergraduate learning center, which would eventually include computer controlled programmed learning, and the full panoply of AV and video resources. "The need is for new environments for learning . . . to make possible new approaches to teaching, to scientific innovation, to exploration of independent study, and to systematic evaluation of new learning methods . . . plus a faculty-student carrel which is original with us . . . a semi-enclosed room with an opening instead of a door, furnished with a table for five. Noise level will be minimized by floor carpet and acoustical treatment."

Stone, C. Walter. *A Library Program for Columbia.* Pittsburgh: 1965, 49 pp. (Obtainable from Nettie Taylor, State Office of Education, Baltimore, Maryland.)

A proposal for an advanced library-communications system for Columbia City, a planned city of 150,000 people half way between Washington and Baltimore.

Bergen, Daniel and E. D. Duryea, editors. *The Library and the College Climate of Learning.* Syracuse: Syracuse University Schools of Library Science and Education, 1966.

Includes an address by Patricia Knapp, "Involving the Library in an Integrated Learning Environment."

Shores, Louis. "The library junior college," *Junior College Journal* XXXVI (March 1966), pp. 6-9.

"Oral communication of facts, by the teacher, is steadily being replaced by bibliographic guidance to a variety of sources. This stimulates the student's independent search for and discovery of facts and concepts at the pace indicated by his individual readiness. As independent study becomes ever the dominant mode of learning, the classroom teacher takes on more and more of the bibliographic competence of the librarian. In the process the librarian assumes ever more instructional responsibility. . . . The true college is a collection of books; the true faculty is a group of teachers who can interpret this collection of books to students. . . . The library serves a unique, instructional role. It is best qualified to teach that 'half of knowledge which is knowing where to find it.' And as for the other half, it is the only college teaching unit which can provide an unlimited interdisciplinary approach to knowledge. . . . Reorganization of our very large institutions into smaller, manageable colleges would restore some of the intimacy inherent in a good learning environment. The Library-College is, therefore, a small college with an enrollment of not over 1,000."

Shores, Louis, "The Library College Idea" *Library Journal XVI* (September 1, 1966), pp. 3871-5.

Shores, Louis, Jordon, Robert and Harvey, John, *The Library-College*: Philadelphia: Drexel Press, 1966.

### Curriculum Materials for the Library-College

Reading with a Purpose Series, American Library Association. 1926-1934. (75 to 100 individual reading guides.)

Meiklejohn, Alexander. *The Experimental College.* New York: Harper, 1932, 421 pp.

Johnson, B. Lamar. *Vitalizing a College Library.* Chicago: American Library Association, 1939, 122 pp.

Johnson, B. Lamar. *The Librarian and the Teacher in General Education.* Chicago: American Library Association, 1948.

Wilson, Louis Round. *The Library in College Instruction.* New York: H. W. Wilson, 1951, 346 pp.

Maxfield, David K. *Counselor Librarianship: a New Departure.* Urbana: University of Illinois Library School, 1954, 39 pp.

Reading for an Age of Change Series. American Library Association. 1962-     (10 reading guides).

Leuba, Clarence. "Using groups in independent study," *Antioch College Reports,* No. 5, 1963, pp. 1-4.

Knapp, Patricia. *Independent Study and the Academic Library.* Special Reports Series. E. R. I. C. (Educational Research Information Center) Washington: U. S. Office of Education, 1964.

Index

# The Library-College Index

282

## DREXEL PRESS PUBLICATIONS

### Drexel Library Quarterly

Each issue will remain in print, and subscriptions beginning with Vol. 1, No. 1 are available. Annual subscriptions are available at $10, and a single issue costs $3. Donald Hunt, Editor. Orders may be addressed to *Drexel Library Quarterly,* Graduate School of Library Science, Drexel Institute of Technology, Philadelphia, Pennsylvania 19104.

Vol. I No. 1. Library Public Relations, edited by Donald Hunt.
No. 2 Legal Bibliography Briefed, edited by Morris Cohen.
No. 3 Charging Systems, edited by Donald Hunt.
No. 4 Government Publications, edited by Kathryn Oller.

Vol. II No. 1 Book Selection for Children, edited by Rachael DeAngelo.
No. 2 Film Service in Public Libraries, edited by Eugene Pringle.
No. 3 College Library Standards, edited by Felix Hirsch.

### Drexel Library School Series

The following issues of the *Drexel Library School* Series are in print or will be published soon. All other numbers are out of print. John Harvey, Editor. They may be ordered singly or by standing order for the Series and are available postpaid from the Bookstore, Drexel Institute of Technology, Philadelphia, Pennsylvania 19104.

No. 7 Children's Book Fairs
Rachael W. DeAngelo, Editor, 1963, 32p. Second Printing. $1.00

No. 11 Simplifying Work in Small Public Libraries
Donald D. Dennis, 1965, 85p. Third Printing. $2.50

No. 12 Church Library Guide
Joyce L. White and Mary Y. Parr, Editors, 1965, 50p. Second Printing. $2.50

No. 13 Problems of Library Service in Metropolitan Areas
Dorothy Bendix, Editor 60p., September, 1966.

No. 14 Project History Retrieval
Elizabeth Ingerman Wood, 1966, 105p. Hardbound. $3.00

No. 15 Problems of Library Work with the Undereducated
Dorothy Bendix, Editor, 55p., August, 1966.

No. 16 The Library-College
Louis Shores, Robert Jordan, and John Harvey, Editors, 250p., Hardbound. October, 1966.

No. 17 Thesaurus of Information Science Terms
   Claire Schultz, 1965. 50p. $3.00

No. 18 Information Use Studies Bibliography
   Richard A. Davis, Compiler. 1964. 80p. Third Printing.

No. 19 A Graph Theoretic Analysis of Citation Index Structures
   Ralph Garner, 100p., November, 1966

No. 20 Public Library Architecture, Principles and Case Studies
   150p., November, 1966

No. 21 "Sometimes Students Do Really Outstanding Papers Which
   Ought to Be Published . . ." Twelve A+ Papers.
   Betty M. Brown, Compiler, 120p. December, 1966

No. 22 Directory of Church Libraries
   Dorothy Rodda and John Harvey, Compilers. 200p. December, 1966.

No. 23 Directory of Library Periodicals. Second Edition.
   Betty Brown and Nancy Shelley, Compilers. 150p. December, 1966.

### Drexel Information Science Series

John Harvey, Editor. All numbers of this series are in print and may be obtained from the publisher, Spartan Press, 1106 Connecticut Avenue, N.W., Washington, D. C. or from the Bookstore, Drexel Institute of Technology, Philadelphia, Philadelphia, Pa. 19104.

No. 1 Technical Information Center Administration I 1964
   Arthur Elias, Editor, 1964, 171p. $6.50

No. 2 Technical Information Center Administration II 1965
   Arthur Elias, Editor, 1965, 161p. $6.75

No. 3 Data Processing in Public and University Libraries
   Joseph Becker, Ralph Parker, and John Harvey, Editors, 250p., September, 1966.

No. 4 Technical Information Center Administration III 1966
   Arthur Elias, Editor, 160p. December, 1966

### DREXEL INSTITUTE OF TECHNOLOGY
### GRADUATE SCHOOL OF LIBRARY SCIENCE

#### 1966-67 Conferences

September 24-December 3    Library Workshop for School Administrators
led by Rachael DeAngelo, Professor

October 10-28 and
May 1-19, 1967    Seminar in Search Strategy
led by Claire K. Schultz, Visiting Associate Professor

| | |
|---|---|
| October 18-November 29 | Fourth Annual Seminar in Synagogue Librarianship led by Sidney Galphin, Adjunct Instructor |
| November 8-11 | Workshop on Library Association Administration led by Bill M. Woods, Special Libraries Association |
| December 18-21 | Library-College Conference led by Theodore Samore, Univ. of Wisconsin Library School, Milwaukee |
| January 2-June 12 1967 | Medical Librarianship Course taught by Robert Lentz, Adjunct Assistant Professor |
| March 4 | Third Annual School Library Student Assistants Conference Cosponsored by the School Librarians Association of Phila. led by Ruby Boyd, President |
| April 1 | Fifth Annual Church Library Conference led by Joyce White, Librarian, Penniman Library, University of Pennsylvania |
| April 2-June 14 | Mass Media of Communication Course taught by Ralph Collier, Adjunct Instructor |
| April 22 | Critique in America Today Conference led by Ralph Collier |
| June 13-16 | Technical Information Center Administration Conference IV led by Arthur Elias, Adjunct Associate Professor |
| July 17-28 | Seventh Annual School Librarianship Workshop led by Beatrice Downin, Director of School Libraries, Abington Township, Pennsylvania |
| September 19 | Ninth Annual Book Repair and Processing Demonstration led by Robert Heald, Gaylord Brothers Representative |

For further information please contact Margaret Warrington, Administrative Assistant.